Devotional Cultures of European Christianity

Devotional Cultures of European Christianity 1790–1960

Henning Laugerud & Salvador Ryan

EDITORS

FOUR COURTS PRESS

Set in 10.5 on 13.5 AGaramond for
FOUR COURTS PRESS
7 Malpas Street, Dublin 8, Ireland
www.fourcourtspress.ie
and in North America for
FOUR COURTS PRESS
c/o ISBS, 920 N.E. 58th Avenue, Suite 300, Portland, OR 97213.

ISBN 978-1-84682-303-9

SPECIAL ACKNOWLEDGMENT

Published with the financial support of The Scholastic
Trust, St Patrick's College, Maynooth; Bergen Museum,
University of Bergen; Department of Linguistic, Literary
and Aesthetic Studies, University of Bergen.

European Network on the Instruments of Devotion (ENID)

www.enid.uib.no

Printed in England by
CPI Antony Rowe, Chippenham, Wiltshire.

Contents

Contributors

HENRIK VON ACHEN is Professor of Art History at Bergen Museum, the University of Bergen.

ARNE BUGGE AMUNDSEN is Professor of Cultural History and Head of the Department of Culture Studies and Oriental Languages at the University of Oslo.

DAVID J. BURN is Professor of Musicology at the Catholic University of Leuven.

SHERIDAN GILLEY is Emeritus Reader in Theology of the University of Durham.

E. FRANCES KING is a research associate in the School of Sociology, Queen's University Belfast.

EWA KLEKOT is Assistant Professor at the Institute of Ethnology and Cultural Anthropology, Warsaw University.

GEORGIOS KORDIS is Professor at the School of Theology, University of Athens and visiting professor at Yale University. He is also an iconographer.

HENNING LAUGERUD is Associate Professor at the Department of Linguistics, Literary and Aesthetic Studies, University of Bergen.

SARAH F. MACLAREN teaches sociology at the Rome Centre of the Loyola University of Chicago.

BRENDAN McCONVERY teaches sacred scripture at the Pontifical University, St Patrick's College, Maynooth.

PETER McGRAIL is Associate Professor in the Department of Theology, Philosophy and Religious Studies, Liverpool Hope University, and Assistant Director of Liverpool Hope University's Institute for Pastoral Theology.

PETER DE MEY is Professor of Systematic Theology at the Catholic University of Leuven and Director of the Centre for Ecumenical Research of the Leuven Faculty of Theology.

SALVADOR RYAN is Professor of Ecclesiastical History at the Pontifical University, St Patrick's College, Maynooth.

ELI HELDAAS SELAND is currently completing her PhD in art history at the University of Bergen.

Acknowledgments

The editors would like to thank Kristian A. Bjørkelo for his assistance with the editing of this volume. Warm thanks are also extended to the following for their very generous financial support: Maynooth Scholastic Trust, St Patrick's College, Maynooth, Ireland, and also Bergen Museum and the Department of Linguistic, Literary and Aesthetic Studies, both at the University of Bergen, Norway.

Many of the following contributions were first presented as papers at a five-day workshop for the European Network on the Instruments of Devotion (ENID) held at St Patrick's College, Thurles, Ireland, which culminated in an international conference on 'The Material Culture of Catholic Devotion, *c*.1850–*c*.1950' on 18 January 2008. We would like to express our sincere gratitude to the staff of St Patrick's College, Thurles, for their warm hospitality and for their willingness to host these events.

Finally, we would like to thank Four Courts Press for its cooperation and professional assistance in preparing this volume for publication, and to Cyprian Love OSB, Glenstal Abbey, Co. Limerick, for agreeing to read a draft of this work prior to publication.

Henning Laugerud & Salvador Ryan

Introduction

HENNING LAUGERUD & SALVADOR RYAN

This volume takes as its theme the devotional cultures of European Christianity, from the dawn of the French Revolution to that later revolution which was the Second Vatican Council. At one level it deals with what might be called, in devotional terms, a 'long nineteenth century'. This term, of course, as used by Eric Hobsbawm, begins in 1789 and ends at the outbreak of the First World War, and this chronology, with some variations, has been generally adopted since. However, an argument might be made that, in devotional terms at least, the 'long nineteenth century' did not end at the outbreak of the Great War; certainly when applied to Catholicism, the devotional world forged in the late-eighteenth and nineteenth centuries continued to make a great deal of sense at a popular level through the 1960s and, even, to a lesser extent perhaps, beyond. This can also be justified when we are talking about the protestant or reformed churches in northern Europe. The nineteenth-century practices, ideals and theologies were hardly challenged until well into the 1960s.

The Catholic revival of the nineteenth century might be said to have its roots in the revolutionary period of the 1790s when a particular reading of the 'Enlightenment' had 'Reason' enthroned as a goddess in the cathedral of Notre Dame in 1793 and two successive popes were arrested by Napoleon some short years later – Pius VI and Pius VII, the latter held for six years. In fact, the years of turmoil through the 1790s actually led to a great deal of clandestine creativity among members of the laity, as familial reading and interpretation of the lives of the saints, lay instruction in catechism and the recitation of the rosary supplemented for the Eucharist in the absence of clergy; some other prominent members of the laity celebrated what were called 'white masses', complete with vestments, rubrics and Gregorian chant, excepting, of course, the consecration. In addition, more extreme examples of lay activism would see angry groups accost local officials and forcibly compel them to restore confiscated religious statues and other sacred objects. After the downfall of Napoleon, the status of the papacy was enhanced rather than diminished, and the example of Pius VII's fortitude in captivity certainly contributed to the credibility of an emerging wave of Ultramontanism.

This, of course, is the paradox of the nineteenth century: on the one hand, it is an age that witnesses the onward march of secularism and the end of the thousand-year-old or so Papal States, leaving a pope (Pius IX) who regards himself as a 'prisoner' in the Vatican; on the other, papal infallibility is solemnly defined in what might be regarded as the zenith of the ultramontane movement. It is an age of deep scepticism towards religious faith, fuelled, in part, by developments in science and the rise of

critical biblical and historical scholarship; yet, it is also an age in which reports of
Marian apparitions proliferate, often associated with unlettered and unsophisticated
visionaries. Indeed, in some quarters, where reason abounded, anti-intellectualism did
much more abound. These trends within Catholicism might be regarded as evidence
of a reactionary church responding to the challenges of Reason, Revolution and
Risorgimento; a last-ditch attempt to stem the tide of modernity such as that found in
the Syllabus of Errors of 1864. However, this view, which tends towards an interpretation of the developments in devotional culture as directed 'from the top down', as
part of some ultramontane 'master plan', surely misjudges the dynamism within
popular piety, which is more than capable of accepting or rejecting devotional innova-
tions on their own merits or usefulness.

The challenges of secularization in the nineteenth century were, moreover, shared
across denominational divides. Indeed, industrialization and the advent of secular
socialism would contribute to a weakening of religious practice among males, leading
to the increasing feminization of religion. This was especially evident in the explosion
of female religious orders within Catholicism, but also the important roles that
women enjoyed within religious movements such as Haugeanism in Norway, the
subject of the first essay in this volume. Many women within the Haugean movement
had leadership roles and acted as counsellors and preachers, often travelling long
distances alone, in an age when this was altogether uncommon. Sara Fiona Maclaren's
essay in this volume highlights particularly how the spiritual strength of women such
as Blessed Anna Maria Giannetti Taigi (1769–1837) and Blessed Elisabetta Canori
Mora (1774–1825) would be held up as models to be emulated.

In short, the piety of the Catholic 'long nineteenth century', perhaps not to
everyone's taste today – with its sentimentality and saccharine 'devotions' – could
claim at least to be broadly based. Shrines such as Lourdes, examined in one of the
essays here, were not solely the pilgrimage destinations of the peasant, but increasingly
that of the well-heeled pilgrim who could afford to make the trip; the Stations of the
Cross might appeal to the imagination of an unlettered Irish devotee in a newly built
post-Emancipation church in Ireland, but could also inspire the work of a gifted
Hungarian composer such as Franz Liszt, who created his work not at a remove from
the sentiments behind the *Via Crucis*, but rather by drawing deeply from his own
personal devotion to Christ's passion; images of the Sacred Heart could usefully stop
an enemy's bullets but could also say something theologically significant about the
breadth of God's salvation in the Jesuit-Jansenist debate. This was, indeed, a
devotional culture aimed at a broad church and one which, on the one hand,
excoriated the modern world and its technological creations, and on the other, made
use of these with holy abandon to internationalize its brand.

Both the Orthodox and the Protestant churches would have their own battles to
fight with 'modernity': for the former (at least in the contribution to this volume), that
battle was aimed at recovering the Byzantine painting style from its more recent

Nazarene usurper. In the case of Haugeanism, the battle was as much with what it considered to be a spiritually deficient state church; for some members of the Established Church of mid-nineteenth-century England, the restoration of the Catholic hierarchy would raise its own difficulties, as would the presence of two distinct traditions with their own emblems of identity in twentieth-century Northern Ireland. Whatever the geographical location, or social or political context, the deep-seated attachment of individuals and groups to their respective devotional worlds and the extent to which these worlds shaped them cannot be ignored.

THE ANTHOLOGY

The collection is divided into three parts. The first is comprised of five essays that explore the theme of spiritual and devotional renewal in Norway, Ireland, Italy and France. The second part explores questions pertaining to devotional culture in the arts, with specific studies related to aspects of sacred music, iconography and architecture. The final part addresses the use of devotional instruments, respectively hymnody and religious emblems, to identify individuals and groups over and against a specified 'Other', whether that 'Other' be in 1850s' England, 1930s' Spain or 1970s' Belfast.

Part I
In the first essay, Arne Bugge Amundsen introduces the Haugean movement, a hugely influential Norwegian manifestation of pietism. It was led by the young and unlettered Hans Nielsen Hauge (1771–1824), son of a peasant, who became a wandering lay preacher and took it upon himself to travel throughout Norway confronting clergy and their congregations with searching questions surrounding their own spiritual state. He would rail in particular against the Anti-Conventicle Act, passed in Norway in 1741, and would be imprisoned for doing so. Such acts were commonly used by a number of European governments of the period in an effort to halt the adverse effects that pietistic movements were perceived to be having on the state churches. The Anti-Conventicle Act ensured that the clergy of the Danish-Norwegian state church had preaching rights and the right to supervise private religious meetings.

Hauge travelled enormous distances on foot, setting up small Haugean cells wherever he went, and appointing elders to represent him in his absence. While many aspects of Haugean communities have been examined in the past, Amundsen sets about exploring a somewhat neglected aspect of the movement: its devotional culture. Three years before his death, Hauge would circulate a 'spiritual testament' that was drawn up to ensure that the movement would not depart from his ideals. Here, he outlines the devotional character of the movement and its tradition of reading, singing and praying. It also communicates the essential conservatism of Haugean ideals: members were to continue to predominantly use the Bible, works with biblical extracts and the catechism, and Hauge cautioned against the development of novel features. His followers would eventually be fully integrated into the Norwegian Lutheran Church.

Hauge was also the enthusiastic writer of a large collection of spiritual letters, which seem to have been accorded an authoritative status from early in the movement's history. Letters to Hauge from his followers and the responses to these were often included in later printed editions of Hauge's works. In an almost Pauline fashion, letters addressed to individuals were often copied and more widely distributed among believers as spiritually edifying works. Moreover, Amundsen shows how Hauge was to use his printed works as 'interactive' texts, responding to critics in subsequent editions. Hauge's achievements in this regard constitute one of the first examples of mass communication in Scandinavia, his output far outstripping the Moravian Brethren in its sheer volume. Haugeanism is a good example, then, of the manner in which revival Christianity, with its pietistic enthusiasm, could reinvigorate an established church.

In the case of mid-nineteenth-century Ireland and England, the so-called 'Devotional Revolution' exerted a profound influence on what was clearly not the established church – the Roman Catholic Church – albeit, in the case of England, one that had just had its hierarchy restored by Pope Pius IX on 29 September 1850. Emmet Larkin's seminal article in 1972 on the 'Devotional Revolution' posited the transformation of post-Famine Irish Catholicism from a faith centred on prayer in the home, pattern days to holy wells and local pilgrimage sites and the practice of a brand of folk religion largely untouched by the ideals of sixteenth- and seventeenth-century Catholic reform, to a more clerically controlled form of Catholic observance. With this came a new emphasis on regular attendance at Sunday Mass and the adoption of Rome-sponsored devotions such as the rosary, the forty hours, benediction, novenas and confraternities; all of which could be associated with the 'Cullenization' of Irish Catholic life under the eponymous Cardinal Paul Cullen, Rome's man in Ireland, through the years 1850 to 1878.

In the second contribution, Sheridan Gilley revisits the devotional world of this 'revolution', emphasizing both its complexity and its vitality, and concurring with recent conclusions that its genesis can be said to actually pre-date Cullen's arrival by some decades, its stirrings to be found perhaps as early as the episcopacy of Archbishop Troy of Dublin in the late eighteenth and early nineteenth century and his promotion of a number of confraternities and sodalities in the diocese. Furthermore, Gilley stresses the primacy of English devotional works in the literature of the 'revolution', suggesting that it should be viewed not merely a feature of the romanization of Ireland, but also of its anglicization. One of the classic devotional texts of the period was Bishop Richard Challoner's *Garden of the soul*, which continued to be widely used, albeit updated to include additional devotional exercises in later editions.

Gilley cautions that this devotional world should not be regarded simply as imposed from above, and clerically driven. Rather, he argues, many of these devotions became popular for precisely that reason – they were adopted by the people – lay men and women – who found them to be spiritually beneficial and accessed them in a variety of ways. Indeed, for the lay person, there was any number of ways in which one could hear Mass – the Redemptorist, George Stebbing, for instance, published a devotional work in 1913 outlining thirty different ways of doing so. Moreover, for obvious reasons it was the clergy's celebration of Mass which was, in fact, the most constricted. The advent of the modern liturgy in the 1960s would bring an end to much of this devotional world, and Gilley wonders whether, in its modern word-laden form, something valuable has been lost.

Brendan McConvery's essay on the shaping of Irish devotion from 1851 to 1965 traces the impact of the Redemptorist order and, in particular, its parish missions, on Irish popular religious culture. One of the decrees of the Synod of Thurles of 1850, in many respects the Devotional Revolution's ecclesiastical flagship, instructed that bishops were to have parish missions organized in their diocese in an effort to combat error. While the presence of parish missions in Ireland pre-dated the synod by less than a decade, their numbers would increase exponentially in subsequent years, conducted by a number of religious orders including the Vincentians, the Oblates, the Rosminians, the Passionists and the Redemptorists. These missions were often occasions of spectacular outpourings of faith, devotion and, indeed, repentance for sin, the queues for Confession sometimes taking more than a day to process. They would play a hugely significant role in the implementation of Cullen's efforts to re-sacramentalize the Irish. In later years, they would ally themselves to temperance campaigns, the most memorable examples being the 'poitín missions' of the Redemptorists, which often closed with the ritual burning of the equipment for the manufacture of this illicit spirit. In the early years of the Irish Free State, they would help to reconcile within communities neighbours who had found themselves on opposite sides during the Civil War.

Parish missions are perhaps most remembered, however, for their promotion of a lively faith and intense piety and, to assist the attendee in this regard, were enthusiastic purveyors of all manner of devotional objects aimed at helping the individual to continue in this vein after the mission departed. No one could attend a mission without encountering a number of religious goods stalls, which offered a wide variety of crucifixes, medals, scapulars and devotional and catechetical pamphlets. The supply of printed works to assist the devout layperson in hearing Mass or making visits to the Blessed Sacrament that became associated with parish missions further enabled the 'ordinary believer' to participate in the renewal of devotion promoted by Cullen and others. McConvery argues that this kind of 'devotionalism', which would be largely jettisoned in the years after Vatican II, filled a void in a period of theological poverty, which struggled to engage with modernity and, in doing so, fostered both a warm religious fervour and a sense of belonging for many.

In Sarah Fiona Maclaren's essay on Blessed Anna Maria Giannetti Taigi (1769–1837) and Blessed Elisabetta Canori Mora (1774–1825), we see how a particular model of female sainthood is identified by the Catholic Church as a powerful resource in the struggle against modernity. What marks these individuals apart is that neither was a nun; indeed both were wives and mothers. Theirs was a sainthood rooted in the chores of everyday life, which included the care of their respective husbands and children, although this did not preclude either from experiencing mystical revelations or exhibiting the gift of prophecy.

Maclaren situates the recognition of the reputation for sanctity of these individuals even within their own lifetimes in the context of the Catholic Church's efforts at *Christiana Restauratio* after the calamitous events of the late eighteenth century. This restoration would now be achieved by drawing on the strength of faith of the lower classes and, in particular, of women at a time when many of the so-called 'enlightened' elites had turned away from the Church. However, the portrayal of Taigi would change over time in accordance with the prevailing religio-political climate. For instance, during the reign of Pope Pius IX, her prophetic and political qualities would be emphasized over her motherly virtues: she is depicted as predicting the attacks on the Pope and the Church while also presaging the Church's future resurrection and its conquering of the forces of modernity. From the later nineteenth century, however, she will revert to being a model for young women who wish to lead virtuous lives while at the same time rearing their families and caring for their husbands.

In the final contribution to this volume's first section, Eli Heldaas Seland focuses on the phenomenon of Marian apparitions of the nineteenth century and, in particular, the religious medals associated with the burgeoning Marian cult. This essay closely examines the interplay between the images presented on the medals and the principal texts associated with the cults in question. In the case of the medal that would come to be titled 'Miraculous', the visual image, while reminiscent of *immaculata* iconography of the seventeenth and eighteenth centuries, nevertheless departs from this type in some details. Furthermore, a discrepancy between the image depicted and the account of the visionary, Catherine Labouré, of what she actually saw in the year 1830 (namely the Virgin holding a globe representing the world, and particularly France) suggests that what emerges in the material culture of the devotion constitutes something of a compromise (the medal, by contrast, depicts the Virgin with her open hands by her side from which rays of light stream). The image, it is argued, would play a significant role in preparing the ground for the proclamation of the dogma of the Immaculate Conception in 1854.

If Catherine Labouré's medal was used in advance to prepare the way for the proclamation of the Marian dogma, the apparition at Lourdes to Bernadette Soubirous and its associated cult would constitute a veritable celestial rubber-stamping of this development four years later: here, the Virgin identified herself as the 'Immaculate Conception'. The depiction of the figure of Bernadette kneeling before the apparition was also significant: here was a young, pious girl from a poor and unsophisticated background communicating with the Virgin Mary. The same Virgin had stated that she could not promise to make her happy in this life but in the next and, indeed, this visionary would experience much suffering before dying at a young age. Here, then, was someone with whom a majority of unsophisticated Catholics could identify; the favour visited upon this country girl was undoubtedly recognized by church authorities who came to see its potential to unmask the inadequacy of the rationalism and scepticism of the so-called 'enlightened' elites.

Part II

Peter De Mey and David J. Burn's contribution examines the *Via Crucis* of the Hungarian composer, Franz Liszt (1811–86), as a reflection of his own religious sentiments. This complex work was composed in 1878–9, quite late in Liszt's career, although never performed during his lifetime; it followed the death of a dear friend of the composer, Baron Antal Augusz. The composition of the *Via Crucis* expressed, in part, the deep sadness that Liszt experienced after this event. De Mey and Burn closely examine the composer's deep devotion to Christ's passion and the Way of the Cross in particular. In a close analysis of the piece, De Mey and Burn note how Liszt situates his composition within the timeless tradition of the Church, principally by introducing it with Venantius Fortunatus' *Vexilla Regis* with its traditional Gregorian melody. Yet he also employs newer techniques, as exemplified in what would later be termed 'tone-clusters', which he uses for the Fourth Station in which Jesus meets his Mother. Ultimately, De Mey and Burn agree that a purely stylistic analysis of Liszt's *Via Crucis* will always be inadequate, as it belongs to the realm of faith and can only be properly understood when its theological message is appreciated. To this end, De Mey and Burn situate Liszt's work within the broader devotional evolution of the Way of the Cross, which was greatly influenced by figures such as Leonardo da Porto Maurizio (1676–1751) and Alphonsus de Ligouri (1696–1787) in the eighteenth century and, indeed, Liszt's contemporary, John Henry Newman, in the nineteenth (1801–90).

In Georgios Kordis' essay on the painter Fotis Kontoglou (1895–1965), we move to the world of Orthodox Christianity and its tradition of iconography. Here we find an account of how the Byzantine style of iconography, which had been in dialogue with western naturalism since the fifteenth century, was, for a period of the nineteenth century, substituted by the naturalistic Nazarene style, which was now favoured by some Russian monks at Mount Athos and, indeed, by Otto, the new Bavarian king who came to rule Greece. Yet this would later provoke its own reaction. Kontoglou would become acquainted with traditional Byzantine painting on a visit to Mount Athos in 1923 and would begin to employ it in his own work, abandoning the Nazarene style. He would go on, in the post Second World War years, to spearhead a movement to restore traditional Byzantine artistic language in the face of much opposition.

It was, however, theology that Kontoglou would use as the most effective argument for reviving the Byzantine style: these icons, while not possessing the beauty of some Nazarene examples, nevertheless possessed a theological beauty which could not be matched in their expression of the truths and mysteries of the Christian faith. In this way, he would set their spiritual beauty over and against the fleshly concerns of western naturalism. His approach would, to a degree, be vindicated, and in 1963 he would meet with the first monk in Mount Athos to begin to paint in the Byzantine style in over a hundred years. Yet, it was also at a cost, for by too closely identifying the Byzantine style with theological content, artists would subsequently become far less willing to be creative, often slavishly copying earlier examples.

A different kind of revivalism is treated of by Henrik von Achen in his essay on nineteenth-century art and architecture. Medieval revivalism would join the wider struggle of religion with secular forces which so characterized the culture wars of that century in an effort to 're-enchant' a disenchanted world, exemplified best in A.W.N. Pugin's *Contrasts; or, A parallel between the noble edifices of the Middle Ages and corresponding buildings of the present day* of 1836. However, the forces of re-enchantment were much wider too: the promotion of new or revived devotions, the reinvigoration of lay piety in confraternities and sodalities, the wave of reported Marian apparitions giving rise to vigorous and influential cults that would ultimately exert international influence; and, within Protestantism, the ongoing phenomenon of religious revivals. Across denominational boundaries, the explosion of church-building in the nineteenth century is also worthy of note.

This movement was not without its critics, however; Max Weber, for instance, would intimate in the early twentieth century that medieval revivalism was a kind of antiquarianism, the pursuit of which allowed intellectuals to express nostalgia for the genuine faith they no longer possessed. The Liturgical Movement within Catholicism would likewise caution against visualized nostalgia and the resultant danger of petrification of forms and styles. In allowing for the spiritual and ideological conflict between the sacred and the secular, which characterized the period, von Achen nevertheless cautions against forgetting that most ordinary believers lived between these two worlds: it was, after all, the contribution of Pope Gregory XVI's 'infernal machines', trains and the railway systems, which would go on to open up many burgeoning sites of pilgrimage to the devoted masses. Likewise, the industrialized world of mass production would also ensure that millions of devotional items would reach their 're-enchanted' users in time for them, in turn, to pray for protection against this same secularized world! The dynamic between these 'two worlds', therefore, remains a fruitful subject that will require a great deal of further research.

Part III

The construction of the 'Other' by means of religious texts, emblems and iconography is the subject of the final three contributions of this collection. Peter McGrail begins the discussion with a treatment of hymn production among English Catholics and

Protestant communities across the 'long nineteenth century', which is understood here to reach the 1960s and the era of Vatican II. What both sets of hymns share is an effort to map out a particular account of English history and national identity: on the one hand, the elect nation which had successfully withstood papally sponsored attempts to overthrow the ideals of religious and political liberty, and on the other, the 'dowry of Mary' whose Catholics would always remain loyal to Rome in the face of the depredations of the Protestant reformers.

Events of the nineteenth century – especially the relaxation of the penal laws against Catholics and the restoration of the English Catholic hierarchy in 1850 – led to renewed fears among many Protestants, which would, in turn, influence the hymns used, adapted and newly composed. However, by and large, the sectarian nature of English Protestant hymnody would wane across the nineteenth century, becoming more devotional in tone under the influence of American evangelism. However, it was just at this point that Catholic hymnody actually began to draw the 'Other' in more clearly defined terms. Centred on similar events such as Catholic Emancipation and the restoration of the hierarchy, a degree of triumphalism now entered the type of Catholic hymn used: here was England being restored again after the rupture of the Reformation. Here too, contemporary English Catholics, steadfast to the last, could identify themselves with those who had given their lives in martyrdom in the sixteenth and seventeenth centuries. Those who, on the other hand, were considered to have rejected all that Catholicism held dear, were those 'wicked men' who blasphemed figures such as the Virgin Mary in John Wyse's well-known *I'll sing a hymn to Mary*.

The final two essays of the volume concern themselves with religious emblems that came to acquire political associations. Ewa Klekot addresses the topic of *detentebalas* or 'stop-bullets', which are also known as scapulars of the Sacred Heart, and which were used during the Spanish Civil War by the counter-Republican forces. These items, depicting the burning heart of Jesus surrounded by thorns, were accompanied by the words *Détente! El corazón de Jesús está conmigo!* ('Stop! The Heart of Jesus is with me!'). Klekot traces the history of the development of Sacred Heart iconography before examining its emergence as a protective talisman – from efforts to stave off plague in Marseilles in 1720 to the adoption of the Sacred Heart as a royalist symbol during the French Revolution. The Sacred Heart would subsequently take its place in some of the long-running struggles, religious and political, in France: between republic and monarchy, but also between Jansenists and Jesuits (the widely extended arms of the Sacred Heart image at Montmartre epitomizing a visual rejection of the Jansenists' preferred narrow road to salvation). Its monarchist associations would allow it to traverse the Pyrenees easily and play a significant role as a counter-Republican emblem in the Spanish Civil War, where it was enthusiastically adopted by Carlist forces in a struggle which was to exhibit many of the connotations of religious crusade, acts of consecration to the Sacred Heart being taken on the feast of St James the Moor-slayer. Devotion to the Sacred Heart had been criticized for its perceived anti-intellectualism in the nineteenth century; yet Pope Leo XIII expressed a wish that the Sacred Heart image would be regarded as a new 'Labarum' in the struggles against what by him and many others was regarded as the 'Other': the forces of modernity, both political and religious. We can see that many of the themes of this volume coalesce in this hugely popular image.

E. Frances King closes the volume with an essay that focuses on the use of religious emblems and their associations with cultural identity in Northern Ireland. Here, King argues for a greater degree of attention to be paid to the material culture of religion and its role in creating what she calls a 'visual apartheid' in Northern Ireland. This essay is based on an oral-based study that King conducted across different communities and which explored their associations with and reactions to a wide range of religious and devotional objects. The interviewees displayed a keen awareness of the religious objects of the 'Other' within their wider communities and how their own identities were partly shaped using these objects as points of reference.

King surveys the nineteenth-century development of what might be called an 'international style of Catholic art', epitomized in statues, prayer cards, rosaries and medals and widely available to purchase at religious goods shops and mission stalls, as outlined elsewhere in the volume by Brendan McConvery. This was paralleled within Protestantism in its mass-production of cheaper copies of the Bible throughout the nineteenth century and also the manufacture of religious texts and mottoes, which might be embellished and mounted for display in the home. After Partition in 1921, the differences in material religious culture came to matter a great deal in Northern Ireland and became markers of difference between religious communities. These objects, insignificant as some of them may seem, would actually become inextricably entangled with ethnicity, influencing both the public and the private lives of families and communities and becoming vital material links in the chain of religious memory. Just as Eli Heldaas Seland reminds us in her essay on religious medals, these items are of no little account, and are overlooked at the cultural historian's peril: even the least of these items, when viewed with care, can reveal layer upon layer of unspoken meaning.

This is the second volume of essays published by the European Network on the Instruments of Devotion (ENID) in recent years.[1]

---

1 Henning Laugerud and Laura Katrine Skinnebach (eds), *Instruments of devotion: the practices and objects of religious piety from the late Middle Ages to the 20th century* (Aarhus, 2007).

PART I

Devotional geographies

1 The devotion of the simple and pure: devotional culture in the Haugean movement in Norway, 1796–1840

ARNE BUGGE AMUNDSEN

When describing the formation of the nineteenth-century religious devotional culture in Norway, one of the most relevant points of departure is the dominant element of Norwegian pietism in the period – the so-called Haugean movement, named after the lay preacher Hans Nielsen Hauge (1771–1824). At the margins of Christian Europe, eighteenth- and nineteenth-century Norway was the scene of a successful and rapidly expanding pietist devotion, a devotion and a devotional culture more or less accepted as a national, self-explaining religious culture. At the very beginning of this historical and cultural process we find Hauge and the religious movement created by him and his associates. By following the footsteps of this movement, a subversive but also self-confident and egalitarian Norwegian religious culture can be traced.

Hauge was a peasant's son from Rolvsøy in Tune parish, a district some one hundred kilometres south-east of the present Norwegian capital, Oslo.[1] After what has been called his 'vocation' or 'conversion'[2] – an experience of deep ecstatic and super-natural character – on 6 April 1796, the 25-year-old man started his career as a wandering lay preacher, craftsman, merchant, author and publisher. His message comprised Puritan, pietist and spiritual ideals. Hauge's main perspective was that the 'hypocrites', the non-repentant sinners of all classes and occupations, would use services and sacraments as the means for guaranteeing their own salvation – which, according to Hauge, was a treasonous strategy leading them to eternal damnation.[3] His own ideal was a pure community of true and simple believers all over the country. Within this community, Christians would organize their own 'gatherings' or conventicles, in which they would share the word of God and give each other spiritual advice, sing hymns and speak about the future status of the individual believer.

---

[1] There are many more or less scholarly biographies and analyses of Hans Nielsen Hauge. Among the most important are: Anton Christian Bang, *Hans Nielsen Hauge og hans Samtid* (Christiania, 1874); H.G. Heggtveit, *Den norske Kirke i det nittende Aarhundrede*, I–II (Kristiania, 1905–20); Andreas Aarflot, *Norsk kirkehistorie*, II (Oslo, 1967); Andreas Aarflot, *Tro og lydighet. Hans Nielsen Hauges kristendomsforståelse* (Oslo, 1969); Andreas Aarflot, *Hans Nielsen Hauge. Liv og budskap* (Oslo, 1971). [2] The concepts have been given quotation marks due to the fact that there has been considerable debate as to the character and interpretation of what happened on this specific occasion, Arne Bugge Amundsen, '"En lidet forsøgt og mindre skriftlærd dreng": Hans Nielsen på Hauge' in Svein Aage Christoffersen and Trygve Wyller (eds), *Arv og utfordring. Menneske og samfunn i den kristne moraltradisjon* (Oslo, 1995); Arne Bugge Amundsen, 'Apokalyptikk på norsk – fra Draumkvedet til Hauge', *Humanist. Tidsskrift for livssynsdebatt*, 2–3:99 (Oslo, 1999) and Arne Bugge Amundsen, 'Hans Nielsen Hauge i dobbelt grep', *Humanist. Tidsskrift for livssynsdebatt*, 1:01 (Oslo, 2001). [3] Hauge is very explicit on this topic, especially in his early writings, for example, Hans Nielsen Hauge, 'Reflections on the miserable status of this world' ('Betragtning over verdens daarlighed', 1796) in Hans Ording (ed.), *Skrifter*, I–VIII (Oslo, 1947–54), I.

HAUGE'S TRAVELS AND OTHER ACTIVITIES, 1796–1824

Regarded as isolated phenomena, Hauge's message and ideals were neither original nor surprising in the late eighteenth century.[4] On the contrary, official theology, ecclesiastical laws and even members of the royal family in Denmark-Norway had supported moderate pietistic ideas and practices for decades. The idea of an official church life dominated by a majority of 'sleeping sinners' was a traditional topos in pietistic rhetoric, as was a critical position towards collective religious rituals and services, and attacks on the 'greedy and hypocritical clergy'.

What *was* original, however, was that these ideals were formulated, propagated and aggressively distributed in print by a commoner, a young peasant lacking all formal education and with no position in the civil or ecclesiastical hierarchy. When Hauge in 1796 set out as a wandering lay preacher to all parts of the country, opposing the sermons and ideals of the clergy, confronting members of congregations with intense questions about their spiritual status, and gathering sympathizers for separate and private meetings, then he not only provocatively attacked traditional authority, but also roused suspicions of a peasant riot.[5]

The authorities soon found laws under which to accuse him and to define his misdeeds. When he opposed the Anti-Conventicle Act of 1741, Hauge and his followers were accused of economic and social criminality; they were defined as vagrants and as such accused of criminal activities.[6] In addition, rumours began to spread concerning the illegal distribution of money and estates among the members of the 'holy community', the egalitarian community of the true believers.

Hauge's activities were indeed surprising, and not only in the eyes of the authorities. In 1796, he began his first mission in his own neighbourhood, a mission that soon expanded to the proximate districts. He also arranged for a first trip to Oslo in order to have his recently finished manuscripts printed there. In 1798, he visited the inland districts of southern Norway and travelled to Bergen, the most important commercial city in Norway. In 1799, he was arrested in the city of Trondheim and accused of vagrancy and of having violated the Anti-Conventicle Act.

After his release in 1800, he decided to go to Copenhagen, the Danish-Norwegian capital, where he hoped to present his case to the central authorities. On his return to Norway, he established a paper mill in Eker, close to the city of Drammen. This mill received its formal privilege in 1801 and soon became a Haugean ideal community based on religious, social and economic equality of all members.

---

4 Trygve Riiser Gundersen, "'Disse enfoldige ord": Hans Nielsen Hauges forfatterskap' in Egil Børre Johnsen and Trond Berg Eriksen (eds), *Norsk litteraturhistorie. Sakprosa fra 1750 til 1995*, I (Oslo, 1998).   5 In fact, such a riot had occurred not many years before Hans Nielsen Hauge arrived on the scene. Christian Jensen Lofthuus (1750–97) had been the leader of a peasant revolt, but he was arrested in 1787 and in 1792 sentenced to life imprisonment.   6 The Anti-Conventicle Act of 1741 was the result of a rather tumultuous period during the reign of King Christian VI (1730–46), when Pietists, Moravians and even Anabaptists propagated their ideals in Denmark and Norway. The act stated that private religious gatherings should be the object of the control and inspection of the Lutheran clergy.

1.1 The paper mill in Eker was established as a Haugean ideal community in 1801 (xylography by Johan Nordhagen).

In 1804, Hauge was arrested for the last time. After 1810, he was allowed to leave the prison for long periods of time, but the first judgment was not passed until December 1813. Hauge was then sentenced to two years imprisonment for having violated the Anti-Conventicle Act of 1741 and offending the ecclesiastical authorities. He appealed this decision and, on 23 December 1814, the final ruling was set as a fine of 1,000 riksdaler, a quite substantial amount of money at the time. The fine was paid by Hauge's sympathizers and friends.

Hauge's health was severely damaged during his stay in prison and he settled as a farmer in Aker outside Oslo during the last years of his life. He was no longer able to travel, but was visited by his many followers, and even by curious visitors and former critics. He also married twice and was the head of a small patriarchal household until the time of his death in 1824 at the age of 53.

THE DEVELOPMENT OF A MOVEMENT

These short biographical notes on Hans Nielsen Hauge relate to a much wider set of actions and actors. Ever since his first mission in 1796, Hauge had become the spiritual leader of a growing group of followers. A map covering his many travels in Norway and Denmark reveals overwhelming physical and mental activity. It has been estimated that Hauge travelled about 6,500km between 1796 and 1804, most often on foot.[7]

It was undoubtedly the growing number and expanding geographical distribution of his followers that in the end forced the authorities to act against Hauge; they had to cope with the fact that this lay preacher had created a movement, a more-or-less organized group of people who obeyed his words and followed his example. Small cells of Haugeans existed all over the country, repeating the words of their leader and propagating his message. It became known that Hauge himself in February of 1802 had officially appointed about thirty people – men and women – to represent his leadership in different parts of the country. This system of 'elders' was to become a very significant element of the Haugean movement, even in the years after his death in 1824.[8]

After 1824, however, the leadership within the movement became more diffuse and complex. The Haugeans had no formal definition of membership, while both local and regional leadership was based on quite informal structures and strategies. This makes describing the movement numerically or even qualitatively quite difficult. There were groups who regarded themselves as Haugeans who were not accepted as such by the majority of Hauge's followers.[9] And when the ideas of more formal religious organizations became accepted in Norway in the 1840s, the new organizations of so-called inner mission[10] or of missionary activities abroad only partly covered the groups of old Haugeans. For all intents and purposes, the Haugean movement dissolved around 1840, when most of the leaders who had once lived in close contact with Hans Nielsen Hauge had become too old to sustain authority or had died.[11]

HAUGE STUDIES – RELIGIOUS AND SECULAR

Most of the religious organizations established in nineteenth-century Norway nonetheless consider Hans Nielsen Hauge and the Haugean movement to be a very important part of their ideological and historical origin and development. This made what could be called the Haugean mythology a very prolific one at a quite early stage.[12]

---

7 His description of his many travels, published in 1816, still makes very interesting reading: H.N. Hauge in Hans Ording (ed.), VI, pp 1–93. 8 A. Aarflot, *Hans Nielsen Hauge. Liv og budskap*, p. 30. 9 Some of these groups are mentioned in Arne Bugge Amundsen, '"Mig Engelen tiltalte saa …": Folkelige visjoner som kulturell kommunikasjon' in Arne Bugge Amundsen and Anne Eriksen (eds), *Sæt ikke vantro i min overtroes stæd. Studier i folketro og folkelig religiøsitet. Festskrift til Ørnulf Hodne på 60–årsdagen 28. September 1995* (Oslo, 1995). 10 'Inner mission' relates to organized activities within the Lutheran church aiming at strengthening the religious belief and confession of its baptized members. 11 The Norwegian Foreign Mission Society was established in 1842. In that same year, the Norwegian parliament withdrew the Anti-Conventicle Act from 1741, and in 1845, passed the rather liberal Dissenter Act, which made it possible to leave the Lutheran state church of Norway on an individual basis and still remain a subject of the Norwegian state. 12 Arne Bugge Amundsen, '"The living must follow the dead": in search of "the religious person" in the nineteenth century', *Arv. Nordic Yearbook of Folklore*, 53 (1997), and '"The Haugean heritage": a symbol of national history' in Jens Braarvig and Thomas Krogh (eds), *In search of symbols: an explorative study* (Oslo, 1997).

More secular approaches to Hauge and his movement have also emerged, at least in the twentieth century. There have been attempts at interpreting Hauge as the leader of a peasant revolt that was quickly suppressed, but which continued to be an inspiring element in the liberation of the Norwegian peasant during the nineteenth century.[13] More recent studies, using Weberian theories of the relationship between Protestant ethics and capitalist standards, have seen Hauge and other prominent Haugean leaders as examples of the development of modern values and strategies in the economic and industrial fields.[14] Another very recent perspective involves a perception of Hauge and his movement as being part of the new public sphere of the late Enlightenment period in Norway.[15]

To investigate the devotional culture of the Haugean movement, however, is a rather new approach in Haugean research. Of course, questions concerning what made Hauge and the Haugeans different from traditional state church piety or of how the Haugean movement influenced the later devotional development of Norway have been part of earlier studies. But the Haugean devotion as such has only to a small degree been scrutinized. One obvious reason for this is that this was a religious movement of few traditional devotional instruments: they met in private homes, had no artists or craftsmen expressing their religious convictions, and they were highly sceptical about 'the outward' in all spheres of life – true piety was a question of the inner spirit. The defining characteristics of the Haugean devotion, therefore, need to be pursued along other lines of investigation.

DEVOTION ON THE EDGE OF LAW AND ORDER

To understand the devotional characteristics of the Haugean movement, it is important to take into consideration how Hauge and the Haugeans conceived of themselves as opponents to the devotion à la mode in upper class religion. They actively resisted changes in the religious literary and ritual fields that were initiated from above. To a certain extent, this opposition, from an early stage, developed into a question of law and order and of course of the political development of the absolutist state of Denmark-Norway. Thus, political discussions became a central part of the relationship between this religious movement and its social and cultural surroundings. In fact, the printed and unprinted reactions, reflections and discussions concerning how the civil and religious authorities should encounter this new movement were openly political: the issues addressed in these reflections and discussions related explicitly to the question of the basic organization of society.

---

13 Halvdan Koht, *Norsk bondereising. Fyrebuing til bondepolitikken* (Oslo, 1926). **14** See, for example, the different contributions in Svein Aage Christoffersen (ed.), *Hans Nielsen Hauge og det moderne Norge* (KULT's skriftserie, 48) (Oslo, 1996) and Inger Furseth, *People, faith and transition: a comparative study of social and religious movements in Norway, 1780s–1905* (Oslo, 1999). **15** Especially T.R. Gundersen, '"Disse enfoldige ord": Hans Nielsen Hauges forfatterskap' and Trygve Riiser Gundersen, *Om å ta Ordet. Retorikk og utsigelse i den unge Hans Nielsen Hauges forfatterskap* (Sakprosa 3) (Oslo, 2001).

The Haugean movement obviously confronted liberal voices with the limits of their tolerance – how far were the liberal politicians willing to go in questions concerning the freedom of belief? – while, on the other hand, it inspired politically radical minds to go even further in *their* critique of the absolutist establishment. Even conservative combatants used the Haugean movement as an argument in their fight against radicalism and tolerance; if the state did not accept the right of the Haugeans to exist and publicly argue their cause, why should the authorities tolerate all those 'free spirits' furiously attacking the king, the clergy and the Christian religion?[16]

But how did Hauge and the Haugeans reflect when confronted with such matters? Closely reading the historical sources, it is hard to find direct political arguments or reasoning in the first years of the Haugean movement. Hauge himself was mostly engaged by explicitly religious matters; he travelled and distributed his message in print and speech. Moreover, during all his years as a lay preacher, he insisted on his followers obeying the law and order set by the king.

As with all radical preachers, Hans Nielsen Hauge found a way out of the dilemma of secular obedience: the king's laws should be respected, but in instances where conflicts arose the true believer was expected to obey the heavenly Lord rather than the earthly king. In other words, Hauge advocated a relative obedience in religious matters.[17] On a more specific level, Hauge seems to have neglected (among other things) – more or less consciously – the so-called Anti-Conventicle Act from 1741, which gave the clergy of the Danish-Norwegian state church the privilege not only of preaching publicly, but also of controlling private religious meetings and collective religious activities.[18]

During Hauge's imprisonment between 1804 and 1814, his followers continued the building of the movement. Among the most important instruments of this continuous movement building was the use of lay preachers circulating between small cells of sympathizers all over the country. In this period, the conscious violation of the Anti-Conventicle Act from 1741 became a more central element, even among the Haugeans themselves: they obeyed the king and his laws, but this specific law was against the will of the Lord and should therefore be regarded as something constructed by the 'worldly' clergy.[19] Their own spiritual community was one with no other clergy than the Haugeans themselves. In their own view, this was not separatism but a concentration of spiritual power of high value for the whole society: if all members of society were like the Haugeans – dedicated, pious and egalitarian – Norway would face a prosperous future as a nation.

---

16 The discussions among the publicly critical officials and others are presented in Anja Brekkan, 'Ett religiøst syn. Én motstander. Opplysningsteologiens kritikk til Hans Nielsen Hauge' (MA, U Oslo, 1999) and Anders Lindbeck, 'Presteskapet sitt syn på Hans Nielsen Hauges religiøse vekkelse, i, 1804' (MA, U Bergen, 1999). **17** Arne Bugge Amundsen (ed.), *Norges religionshistorie* (Oslo, 2005), pp 314f. **18** Ibid., pp 300f. **19** Einar Molland, *Norges kirkehistorie i det 19. århundre*, I (Oslo, 1979), p. 95.

HAUGEANS AS POLITICIANS

In some parts of the country, the Haugeans socially seem to have represented the economic and social elite among the local peasants, experienced in religious and practical affairs, and hence trusted by the local communities. In social and economic respects, they were far from marginalized. What is even more interesting is the fact that the first generation of Haugeans was elected as political representatives in the first decades of the new Norwegian democratic system. A central concern for these Haugeans seems to have been to contradict any allegation of separatism or marginalization.[20]

In the same year as the final verdict fell on Hauge, Norway was given a rather liberal and democratic constitution. As a consequence of Denmark-Norway having been allied with France and as a result of the negotiations in Kiel in 1813, Norway was separated from Denmark and given as compensation to Sweden, which had lost Finland to Russia a few years earlier. The Kiel treaty was met with considerable resistance in Norway, and the Danish prince and governor in Norway, Christian Frederik, organized a Norwegian parliament during the spring of 1814. This riot parliament signed a separate Norwegian constitution on 17 May, and elected Christian Frederik as king. The Swedish authorities, of course, did not accept this, and after a short war in the autumn of 1814, King Christian Frederik resigned from his throne, and the parliament was forced to elect (recognize/acknowledge?) the Swedish king as Norwegian king.[21] Despite the Swedish occupation, Norway was allowed to keep its new constitution. In the new parliament (the so-called *Storting*), members from different parts of society were represented: military officers, civil servants, the clergy, urban citizens and peasants were elected according to their social position. After a few years, Haugeans became an important part of the peasant representatives in the Storting.[22]

A few years after their leader had been found guilty of having violated the law, the Haugeans found themselves to be a prominent part of the political establishment. In the debates at the Storting, the Haugean representatives met with many of their former oppressors or opponents.[23] First and foremost, the Haugean politicians concentrated on one specific issue: the withdrawal of the Anti-Conventicle Act of 1741. This strategy was mostly of a symbolic nature. The Haugeans wanted to remove the last sign of what they regarded as the religious oppression of the Norwegian state. During the 1830s, discussions and conflicts surrounding the Anti-Conventicle issue increasingly developed into a right–left controversy in the parliament, and in 1842 the Anti-Conventicle Act became history – the law was formally withdrawn by the king

20 Arne Bugge Amundsen, 'Haugeanism between liberalism and traditionalism in Norway, 1796–1845' in Jonathan Strom (ed.), *Pietism and community in Europe and North America, 1650–1850* (Leiden and Boston, 2010). **21** Ole Feldbæk, *Danmark-Norge, 1380–1814 4. Nærhed og adskillelse 1720–1814* (Oslo, 1998), pp 353–75. **22** Three members of the national assembly in 1814 were Haugeans, see H.G. Heggtveit, *Den norske Kirke i det nittende Aarhundrede*, II, pp 808ff. **23** E. Molland, *Norges kirkehistorie i det 19. århundre*, I, pp 170–5 and Åge Skullerud, *Bondeopposisjonen og religionsfriheten i 1840–årene* (Oslo, 1971).

and his government. The Haugeans celebrated what in their view was a tremendous victory.

The Haugean political strategy had been successful. To obtain this, the Haugean representatives had had to establish short-term alliances with different groups of liberal representatives. These liberals, however, continued their political crusade against what they regarded as generally oppressive regulations of religious activities. In their opinion, a modern state should not regulate the citizens' religiosity or lack of religiosity. Religion belonged to the private sphere, and any decent religious viewpoint and activity should be tolerated by the state.[24]

In 1845, the liberal majority of the Storting reached another victory: the Dissenter Act, which allowed any adult Norwegian citizen to leave the Lutheran state church without losing civil rights, was accepted by the king. During this political process, the Haugeans turned their backs on their former liberal allies and started a political campaign against any further liberalization of the legislation on religious matters. In 1845, they lost this fight, and, as it turned out, this also marked an end to a distinct Haugean group of parliamentary members. Within a few years, the Haugeans had left or lost their political positions. This took place parallel to the falling apart of the Haugean movement.

THE HAUGEAN IDEOLOGY

Haugean parliamentary activities in the first decades of the nineteenth century seem to have been dominated by ambivalent political strategies. Their representatives were consequently neither liberal nor decidedly conservative. The Haugean politicians were definitely not liberal in their more general views on religion and society; rather, they were traditionalists. Confronted with the possibility of the Lutheran state church not being the only reference of religious activities but being reduced to only one among many religious communities in Norway, they showed their close ideological ties to traditional rural values.

It is probably impossible to identify any Haugean political ideology as such; nevertheless, it is possible to identify some dominant features of Haugean political thinking. Firstly, the memory of their own recent history contributed heavily to the fact that they identified the struggle against the Anti-Conventicle Act as the most important measure of their political success. Secondly, the Haugeans felt obliged by the intention and wording in the so-called 'spiritual testament' of their own leader from 1821. The Lutheran state church was recognized as a suitable formal structure in so far as it was

---

24 These liberal politicians made a very relevant point: in 1814, the constitution fathers actually had decided that Norway should have total freedom of religion, and that no citizen should be forced to be a member of a Lutheran state church. No one could really explain why this paragraph had been omitted from the final version of the constitution: see Arne Bugge Amundsen & Henning Laugerud, *Norsk fritenkerhistorie, 1500–1850* (Oslo, 2001), pp 294ff.

upheld by a Christian monarch and did not interfere in the movement's spiritual matters. To accept total religious freedom would be to make way for free-thinking and non-Lutheran activities and this would be far from the intention of Hauge.

Following these lines of thought, the Haugeans had managed to establish themselves as a mainstream religious culture, accepted by the Norwegian state in their devotional separatism.

THE 1821 'SPIRITUAL TESTAMENT' OF HAUGE

Looking more closely into the matter, it is quite obvious that the first generations of Haugeans acknowledged as undisputable their leader's will. Until his death in 1824, Hauge was regarded as the dominant leader and patriarch of the movement. He sent letters to his followers, published further books for them to read and, not least, he was constantly worried about the future of his own movement. His health was quite poor after his ten years in prison, so on several occasions he expected to die. In 1821, he wrote and circulated his last will – his 'spiritual testament to his friends' – a document of nine pages.[25] In this testament, Hauge instructed his followers to be of one spirit in the future, to respect the leaders appointed by Hauge and not least to 'stay quiet'. His movement should not develop in any revolutionary directions after his own death. This seems to have been the political manifesto of the Haugeans elected for the Storting, but the 'spiritual testament' – also reveals a more thorough description of the devotional culture of the movement.[26]

The testament is introduced by the self-conscious formulation: 'May the Spirit of Grace and Sanctification which has followed me and has been received by you, still be with you and with all future believers in The Spirit and the Holy Word of the Lord.' This is an expression of the 'apostolic' position of the writer. He expresses himself as and obviously also identifies himself with the apostles of Jesus. This position is further developed by the statement on which writings Hauge's followers were to accept and use in their devotion: the Bible, books with extracts from the Bible and the Lutheran Catechism. For the future, the Haugeans were not allowed to recommend, write or publish new books without these being thoroughly and critically examined 'in the congregation by the elders'.[27]

Hans Nielsen Hauge believed his followers to be not only a 'movement', but a, or even *the*, Christian congregation. This is why not only does he order the 'elders' to continue but also why a central part in the testament is concerned with how to avoid schismatic and heretical deviations from the religious truth as presented by Hauge

---

25 H.N. Hauge in H. Ording (ed.), *Skrifter*, VIII, pp 241–9.   **26** The second 'edition' appeared in 1849 and the third in 1875: H.N. Hauge in H. Ording (ed.), *Skrifter*, VIII, pp 234f.   **27** In February of 1802, Hauge officially appointed about thirty people – men and women – to represent his leadership in different parts of the country. This system of 'elders' was to become a very significant element of the Haugean movement even in the years after Hauge's death in 1824, A. Aarflot, *Hans Nielsen Hauge. Liv og budskap*, p. 30.

during his lifetime. Any deviations should be handled by what he calls 'church disci-pline' – not by the ministers but by the 'elders'. Thus, the Haugeans would function as any other regular congregation. Also, as seen from the inside, Hauge wanted order and simplicity. To avoid any provocation there should be no more than two or three persons preaching the Word of God and admonishing the believers when the Haugeans gathered. On such occasions, the preachers should be appointed by decision of the 'elders' or by common agreement, and they should present their messages in due order.

In the various parts of his testament, Hauge also described devotional standards. His movement or congregation was a reading, praying and singing community dominated by mature and experienced spiritual leaders who controlled the message and the members. Nothing 'new' was allowed to develop, only repetitive manifesta-tions of 'the Spirit of Grace and Sanctification which has followed me and has been received by you'.[28]

Only after having described the structure, culture and devotional standards of the Haugeans[29] did Hauge turn to the relationship between his followers and the estab-lished Church. In the fifth paragraph he introduced this issue by declaring that 'we' have been permanently loyal to 'the Evangelical [religion] according to the right Confession of Augsburg or the religion of the state'.[30] Consequently, their opponents are mistaken if they regard them as a 'sect'. To counteract such allegations, Hauge suggested two possible strategies. The first strategy was to be known as 'the true pious sect' famous for the Christian deeds and beliefs of its members. The second strategy was to continuously respect the ministers of the state church. This strategy is formu-lated in a rather passive way: the Haugeans should 'receive' from the ministers anything that 'belonged to their public office', that is, to go to church, to marry in church, to be buried in the churchyard 'and everything else according to good order'.[31]

The passive expressions in the testament give no specific accreditation to the ministers or the 'religion of the state' as such. This is equivalent to the relative obedience to the king and public law and order advocated in the 'political' field of the Haugean movement. The clergy and the public church services should be respected – as far as this respect could be kept. The ministers did their job, and if they did not provoke or oppose the Haugeans there was no reason that the Haugeans should oppose them. But the services of the state church were only an empty framework for the true believers; their basic commitment was the spiritual friendship and the 'gatherings' of the movement.[32]

In Hauge's own writings, the 'ministry of all believers' is the main perspective, and besides the perspective of law and order he pays no attention to the 'special ministry'

28 H.N. Hauge in H. Ording (ed.), *Skrifter*, VIII, p. 241. **29** Hauge of course did not refer to his supporters as 'Haugeans'. The expressions used in the testament from 1821 – in addition to 'the congregation' – are 'friends' and 'fellow believers'. **30** H.N. Hauge in H. Ording (ed.), *Skrifter*, VIII, p. 243. **31** H.N. Hauge in H. Ording (ed.), *Skrifter*, VIII, pp 243f. **32** A.B. Amundsen (ed.), *Norges religionshistorie*, p. 316.

of the clergy. Furthermore, there are hardly any references to liturgy, church symbols or rituals in Hauge's message. On the contrary, in his testament from 1821 he describes his followers' identity in this way: 'As you all know, we definitely do not have any signs or ceremonies amongst us; our intimate community is based on personal communication, on deeds and partly on recommendations.'[33] The implications of this way of describing the cultural and devotional identity of the Haugeans are examined below.

HAUGEANISM AS STRATEGY OF SPIRITUAL EQUALITY

Our concern will be with the following fundamental problem: what was Hauge's message really about? This may seem like a simple or even trivial question, but the answer is not immediately clear. A message is, of course, not an isolated phenomenon but is closely related to both the messenger and the recipients. And since Hauge's message must be described as having been a noteworthy success, it seems obvious that what he said was something that could be accepted by many of those who received it. This acceptance affected them to the extent of changing their own behaviour and even, in many cases, of being willing to suffer persecution and to endure civil penalties as a consequence.

When reading Hauge's sermons and other printed material referring to his message, it is difficult to understand how they had such a radical effect on those who listened to him. His sermons are most often literal readings of verses from the Bible, while the main elements of many of his books are extracts from canonical works within traditional pietistic literature.[34]

Much of what Hauge preached and wrote must have been known and accepted by his listeners even before they encountered him and his message. He used the rhetoric and the formal phrases already well known from the conservative religious books distributed among the peasants at that time. Contemporary and educated observers regarded Hauge as old-fashioned and as a conservative traditionalist, and most of them were simply unable to understand how such a person was able to inspire his followers. The perspective of these observers was that of either the orthodox clergy or the enlightened authorities.[35]

If we alter our perspective and focus on how Hauge's actual followers described what happened when they met him, we receive quite a different impression – of a man and a message being able to 'move hearts and minds'. He was one of them, the son of a peasant; he dressed like them and had no formal authority. But Hauge was able to emphasize that the ideals and norms of Christian belief were far from the social and cultural realities of the day or what most people acknowledged as their own standards.

Although this was a conventional message, it seems to have been presented in a

---

33 H.N. Hauge in H. Ording (ed.), *Skrifter*, VIII, pp 245f.   **34** A. Aarflot, *Hans Nielsen Hauge. Liv og budskap*, pp 50f, 58ff.   **35** See n. 14.

manner dominated by equality and simplicity – it was a commoner, a peasant, an uneducated person who presented it to his equals. Hauge's communicative strategy had several elements, but one of them was that of filling the gap between the pulpit and the pew, to use David Clark's expression.[36] To the common people he met, Hauge would appear as one of them, not as an ordained minister with an official position in His Majesty's service instructing the commoners to follow ecclesiastical and civil law and order.

Upon arriving in a new location, Hauge usually attended church services. Afterwards, he approached both the vicar and those who had attended the service and asked them specific questions: what does this mean to you? Do you recognize the standards of Jesus in your own lives and minds? According to reports, most of the clergymen reacted with anger and fury upon being confronted with questions of this kind. Most of the congregation also routinely turned their backs on Hauge, but some stayed to listen to him. A common reaction among those who responded positively was to weep, to begin meditating on verses from the Bible or to begin struggling with the burden of their sinful lives. Proceeding from this dialogic strategy, Hauge gathered those who were 'moved' to listen to his more formal sermons and to take part in the singing of hymns and the recital of prayers.

Partly because of such experiences and partly based on his own biography as a spiritual person, Hauge showed a remarkable interest in what today would be called the psychology of religion. His most famous essay in this field was published in 1817 with the title 'On religious sentiments and their value' (Om religiøse følelser og deres værd).[37] Hauge was explicitly aware of the possible reactions to his message and personal behaviour, but at the same time he was eager to warn against 'religious feelings' in general. In his view, religious feelings were of little value without close connection to the standards of the biblical testimony: a true believer would only feel and experience according to the biblical norms. Only when supported by the Bible could psychological reactions to Hauge's sermons and writings be validated. But given this condition, Hauge was of the opinion that religious experiences would strengthen the believers in their daily fight against evil and oppression. His own spiritual biography was, in his own eyes, the most illustrative example in this respect. Accordingly, the main part of his essay from 1817 is his autobiography, which is supplemented by personal testimonies from eighteen of his own followers.

These testimonies demonstrated how individuals reacted both to Hauge's writings and sermons and to meeting him in person. It was above all a question of sharing the Word of God and thus establishing a spiritual equality. By the common reactions to Hauge's message, men, women and even children taking part in the conventicles would suddenly become 'brothers and sisters in Christ'. Local vicars were in principle

---

36 David Clark, *Between pulpit and pew: folk religion in a North Yorkshire fishing village* (Cambridge, 1982).
37 H.N. Hauge in H. Ording (ed.), *Skrifter*, VI, pp 103–217.

also invited to become part of this religious community, but only as an additional 'brother'; this, of course, was impossible for men whose descent and position could never have brought them to join the group of Hauge's followers.[38]

These different elements in Hauge's communicative strategy clearly indicate that it had a single and very simple aim: no listeners would ever remain unmoved by his message, but would be divided into two groups; friends and enemies – not only of Hauge, but of Christ himself. The division resulting from this strategy was a division between believers and unbelievers – just as described in the New Testament.

HAUGEANISM AS A STRATEGY OF INTERNALIZATION

Hans Nielsen Hauge's communicative strategy also placed pressure on traditional pietistic standards and ideals. He told his followers that they must internalize these ideals, and that they must both experience and indicate in practice that Christ was the real master of their lives. This internalization was, in other words, based on a definite concept of individuality: the individual was responsible for his own feelings and acts. It was not enough that he or she follow religious tradition or take part in collective action. Tradition and collectivity were the standards of the 'enemy'. But simple, trusting and repenting individuals who abandoned tradition and collectivity would experience a new religious body – the community of brothers and sisters.[39]

The balance between traditional statements and radical demands on the individual seems to have been the inner structure of Hauge's message. By using conventional statements and arguments in a new setting, he was able to create new arenas and new opportunities for action in a traditionalist peasant society in which the main setting for activity and moral control was the household.

This feat would, however, never have been possible by the use of verbal communication alone. Travelling through most of Norway over a period of more than eight years was impressive enough, but Hauge seldom remained in one location for any length of time. His close ties to cities like Bergen, Trondheim and, partly, Kristiansand and Copenhagen were exceptions to this rule. And even if he had stayed longer in the various places where his message had met with positive interest, the voice and speech of the master would have been difficult to preserve in the years that followed.

The key and solution to this problem was the deliberate use of written communication: printed and unprinted books, pamphlets and letters. I have touched upon several of these above. In what follows, the focus will be more precisely on Hauge's use of written communication as a cultural and devotional tool in building and sustaining a widely spread group of followers and supporters.

---

38 Not until the middle of the nineteenth century did young men from the Haugean culture take up theological studies in order to become State Church ministers.   **39** T.R. Gundersen, '"Disse enfoldige ord": Hans Nielsen Hauges forfatterskap', p. 237.

HAUGE AS A PUBLICIST

Hans Nielsen Hauge was the author of a large number of books and pamphlets.[40] In fact, he started writing his first two books in the weeks and months after his so-called conversion in 1796. He also succeeded in having them printed in Oslo and widely spread among and with the help of his growing number of followers.[41] The very first book appeared as early as the spring of 1796 under the title 'Reflections on the miserable status of this world' (*Betragtning over verdens daarlighed*). He added a short autobiographical text reflecting on the course of his life until his conversion on 5 April 1796. Hauge's next book, entitled 'An essay on the wisdom of God' (*Forsøg til en afhandling om Guds viisdom*), was published in September 1796. In these publications, Hauge was mostly concerned with describing how little 'the world' had to offer searching souls, but that a belief in God was the answer to all the troubles of distressed minds and bodies. Hauge placed his own personal experiences squarely in the centre of this spiritual universe. At the same time, he was forthright in his description of 'the world', which, in his terms, also comprised 'worldly' vicars and 'dead believers' who were not inspired by the true spirit of God.

Two years later, Hauge published two pamphlets: 'A true confession of salvation' (*En sandheds bekjendelse om saligheds sag*) and 'The teaching of the innocent and the strength of the weak' (*De enfoldiges lære og afmægtiges styrke*). These pamphlets are principally made up of Hauge's quite personal sermons; yet many contemporary readers and critics directed special notice to his very aggressive attacks on the Lutheran clergy. In these sections, Hauge continued his critical views found in the 1796 books, but presented them in an even more fluent and explicit way.

In subsequent years, Hauge wrote books in different categories of the Christian faith, such as a hymnal (1799), collections of aphorisms and rules for a Christian life, sermons (1800), a prayer book (1803) and an exposition of Martin Luther's Small Catechism (1804). The estimated number of copies of Hauge's books up to 1805 is approximately 200,000,[42] while the various publications written by Hauge cover about 2,000 pages in a modern edition.

In 1805, as a part of the legal actions against him, the civil authorities ordered that all books written by Hauge be confiscated and destroyed. This ruling remained in force until 1816 when Hauge once again was allowed to publish and distribute his writings. The titles and contents of these late writings shall not be commented on further in this essay, but there is no doubt that Hauge was Norway's most important publicist in the first decades of the nineteenth century. This fact does not refer to him primarily as an author accepted and read by the uneducated elite in contemporary society, but instead to the surprisingly large numbers of his books and pamphlets that were printed and distributed. His readers are not known to posterity to the same extent as the number of his books and editions, but his writings were probably

40 A full text-critical edition of his books is H.N. Hauge in H. Ording (ed.), *Skrifter*, I–VIII.   **41** A. Aarflot, *Hans Nielsen Hauge. Liv og budskap*, pp 235ff.   **42** A. Aarflot, *Hans Nielsen Hauge. Liv og budskap*, p. 32.

distributed among his sympathizers by wandering preachers and in the Haugeans' local 'gatherings'.

THE MASTER'S VOICE

This surprisingly high level of literary activity should be considered more closely. What was the reason for the obvious risks – both economic and legal – taken by Hauge and his followers in the years between 1796 and 1805? Both he and they had to raise considerable amounts of money in order to have all the books printed, bound and sent around the country. At an early stage it also became publicly known that the civil authorities regarded Hauge's books as being intimately related to his illegal activities as a wandering preacher, as the leader and motivator of suspect economic transactions, and as a revolutionary critic of the social order.

I believe that a very central and quite simple motive for Hauge and his followers was their eagerness to make these teachings known to as many as possible. Between 1796 and 1804, Hauge travelled more or less continuously, as did a small group of supporting preachers who were inspired and partly led by him. These preachers usually brought some of Hauge's books with them and left them behind as offprints of his message. All these books were obviously meant to be used in a practical, pious life: the sermons were to be read, the hymns to be sung, the exposition of the catechism to be studied and learned by heart.

This is, culturally speaking, a very important element in the use of Haugean literature. It was not just a question of producing 'books' in general, but of producing books meant to constitute the communal aspects and formalize the rituals of the new and holy community. The Haugean conventicles had a full-scale literary supply: sermons, hymnals and catechisms.[43]

There is, however, another motive lying deep in this strategy of writing and publishing among the Haugeans: having Hauge's followers read his printed messages made it possible to keep the group ideologically and practically integrated. They all read the same books in which the 'voice of the leader' could be found. Even if he was present physically for only a few days, or – at a later stage of his career – was prevented from communicating with his followers in other ways, his writings still meant that he could be heard and accepted as their inspirational leader.

HAUGE'S BOOKS AS COMMUNICATIVE INSTRUMENTS

In order to understand more precisely how Hans Nielsen Hauge's printed books were able to operate as communicative instruments, it is necessary to take a closer look at their specific contents.

---

43 T.R. Gundersen, '"Disse enfoldige ord": Hans Nielsen Hauges forfatterskap', p. 235.

1.2 There probably exists no contemporary portrait of Hans Nielsen Hauge. The sculptor
Thorsten Fladmoe used Hauge's son as a model for this portrait bust in the 1870s (xylography
by Johan Nordhagen).

In his first book, 'Reflections on the miserable status of this world', printed in the
spring of 1796, Hauge includes an autobiographic text. The first edition of the book
also reflects many other features which indicate that he had a primarily local reading
public in mind when he published it. He refers to 'what is commonly known in these
districts',[44] and he quotes from a letter which he had sent to the local vicar, the
scandalous Gerhard Seeberg[45] who, a few months earlier, had been forced to leave his
position on the basis of disobedience and unworthy behaviour. It was obviously
important for Hauge to keep his former patron at a distance. In addition to these
features, Hauge's first printed book included a religious song.

44 H.N. Hauge in H. Ording (ed.), *Skrifter*, I, p. 75.   **45** On Seeberg, see S.G. Eliassen, 'Gerhard Seeberg –
en prest og hans menighet' in Arne Bugge Amundsen (ed.), *Presten – lærer, kollega, lovbryter. Studier i Østfolds
prestehistorie på 1700– og 1800–tallet* (Sarpsborg, 1992).

In short, Hauge used the book in order to acquaint his neighbours and others living in the districts around his father's farm with what had actually happened to him and to make his position clear: he was *not* one of Gerhard Seeberg's fanatical followers, but had experienced and discovered something for himself. Hauge could later report that it was the autobiographical section of the book that had made the deepest impression on his readers.[46] Local references became less and less important to him, however. Consequently, the five new editions of the book, published between 1798 and 1804, must have had their major potential not in the implications of the local rumours about Hauge and Seeberg,[47] but in the autobiographical section. And Hauge used this book interactively. In the second edition (1798), he added some pages that were meant to show his critics that his message was consistent with the Holy Scripture.[48]

In his next book, 'An essay on the wisdom of God' (1796), Hauge published another song and again included several pages of direct comment to the critics of his first book.[49] In 'A true confession of salvation' (1798), Hauge continued the public narrative about himself. This book was written in his parents' home in Tune, and he explicitly refers to the fact of his recent arrest in Fredrikstad. He actually goes even further, by presenting his version of what had happened when the local civil and ecclesiastical authorities interfered with one of his conventicles and decided to arrest him. These authorities are mentioned by name and described as enemies of Hauge's good and righteous cause. He also publishes his letter of appeal concerning his release from prison – and by writing this book after he was freed, Hauge demonstrates that his cause *was* just and his enemies *were* wrong.[50]

Here also, Hauge alludes to a specific group of readers for the first time: he has established his group of 'brothers in Christ'.[51] In his second book from 1798, 'The teaching of the innocent and the strength of the weak', this is even more explicit. He once again refers to 'his brothers', and he asks them to pray for him: 'If God should permit my enemies to force me to leave you and depart to where I seldom or never will be able to see you physically, let our eyes of belief and our spiritual community in the love of Jesus Christ be so invincibly strong that we shall never be parted in this world – and let us be congregated in Heaven!'[52]

These examples from the early books by Hans Nielsen Hauge clearly indicate the very impressive personal and communicative element in his texts. His books were part of a communicative strategy embracing both specific readers and potential readers. Furthermore, several of the books constituted running commentaries on Hauge's own biography – his battles with his enemies and his hopes and victories as a preacher. In this way, Hauge's texts obviously 'construct' the individual reader. 'The reader', as an ideal identity, is implicated in both the form and the content of the texts. At the same time, Hauge's texts remain close to his and his readers' biographical realities: the

---

46 H.N. Hauge in H. Ording (ed.), *Skrifter*, I, pp 67, 71.   **47** The letter to Seeberg was, accordingly, omitted in later editions: H.N. Hauge in H. Ording (ed.), *Skrifter*, I, p. 267.   **48** H.N. Hauge in H. Ording (ed.), *Skrifter*, I, p. 72.   **49** Ibid., pp 233–7, 248f.   **50** Ibid., II, pp 33–7.   **51** Ibid., p. 52.   **52** Ibid., pp 57f, 82f.

'brothers and sisters' using the texts are real people as well as ideal individuals. Thus, Hauge's texts communicate with his readers and through his readers. They are bound to specific historical and biographical realities, but have at the same time a potential for exceeding the limits of these realities.

Another very important aspect of the Haugean movement was the writing that took place apart from the printing offices. In addition to being an author of printed works, Hauge was a devoted writer of letters. Throughout his entire career as a lay preacher, he wrote letters to individuals and to collective groups. This writing of letters was never a casual activity, and was not regarded as such by those who received them. Hauge's letters have been preserved due to the quite extraordinary reverence with which they were regarded in the preacher's lifetime and, especially, after his death in 1824. Several of his followers created small individual collections of letters, originals or copies, and kept them as spiritual legacies for the generations to come.

The scholarly edition of Hauge's letters appeared in four volumes between 1971 and 1976. The letters[53] cover the period between 1796, the year of Hauge's 'conversion', and 1824, the year in which he died. The four volumes contain a total of around 1,100 printed pages, 947 of which consist of the printed text of 511 Hauge letters.[54]

There are several very interesting links between Hauge's printed works and his letters. For instance, in his 'journal' entitled *The Basis of Christian Wisdom*, the first and second sections of which were published in Copenhagen in the autumn of 1800 and the third section in Kristiansand in 1804, Hauge printed several letters – some sent by him to his followers and others from his followers either to him or to each other. In addition, most of the eighteen testimonies by Haugeans printed in Hauge's 1817 essay on religious sentiments were from letters sent to Hauge. In this way, 'the Haugean letter' seems to have been given some authoritative formal standard at a quite early stage in the development of a devotional and cultural practice within the movement.

In the preface to *The Basis of Christian Wisdom*, dated Copenhagen, 5 September 1800, Hauge describes his motives for making these letters public.[55] By reading them, true believers should be even more enabled to punish evil and to do good. At the same time, the readers would better understand and realize the torments of contemporary Christians. Hauge's introduction to these letters gives a virtual impression of their being apostolic, with many references and allusions to New Testament letters. The first of them was originally written by Hauge himself in Bergen on 15 July 1799.[56] This

---

53 The term 'letter' is used somewhat freely in this edition; in some instances, the editor has also included printed material and some petitions to the civil authorities: Hans Nielsen Hauge in Ingolf Kvamen (ed.), *Brev*, I–IV (Oslo, 1971–6).   **54** A more detailed analysis of both Hauge's letters and the Haugean letters can be found in Arne Bugge Amundsen, 'Books, letters and communication: Hans Nielsen Hauge and the Haugean Movement in Norway, 1796–1840' in Arne Bugge Amundsen (ed.), *Revival and communication: studies in the history of Scandinavian revivals, 1700–2000* (Lund, 2007).   **55** H.N. Hauge in I. Kvamen (ed.), *Brev*, II, p. 165.   **56** Ibid., pp 189–92.

letter and those following it are given a very ambitious title; they are 'letters of faith, written in order to enlighten, comfort and convince the readers about the present condition, anxiety and oppression of the true believers'.

In the first letter, Hauge addresses his readers as 'beloved confessors of the Word of God'. He argues that a very important sign of the approaching last days of this world is the heavenly spirit's promise of enabling the believers to act as prophets – just as in the days of the Apostles. The true believers should therefore attempt to convince as many people as possible of the necessity of repentance and of leading a life in harmony with God's will. Regardless of the fact that God would send the spirit of truth to his children, their enemies were everywhere. At this point in the letter, Hauge begins to describe more specific events. He was occupied with printing and preaching in Bergen at this time, while some of his followers in and around Oslo had been imprisoned – merely because they had begun to talk to people after church services and admonish them about the true meaning of God's Word. According to Hauge, this must have happened without the consent of the just and godly king in Copenhagen and his godly laws. The ironic consequence of this injustice was that while decent, hard-working Christians were imprisoned and thus unable to maintain their own incomes by carrying on their normal businesses or by farming, the godless and lazy among the inhabitants of the city would now have to work to produce their own food.

INTERACTIVE HAUGEAN LETTERS

Letters written by Hauge's followers or sympathizers also circulated outside those printed in Hauge's own publications. The first generations of Haugeans started to compile collections of letters that had circulated among them. In the 1980s, the National Archives of Norway was able to distribute a preliminary version of the 'Haugean letters, 1760–1840' in which 815 letters make up 1,343 pages of transcripts. The letters refer to different periods, circumstances and needs within the groups of Haugeans. Important shifts of interest can be identified during, for instance, the period of Hauge's long imprisonment in Oslo, at the time of his release, and, not least, around the time of his death in 1824. What is even more interesting, however, is that these letters in many ways represent the reception of the letters from Hauge himself. In this collection, we find many of those letters that Hauge wrote, responded to or commented upon. This emphasizes the importance of the writing of these letters, especially in the first period of the Haugean movement, 1798–1804. The letters to and from Hauge and his followers might be said to fill the communicative vacuum between Hauge's personal contribution by means of the conventicles, his conversations and his sermons, and the distribution of his many books and pamphlets.

In part, the Haugean letters provide the contextual evidence of how the books were distributed around Norway and Denmark in order to preserve the spirit of their leader among the believers and to establish Hauge's reputation as a credible layman and preacher. The letters also seem to have accompanied the transport of money, books and goods between the different Haugean circles and societies.

A further important aspect of these letters is that they have 'transported' Hauge's and the other Haugean preachers' admonitions and advice to individuals and collectives. Few of the letters could be described as being private in a modern sense of the word. On the contrary, many of them are addressed collectively to and from 'friends' or 'brothers and sisters'. And even those letters which might at first glance appear to be addressed to individuals may have been copied and distributed within the group of believers as examples of good advice or relevant experiences.

Another aspect of Hauge's activity concerns the spreading of news through the letters. A feature of his own letters, but which is perhaps even more predominant in other Haugean material, is the spreading of information about the 'enemies' – all those persons, authorities and institutions who tried to obstruct and hinder the distribution of the Word of God. But the letters also carry messages concerning successes and victories – and of tragedies, such as of believers becoming 'cold' or of the death of central persons within the movement.

THE DEVOTION OF THE SIMPLE AND PURE

This essay comprises a brief overview of some central elements in the devotional culture of the Norwegian Hauge movement. As shown in the first part of this essay, the Haugean movement had a distinct 'political' element aimed at making its own religious culture legal, respectable and dominant within the Lutheran state church. This 'political' element should not be isolated from the development of the movement's devotional culture.

The Haugean devotion was at once both radical and traditionalist. It was 'a peasant devotion' in the respect that it was constructed on the basis of a peasant culture of farmers, households and rather simple social structures. It was also an 'anti-elite devotion' in the sense that it expressly opposed the devotion of the educated, modern and sophisticated urban elite, which was dominated by rationalist theology. Both the peasant and the anti-elite characteristics of the Haugean devotion were traditional. The most radical element of the movement was perhaps the 'anti-clerical strategy'. Important elements of this strategy were the political struggle against the Anti-Conventicle Act and the rather aggressive tone when the authority and message of the Lutheran clergy was commented on. These elements indicate that Haugeans both theoretically and practically favoured separatism and combined it with a radical reinterpretation of the basic elements of the Christian culture and devotion.

As seen from the interior perspective, the Haugean devotion in most ways duplicated or copied central elements in the Lutheran state church. A practicing Haugean was a reading, listening, singing and praying believer. But he or she had devotional instruments of his or her own: a master's voice in different media. And even if the

Haugeans following Hauge's testament from 1821 continued to visit church services and passively accept the authority of the clergy, this was not the inner circle of their religious practice. Their real church was the household, the religious and social community of every producing unit in pre-modern Norway. In this inner circle, according to Hauge's testament, 'we definitely do not have any signs or ceremonies amongst us; our intimate community is based on personal communication, on deeds and partly on recommendations'.[57]

A further radical element of the Haugean devotional culture was the communicative structures and strategies in this early Norwegian revival movement. This must be one of the first substantial examples of popular mass communication, at least in Scandinavia. Hauge and the Haugeans can, of course, be said to have had predecessors and these were primarily among the Moravians. But while the Moravians for the most part developed as an urban elite movement in eighteenth-century Scandinavia, the Norwegian Haugeans were definitely and culturally rooted in rural society and among common people, farmers and craftsmen. And we must not forget that the Moravians never attained the same level of mass communication as the Haugeans. To have published some 200,000 books and pamphlets between 1796 and 1804, and to have distributed them among a Norwegian population totalling about 900,000 people is in itself a remarkable achievement that most certainly should allow for the use of the epithet 'mass'.[58]

It does not take much imagination to understand that the Danish-Norwegian authorities regarded this movement as a new and threatening phenomenon: against good taste, enlightened religion, acceptable devotion and peace and order. In just a few years, Hans Nielsen Hauge and his followers managed to construct – from scratch – complex and well-functioning communicative lines and the structures between them.

These lines of communication were vital to the Haugean movement and to the development of its cultural and devotional identity. The members were 'not of this world', but were still 'in this world'. The establishment of a separate public sphere controlled by the Haugean leaders was an important move in this strategy: nothing was hidden or secret, but the ability to grasp the inner meaning of their communication was possible only among the true believers. This was 'devotion at the edge' – open, inclusive, readable, but only to the pure and simple.

57 H.N. Hauge in H. Ording (ed.), *Skrifter*, VIII, pp 245f.   **58** Some of the effects of this mass distribution have been investigated by Lars Ørstavik, '"Haugianismens sorte epidemi". Studier i Hauge-ovringa på Sunnmøre, 1799–1805' (MA, U Bergen, 1982) and Jostein Fet, *Lesande bønder. Litterær kultur i norske allmugesamfunn før 1840* (Oslo, 1995).

2 Devotions and the old rite

SHERIDAN GILLEY

Most Roman Catholics in the British Isles in the modern period have been of Irish birth or descent, and so I wish to begin with some reflections on the recent historiography of the Catholic Church in nineteenth-century Ireland. In 1972, the veteran historian of Irish Catholicism, Emmet Larkin, wrote an iconoclastic article in the *American Historical Review*, advancing *inter alia* two important ideas.[1] The first, which drew upon the then unpublished research of another scholar, David Miller,[2] was that the norm of religious practice for Ireland for most of the twentieth century, in which over 90 per cent of the Catholic population attended Mass every Sunday, was a comparatively modern phenomenon, and that as recently as the 1830s and 1840s, the percentage of Catholics who went to Mass every week had been much lower, perhaps as little as 30 per cent in much of northern and western Ireland, where parishes were large and priests were few. The more recent state of things had been partly the consequence of the Irish Famine of 1846–9, in which more than a million people had died and more than a million had emigrated, largely to North America. The Famine bore most lightly upon the prosperous middling farmer class in eastern Ireland which sent its sons and daughters into the Church; it bore most heavily upon the poorest, the rural labourers and smallholders or cottiers of Connaught and Ulster, among whom regular church attendance was weakest. Because of the Famine, there was a state of things in Ireland that was rare elsewhere in Europe: a still burgeoning population in 1840 entered upon more than a century of decline, converting a low ratio of priests and religious to an expanding population before 1840, into an improving ratio of clergy to a declining population after it.

Larkin's second principle was just as startling as the first, and this was the transformation of the character of Irish Catholicism itself, a point made in other ways by historians like Sean Connolly.[3] Irish Catholics were undoubtedly Catholics by conviction before the Famine, but they were Catholics of a particular kind. The religion of much of the Irish-speaking population was more based upon prayer in the home and upon such extra-ecclesiastical foci as holy wells and patterns or pilgrimages to ancient shrines in a sacred landscape, than upon the Mass and devotions in the chapel. Weddings and wakes were religious occasions, but could erupt into an indecency or violence beyond the reach of the clergy. At the Glendalough pilgrimage, on an ancient Irish holy site near Dublin, immense crowds assembled around tents

---

1 Emmet Larkin, 'The Devotional Revolution in Ireland, 1850–75', *American Historical Review*, 77:3 (June 1972), 625–52. 2 D.W. Miller, 'Irish Catholicism and the Great Famine', *Journal of Social History*, 9:1 (1975), 81–98.
3 S.J. Connolly, *Priests and people in pre-Famine Ireland, 1780–1845* (Dublin, 1982).

and booths: there was 'Dancing, drinking, thimble-rigging, prick-o'-the-loop, and other amusements', and the massed ranks of devout young and aged penitents walked their rounds saying their prayers, before the faction fighting between rival groups and villages began in the afternoon.[4] In short, bar a few broken heads, a good time was had by all. In the west especially, there was still the custom of 'stations', that is, Masses said in private houses, while popular folklore retained pre-Christian elements untouched by the Reformation or Counter-Reformation. The trauma of the Famine, however, showed that this folk magic did not work, and delivered the coup-de-grâce to the older native culture, as to the language which embodied it, and what then occurred was a 'Devotional Revolution' built around Sunday Mass attendance and centred upon ever more lavishly decorated shrine chapels under clerical control. David Miller has recently suggested that the cycle of occasional sacramental conformity common before the Famine fitted in with the seasonal patterns of, for example, the movements of herds between highland and lowland pastures; regular Sunday Mass attendance harmonized with the new weekly commercial rituals of the market town.[5] In a more directly historical explanation, Larkin especially associated the 'Devotional Revolution' with the long archiepiscopate at Armagh and then Dublin of the neo-ultramontane Paul Cardinal Cullen, Rome's man in Ireland, the first Irish cardinal, between 1850 and 1878, and with his imposition of a firmer ultramontane discipline on the Irish Church, and his exorcism of the elusive shadow of Irish Gallicanism.

Change there was, and perhaps the most dramatic aspect of Larkin's richly illustrated article was his descriptive account of the 'Devotional Revolution', drawing on practices that would be still familiar to any old-fashioned Catholic. 'The new devotions', he wrote, 'were mainly of Roman origin and included the rosary, forty hours, perpetual adoration, novenas, blessed altars, *Via Crucis*, benediction, vespers, devotion to the Sacred Heart and to the Immaculate Conception, jubilees, triduums, pilgrimages, shrines, processions and retreats. These devotional exercises, moreover, were organized in order to communalize and regularize practice under a spiritual director and included sodalities, confraternities such as the various purgatorian societies, the Society of St Vincent de Paul, and Peter's Pence as well as temperance and altar societies. These public exercises were also reinforced by the use of devotional tools and aids: beads, scapulars, missals, prayer books, catechisms, holy pictures and *Agnus Dei*, all blessed by priests who had recently acquired that privilege from Rome', while 'the whole world of the senses was explored in these devotional exercises, and especially in the Mass, through music, singing, candles, vestments and incense'.[6]

There are other elements to this argument. Improving standards of living and of popular education in the second half of the nineteenth century brought Ireland nearer to a Victorian moral and church-going norm, making the devotional life with its

---

4 See M.P. Carroll, *Irish pilgrimage: holy wells and popular Catholic devotion* (London, 1999), p. 115.   **5** D.W. Miller, 'Mass attendance in Ireland in 1834' in S.J. Brown and D.W. Miller (eds), *Piety and power in Ireland, 1760–1960: essays in honour of Emmet Larkin* (Belfast, 2000), pp 158–79.   **6** Larkin, 'Devotional Revolution', pp 644–5.

disciplines a vehicle of modernization. Gerard Connolly has argued that much of the Irish Famine influx into Britain, with its low standard of canonical practice, was an embarrassment to English Catholics, whose levels of practice were generally high.[7] But the new Anglo-Irish romanized religious culture could be transplanted to the urban slums of the Irish diaspora, in Britain as in North America and Australasia, where the new shrine church was the one holy place, with no surrounding ancient sacred landscape to sustain it. There was, of course, something of a similar 'Devotional Revolution' among Catholics in England, and as I am going to draw on English material, I would especially point out the Englishness of, for example, the new vernacular hymnody, in Ireland as well as England, preeminently the work of the English Oratorians, Frederick William Faber, Edward Caswall and John Henry Newman, which bore fruit in the Arundel, Westminster and Parish Hymnals in the twentieth century. In Ireland, English was the language of modernity and improvement, and of 'getting on', and the Irish 'Devotional Revolution' was a largely anglophone affair, reflecting the general indifference in the Irish Catholic Church to the dying culture and language of the Gael. Most Catholics in England were of Irish birth or descent, and popular Catholicism in the two islands developed on similar lines, encouraged by Cullen's English counterpart, the ultramontane Cardinal Wiseman, in a process in which the much smaller English Catholic Church played an important part.

Larkin's picture has been modified to show that the 'Devotional Revolution' was well and truly underway, at least among the better off, among English speakers in Ireland, and in the eastern and southern towns, especially in Dublin, among the farming communities of east Munster and south Leinster, and in the chapels of the religious orders, long before the advent of Cullen. Thus, as early as the era of Archbishop Troy, in Dublin, between 1786 and 1823, the Denmark Street Dominicans sponsored a Confraternity of the Holy Rosary, the Carmelites a Confraternity of the Scapular, and the Franciscan Sodalities of the Sacred Cord, while various convents were homes to Sodalities of the Sacred Heart. Elsewhere in the city, the rosary, Stations of the Cross and purgatorian societies flourished, and where they led, the rest of Ireland eventually followed.[8] Much of the church building in Ireland took place before 1840, expenditure afterwards consisting largely in the enrichment of existing structures with new shrines and sanctuaries. And again, as Desmond Keenan has emphasized,[9] Irish Catholicism had the particular advantage over its English counterpart, that while it had lost its cathedrals and parish churches to the Protestant Church of Ireland, it retained the full medieval hierarchy of twenty-two archbishops and bishops and its

7 Gerard Connolly, 'Irish and Catholic: myth or reality? Another sort of Irish and the renewal of the clerical profession among Catholics in England, 1791–1918' in Roger Swift and Sheridan Gilley (eds), *The Irish in the Victorian city* (London, 1985), pp 226–54. 8 Dáire Keogh, '"The pattern of the flock": John Thomas Troy, 1786–1823' in James Kelly and Dáire Keogh (eds), *History of the Catholic diocese of Dublin* (Dublin, 2000), p. 228. 9 Desmond Keenan, *The Catholic Church in nineteenth-century Ireland: a sociological study* (Dublin, 1983).

own parochial system, so that it was well placed to reassert itself by the mid-nineteenth century as the Church of the great majority of the Irish people.

Larkin points out the importance of prayer books in this 'Devotional Revolution', and here, as in hymnody, English devotional works were of primary importance, and the 'Devotional Revolution' was not so much the romanization of the Irish Church as part of the anglicization of Ireland. The extra-liturgical diet of English Catholicism centred, according to Mary Heimann, in her classic work on Victorian Catholic devotion, on the Rosary and Benediction, which held prominent places in the standard English devotional work, the eighteenth-century Bishop Richard Challoner's *Garden of the soul*, and these devotions, with vespers, remained central to Catholic life in both England and Ireland. As to the contents of *The garden of the soul*, there is an excellent summary of the book in its edition of 1755 by Heimann:

> The work opens with a summary of Christian doctrine, followed by 'a morning exercise' which includes the Lord's Prayer, Hail Mary, Apostles' Creed and Confiteor, as well as 'acts' of faith, hope and charity. Ten meditations of St Francis de Sales and instructions and devotions for hearing Mass are followed by various psalms; more acts of faith, hope, love and contrition are given, along with 'an universal prayer for all things necessary for salvation'. The Lord's Prayer is explicated and the Athanasian Creed given. Rubrics and prayers for 'Vespers' or Even-song are included, as are those for 'Complin' and 'Benediction of the Blessed Sacrament'. Evening prayers, complementing the 'morning exercise', incorporate an examination of conscience … further 'devotional flowers' … include the rosary, St Bernard's hymn 'Jesus, the only thought of thee …', Ave Maris Stella, various aspirations and ejaculations, 'affections', resolutions and meditations, instructions and devotions for confession, mental exercises to prepare for death, prayers for the dead, and litanies of Jesus and of Our Lady of Loreto. The manual … closes with the Jesus Psalter.[10]

Heimann points out that after 1850, *The garden of the soul* retained its popularity, and the greater part of it remained perfectly intact, even down to the original wording, not least the meditations on that 'most devotional of acts' of hearing Mass. Rather, the editions after 1850 add a good deal of extra material, including 'Stations of the Cross', 'Visits to the Blessed Sacrament', 'Devotions to the Sacred Heart' and prayers for the conversion of England. Heimann therefore downplays, to some degree, the effect of the Devotional Revolution in English Catholicism, pointing out the controversialist and thoroughly papistical character of Challoner's own outlook, in a manner which was not much behind that of the new nineteenth-century Ultramontanes themselves.

Something of the pattern of both change and continuity in the new prayer books

---

10 Mary Heimann, *Catholic devotion in Victorian England* (Oxford, 1975), p. 79.

occurs in a compact little English volume of a thousand pages, *The path to Heaven*, published by Burns and Oates in 1866, in London, with the imprimatur of Archbishop Manning, and the strong commendation of Archbishop Cullen. *The path to Heaven* opens with a summary of what every Christian must do and believe, and as in Challoner, there are extensive vernacular forms of morning and evening prayer; all the common Catholic prayers, like the *Salve Regina* and the *Memorare*, in English and Latin; and prayers for every worldly occasion. Then there are methods prescribed for hearing Mass, and prayers before and during Mass; no fewer than forty-four Litanies, beginning with the Litany of the saints, and including a few young Jesuit exotics like St Aloysius Gonzaga and St Stanislas Kotska; and Vespers, Compline and Benediction in Latin and English. The litanies are a study in themselves. Nine or ten of them bear the name of Jesus, and they are packed with solid theological reflection as well as preaching an ardent piety. Then follow various common canticles and hymns, like the *Magnificat, Te Deum* and *De Profundis*, in Latin and English; the Little Office of the Immaculate Conception; the Jesus Psalter, consisting of '150 invocations of the Name of Jesus, interspersed with verses in imitation of the psalms';[11] the common Latin hymns, also in metrical translation; then twelve sets of devotions, by months of the year, beginning with the Holy Child, Epiphany and Holy Name in January, each section including vernacular hymns; the *bona mors*; prayers to do with the seven sacraments, in the vernacular; meditations for every day of the month, in the vernacular; all the principal Epistles and Gospels in translation, for Sundays and festivals; and a hymnal with 293 hymns, mostly new, nearly all in the vernacular. There is a great deal of direct or incidental doctrinal instruction, touching on every aspect of the faith, from the metaphysical to the practical. The Mass is firmly placed in the context of a much wider daily round of prayer and devotion. Here, then, is God's plenty, and someone knowing little or no Latin had any amount of matter on which to feed his or her soul.

Challoner's *Garden of the soul* was popular in English-speaking Ireland, where the commonest native prayer book was *The key of Heaven; or, A manual of prayer*, with thirty-three Dublin editions by 1839. Much of it is centred on the Mass in relation to the Christian Year, on the rules of the Church for attending it and with prayers for before, during and after it, and with an explanation of its ornaments and ceremonies, including a disquisition on the colours of the seasons. There are common prayers for morning and evening in the vernacular, with the Angelus, the *Confiteor*, 'Devout prayers' for many occasions and states of life, some from the Holy Week liturgy, the litanies of the Holy Name of Jesus, of the Saints, of Loreto, of the Blessed Sacrament and Sacred Heart, reflecting the early advance of the Devotional Revolution, fifteen meditations on the passion, the Jesus Psalter, prayers for the dying and for the departed soul, and the rosaries of Jesus and the Blessed Virgin. I am not sure of the

---

11 The *New Catholic dictionary* (London, 1929), p. 507.

point, but there seems to be nothing specifically Irish: 'The Prayers of St Brigid ... To be said in honour of the sacred wounds of our blessed Saviour', are attributed to St Brigid of Sweden, not St Brigid of Kildare, though it should be stressed that in the Jesuit Diarmuid Ó Laoghaire's great collection of Gaelic prayers and blessings, no fewer than eighty-eight are concerned with serving at Mass.[12] In *The key of Heaven*, a few hymns and canticles like the *Salve Regina*, *Te Deum* and *Veni Sancte Spiritus* are given in translation. The Marian content is already high, though lower than in the edition of nearly half a century later: in 1884, *The key of Heaven: a manual of Catholic devotion*, now included the Ordinary of the Mass, Vespers and Benediction in Latin and English, 'Devotions for Mass in Union with the Blessed Virgin Mary', and the principal epistles and gospels in English. The prayers of St Brigid survive. There is a section of common Latin hymns, also in translation. With its Gothic decorations and capitals it is more obviously a prayer book for public use in church. This is quite a different volume, which is more directly liturgical, with less in the way of private prayer.

   Modern liturgists are accustomed to despise a great deal of this, but in fact this devotional world answers to the modern criteria of accessibility and comprehensibility. Above all, there is the solid historical fact, and this is my major point, that the radically improved rates of Mass attendance in Ireland by the end of the nineteenth century had complicated historical and social causes, but they were also the product of the 'Devotional Revolution'. In short, the Mass did not stand or fall by itself; it was part and parcel of a wider movement of prayer, and of other so-called extra-liturgical devotions. Together with the many devotional foci of statues and altars, they made the church a place of frequent public prayer; and it might be argued that it was when the whole devotional ethos and atmosphere which they fostered in the churches, the 'Catholic atmosphere', was abolished from the 1960s, that attendance at Mass itself began to go into decline. Of course, like the Devotional Revolution itself, the new secularism of the 1960s had complicated social causes; the trouble was that the Church abetted it by secularizing its sanctuaries. Many of the old devotions could be used in either Latin or English. They were, moreover, as much communal as individual, and it was here that I would stress the public and objective character of a great deal of this prayer, in the face of the sort of modern liturgical writing which despises it as privatized and individualist and emotive.

   In the older world, the leading role in collective public prayer often was taken by the members of confraternities and sodalities who seem to have formed the core or cadre of enthusiastic and fervent Mass-goers in many parishes. There was, in short, a sort of sliding scale among parishioners from ardour to indifference, or a set of concentric circles, from an inner one in which Catholicism meant a life centred on the

---

12 See *Ár bPaidreacha Dúchais: Cnuasach de Phaidreacha agus de Beannachtaí Ár Sinsear (Our native prayers: a collection of our ancestors prayers and blessings)* (Dublin, 1975). I am grateful for this information to Revd Gerard Deighan.

church, to one marked by the official minimum of practice, fading to an outer circle in which Catholicism was chiefly a badge of cultural identity, among people who might be reclaimed by a mission. In his study of Irish Catholicism in England, Steven Fielding has suggested that at a sensible guess, in the Catholic parishes of twentieth-century Manchester, 'the devout accounted for 5 per cent of Catholics, those who frequently attended to their devotions amounted to 35 per cent, those who infrequently did so, 40 per cent, whilst those who rarely if ever attended mass came to 20 per cent'.[13]

I am not sure what is meant by 'attended to their devotions', but Fielding usefully draws attention to the variety of religious practice among Catholics in England. The figures for practice were obviously higher for Ireland, and here I draw on a recent essay by Maurice Hartigan on religious practice in the diocese of Dublin. In 1931, the Society of St Vincent de Paul made 70,000 visits to Catholic households in Dublin, and found only one persistent non-attender.[14] Poor man, he must have felt lonely. The first half of the twentieth century was the golden age of the Irish laity. In 1928, there were 450,000 communions at the Jesuit Church of St Francis Xavier, Lower Gardiner Street, where the Workingmen's Sodality, founded in 1872, could claim nine hundred members in 1939. Other churches could boast nearly as many. At the Dominican Church, St Saviour's, the exclusively male Holy Name Sodality had 1,800 members by the 1920s, reaching 3,000 at its Golden Jubilee in 1934. The same Church had a Rosary Confraternity for women, the St Saviour's Chapter of Brothers, affiliated to the Dominican Third Order, the Imeldist Sodality for girls and the Angelic Warfare Sodality for boys. The Vincentian church of St Peter's, Phibsborough, operated the Archconfraternity of the Sacred Heart, founded in 1874, specifically designed to secure attendance at the sacrament, with 4,000 members in 1924. There were no fewer than forty sodality guilds for women, with thirty members each, in the 1950s, at the Carmelite church in Whitefriar Street. The Augustinians at St John's Lane, the Franciscans at Merchant's Quay, and the parishes of St Michan's and St James, had similarly strong lay followings.

One needs to multiply such memberships throughout Ireland. Between August 1927 and July 1928, the *Irish Messenger of the Sacred Heart* received the promise of 644,750 visits to the Blessed Sacrament. In this statistical list, promises of attendance at weekday Mass over the same period came third, after an undertaking to keep an hour of silence, at 379,670, and the reception of Holy Communion came eighth, at 197,025. Hartigan suggests on this basis that the Irish preferred to visit the Blessed Sacrament than to receive it, a plausible conclusion in the light of the seriousness with which reception was regarded, as requiring confession beforehand.[15] Yet even here, the statistics for the reception of communion are impressive, as in the 10,000

13 Steven Fielding, *Class and ethnicity: Irish Catholics in England, 1880–1939* (Buckingham, 1993), p. 55.
14 Maurice Hartigan, 'The religious life of the Catholic laity of Dublin, 1920–40' in James Kelly and Dáire Keogh (eds), *History of the Catholic diocese of Dublin* (Dublin, 2000), pp 331–48.   15 Ibid., p. 336.

communions during the missions in the Dublin pro-Cathedral in 1933. The Eucharistic Congress of 1932 appeared to show Dublin as the most practising Catholic city in the world. It seems to me that the pitch of piety attained with other cultuses – of St Brigid, at Killester, and to such local holy men as Matt Talbot, Fr Charles of Mount Argus, and the Jesuits John Sullivan and Willie Doyle – secured a level of ordinary religious practice hardly attained elsewhere, with the numbers of communions rising during and after the frequent parish missions and retreats, and with the strict policing of the Church's rules on weekly Mass attendance and annual confession and communion by the laity themselves.

Unfortunately Hartigan does not discuss the rules and books of guidance of the confraternities, and we need to know much more about these and their internal organization, and how far they operated independently of the clergy, under some kind of lay control. It would be useful to discover if they were more popular with women, and whether they supplied church choirs and the lay servants of the sanctuary as a semi-professional religious elite. Certainly these must have known their religion extremely well. Above all, the rules of the confraternities urged the frequent reception of communion, partly no doubt as a result of the background of Tridentine teaching, the powerful Jesuit influence, the clergy's pride in the statistics for overall communions, in the rivalry of parishes with one another, and in line with the decree on frequent communion by Pope St Pius X in 1905.

Then there is the issue of the cult of Mary, sometimes alleged to have superseded the Mass itself. The modern Marian revival has been studied largely in terms of the strong papal support that it received, especially from the time of Pope Pius IX's definition of the dogma of the Immaculate Conception in 1854. The doctrine was indeed the lynch-pin of his long pontificate of thirty-two years, the longest in the history of the Church, as the pope found in the figure of the perfect woman his succour and defence against the modern liberal heresies. The other two landmarks of his period of rule, the Syllabus of Errors of 1864 and the opening of the Vatican Council in 1869 were both dated by the feast, 8 December, on the tenth and fifteenth anniversaries of the proclamation of the dogma. Yet the pope appears, from another perspective, to have been only the most significant contributor to a much wider current of Marian piety, stimulated by the numerous appearances of the Virgin to child visionaries, most famously at Lourdes in 1858 and at Fatima in 1917. Marian devotion was encouraged from Rome, but Rome clearly did not create it, and even without papal patronage and approval, it would have happened anyway.

Did Marianism, however, outshine the Mass? Not so, I think, in England or Ireland. Irish devotion to Mary had always been strong.[16] But the expatriate Irish Catholics of New York were scandalized by the saint-based devotions of the equally expatriate Italians, who continued to practise a religion built upon the Madonnas of

---

16 See Peter O'Dwyer OCarm., *Mary: a history of devotion in Ireland* (Dublin, 1988).

their rival homeland villages. The only Marian appearance in Ireland, at Knock, combined the Blessed Virgin and St Joseph with the Mass through their appearance with the sacred host in the form of the *Agnus Dei* above an altar dedicated to the Sacred Heart, and with St John the Evangelist, the main New Testament origin of the Eucharistic teaching of the Church. The high point of Marian devotion in modern Ireland was between 1930 and 1960, beginning in 1930 with the creation of the shrine of Our Lady of Lourdes at Inchicore, by the Oblates of Mary Immaculate, which claimed to have received a million pilgrims during its first two years. The climax of Irish Marianism was the solemn dedication of the Irish Armed Services to the Queen of the Most Holy Rosary in 1951. It has been suggested that the intensity of Irish Marian devotion showed the inadequacy of the parish-based sacramental system to meet the growing hunger of the Irish for spiritual sustenance, with the claim that the cults of Lourdes and Fatima eclipsed the sacraments themselves. Take, however, one of the more significant expressions of modern Irish Marian piety, the Legion of Mary, founded in 1921 by Frank Duff, a Dublin member of the Society of St Vincent de Paul doing good works among the destitute, as in founding hostels for homeless men and women. Duff was inspired by the Marianism of St Louis-Marie Grignion de Montfort, and took the devotion of Mary into the Mass, but this, if possible, was designed to raise the level of Mass attendance, as it urged and implored all its members 'to assist frequently – every day if at all possible – at Mass, and at that Mass to receive Holy Communion',[17] and required daily Mass attendance and the daily reception of communion from its 'Praetorian' elite.

Indeed it could be said that the old rite was never so well-known as by the English-speaking laity in Ireland on the eve of its dissolution. Eamon Duffy has emphasized the accessibility of the medieval rite in an age of illiteracy. The Irish were now literate, and Mass was no longer a distant mystery to anyone who could read an English text and could afford a bilingual Missal, with Latin in one column and the English trans-lation in another. I am not sure when these became widely available, but the English translation of the Holy Week services into English goes back to *The compleat office of Holy Week* translated from a French version by two members of the Blount family in 1670, and I possess a copy of *The office of the Holy Week according to the Latin missal and breviary*, which is dated 1738, and had belonged to the Vaughan family of Courtfield, with all the services in English translation, in parallel columns with the Latin.[18] John Gother's *Instructions and devotions for hearing Mass* (1699) expressed a preference for accompanying the priest 'almost in all he says'[19] over the recitation of the Rosary and *'Particular devotions'*, though he reluctantly recognized that this was not possible for everyone, and he divided his methods of hearing Mass into three, the third and highest method involving the attendant following the priest in every word

---

17 *The official handbook of the Legion of Mary* (Dublin, 1962), p. 170. **18** *The office of the Holy Week according to the Latin missal and breviary* (London, 1738). **19** *Instructions and devotions for hearing Mass* (1699), p. 88.

and action. There appeared in 1708 *The vespers; or, Even-song: with the Holy Mass, in Latin and English together, with the antiphons hymns and prayers.* I have been unable to consult the British Library copy of *The Roman missal in Latin and English* (1737), said to have been destroyed by wartime bombing. *The Divine Office for the use of the laity: (The Mass for every day of the year, vespers and compline)* appeared in four volumes in 1763. This declares that the reader 'will find the *Mass* for every day in the year: *Vespers* and *Complin* for all *Doubles* and *Sundays*, with *Commemorations* of the *Semidoubles*, *Singles* and *Ferias*: The administration of the sacraments of *Baptism*, *Confirmation*, *Matrimony* and *Extreme Unction*: The *Visitation* of the *Sick*, the *Burial-service*, the *Office* for the *Dead*, the *Penitential Psalms*, the *Litany ec.*'[20] *The Roman missal for the use of the laity*, published by Keating, Brown and Keating, appeared in 1815.[21]

By 1800, the ordinary of the Mass, in parallel columns of Latin and English, was printed in editions of *The garden of the soul.* I own and used at Mass for a number of years, until it fell to pieces, F.C. Husenbeth's edition of *The missal for the use of the laity*,[22] with the proper and ordinary in Latin and English, for all the Sunday and Holy Week Masses, as well as the Sanctoral. The collects, epistles and gospels are in English only; the book was inscribed by the future Cardinal Wiseman. Ambrose Lisle Phillipps' *The Catholick Christian's complete manual* also contains a great deal of material from the Missal, including the propers, epistles and gospels in English, though it is less well arranged.[23] Such translations, like Dom Gaspar Lefebvre's *Saint Andrew Daily Missal*, became common in the twentieth century. Ecclesiastical authority in both kingdoms during more than two centuries seems to have given them every encouragement, in the interests of accessibility and intelligibility. This is a remarkable fact, given the high value placed on the very letter of the Latin text, and the (wholly unavailing) ban by the Sacred Congregation of Rites on translations of the Ordinary, 'renewed as late as 1857'.[24] For the true aficionado of the prayer of the Church, there was also the whole three-thousand page translation of the Roman Breviary by John, Third Marquess of Bute, though it seems that this was largely for use in religious communities needing to check the Latin.[25]

I have referred to Challoner's devotions for the Mass, suggesting that not all the pious simply said their Rosaries. My *Path to Heaven* of 1862 recommends that one profitable method of hearing or assisting at Mass 'is to follow the Priest in the Ordinary of the Mass as contained in the Missal; joining with him, as far as the laity may, in the very words of the service, and uniting our intention with him in what he does as Priest for the people'. *The path to Heaven* argues that the Ordinary and Canon

20 *The divine office for the use of the laity: (the Mass for every day of the year, vespers and compline)*, i (London, 1763), pp 6–7. 21 I have not seen this edition. See Dom Alcuin Reid OSB, *The organic development of the Liturgy* (Farnborough, 2004), p. 52, and p. 53 for other examples. 22 This contains a preface of January 1847, *imprimaturs* of 1848 and title pages of 1849 and 1850. Reid, *Organic development*, p. 53, dates the original edition to 1845. 23 Ambrose Lisle Phillipps, *The Catholick Christian's complete manual* (London, 1847). 24 Reid, *Organic development*, p. 52. 25 John, Marquess of Bute, *The Roman breviary* (2 vols, Edinburgh, 1889).

'have been made into almost all languages, and circulated by authority', but it requires a certain mastery of the book to get to the Mass in its separate parts. The *Path* also recommends that one can follow the Mass by 'not using or not confining ourselves to the words of the Ordinary', by reading the Scriptural Sentences supplied for each part, or by a sustained meditation on Our Lord's life or Passion.[26] One complete form of meditation on the Mass is by way of union with the Sacred Heart; another follows some lengthy prayers by Blessed Leonard of Port Maurice. There are special devotions given for use before Mass, at the time and after communion, as well as a particular set of 'Meditations for the Mass' for an intending communicant. Given the speed at which Low Masses were often said, there seems a good deal of printed prayer matter to get through as well as a need to keep one eye on the book and another on the priest, to know where one is, and this is a much more complicated method than just saying the Rosary. But it seems to me to be also a great deal more devout than the manner in which the Mass is often heard nowadays, and certainly the piety reflected is an affective one, ensuring that the liturgy was a prayerful experience and the congregation a devout one, with an overall mood which might be called Evangelical or Romantic, but which was also supplied with a great deal of doctrinal instruction as well.

Indeed, by the twentieth century, there was a flood of writing about the meaning of the Mass, from highly sophisticated works like those by Adrian Fortescue[27] or Maurice Zundel's *Splendour of the liturgy*[28] to the *Thirty ways of hearing Mass*, compiled by the Redemptorist George Stebbing.[29] In short, there was only one way for the clergy to say Mass; but excepting the well-drilled server, the laity at a Low Mass could hear it in any way they chose. In Cardinal Newman's words, 'There is the gentleman with his missal, the old woman with her beads, the pious handmaiden with her crucifix, the child with its pictures'.[30] Newman himself rejoiced in this diversity, reflecting on the variety of lay practice, 'This is a *popular* religion'.[31] The old Church wisely allowed for the variety of human nature and culture, and for varying degrees of enthusiasm and commitment. This means that the testimony of older Catholics is bound to be greatly varied, from 'I said my Rosary' to 'I belonged to a confraternity which went to communion together' to 'I was a server' to my favourite, 'like my father before me, I always carried the ombrellino on Maundy Thursday and Corpus Christi' to 'I just used occasionally to slip in at the back' with a welcome anonymity, now alas also unavailable.

This abundance also seems to have produced a certain permissiveness about how to hear Mass among some of the clergy, but there was also a movement against this. 'There are many methods of assisting properly at Mass', wrote Fr Tanquerey, adroitly facing both ways at once, in his *Doctrine and devotion*, translated from French in 1933.

26 *The path to Heaven* (1862), pp 71–2. **27** For example, Adrian Fortescue, *The ceremonies of the Roman rite described* (London, 1917). **28** Maurice Zundel, *Splendour of the liturgy* (London, 1941). **29** George Stebbing, *Thirty ways of hearing Mass* (London, 1913). **30** Cited in ibid., p. 14. **31** John Henry Newman, *Loss and gain: the story of a convert* (London, 1891), p. 426.

The one which yields the best results to the individual is evidently the best for him. But the method which is more in conformity with the spirit of the Church and which in itself is the most efficacious of all, is that of uniting with the Celebrant of the Mass by reciting devoutly at least some of the time-honoured prayers of the Missal.[32]

There were, no doubt, always those like Gother who held that this was the highest way, but there was also a tendency for apologists for the old rite to emphasize its accessibility and intelligibility, even for those without Latin. 'As for the people', wrote Bishop Hedley of Newport,

> [...] it is abundantly possible for them to understand and follow the Mass without either knowing Latin or possessing minute knowledge of the ceremonies. The Mass has broad features, which are easily brought within the comprehension of the least cultivated minds. It is easy to make the faithful realize what is the central point of the Mass – the consecration of our Lord's Body and Blood. It is easy to point out how certain actions lead up to this, and certain others follow it. The preparation or confession, the reading of prayers and of Holy Scripture, the bringing on and oblation of the Bread and Wine, the Preface, the Sanctus and the Canon – these features, with preliminary explanation, can easily be followed with or without a book. After the Consecration, there is no difficulty in recognizing the 'Our Father', the Agnus Dei, and the Communion. Every Catholic is carefully taught these things from childhood. ... the whole office and rite of the Mass is translated and explained in books of every degree of simplicity or elaborateness. There can be no question, therefore, that the most uninstructed Catholics may, and do, find it perfectly easy to follow the Mass with discernment and devotion.[33]

No one, as far as I know, has analyzed the kind of Mass-based meditations that existed before the Second Vatican Council in lavish overabundance, or what is just as important, their integration with other forms of devotion. There also seems to me to be no doubt that the growth of so-called extra-liturgical devotional societies was extraordinary, providing a solid core of ardent Mass-goers, at least some of whom practised their religion almost as lay religious. Of course, there were other forms of lay participation in the rite, by acolytes and servers, who knew the Mass extremely well, but also, in larger parishes with a *Missa Cantata* or even a High Mass, by choirs singing normally from the west gallery, and by the congregations at such Masses, who had to know at least when to cross themselves and to stand and sit and kneel. The flourishing

32 The Very Reverend Ad. Tanquerey SS, DD, *Doctrine and devotion* (Tournai, 1933), p. 209. **33** John Cuthbert Hedley, *The Holy Eucharist* (London, 1907), pp 201–2.

musical sub-culture, much encouraged in convents, appeared with startling rapidity: the Oratorian hymns seem to have spread almost as soon as they appeared in the 1850s, and appear in the *Crown of Jesus music*, edited by a teacher at Ushaw College, Henry Frederick Hemy, and published by Thomas Richardson and Son in 1864. This contains no fewer than twenty settings for Benediction and numerous settings for litanies, as well as a large vernacular hymnody.

The tendency of what writing there is about this subject stresses that the 'Devotional Revolution' marked the increasing control of religion by the clergy, but I can find nothing compulsory about so-called 'extra-liturgical devotion', unless one joined a confraternity to say one's prayers with other people, in which case they can hardly be called private. The Mass remained the one mandatory service for every Catholic, but no one, to my knowledge, apart from Mary Heimann, has suggested, in the manner of Eamon Duffy's analysis of late medieval religion,[34] that devotions spread not primarily because the pope or even prelates like Cardinal Cullen pushed them, as Larkin argued, but because in part for local and social as well as spiritual reasons, they were intrinsically popular with laymen and women who had control of them themselves.[35] A very good, if older, example is Benediction, in origin a late medieval lay copy of the monastic offices, at first centred not on the Sacrament but on the Virgin Mary.[36]

One last consideration is that belief needs practice to become ingrained. But what sort of practice? The Mass is primarily an action, not a form of words, with holy silences punctuated by bells. It seems to me a rather Protestant notion that one can only understand a thing by following a text. On the one hand, the blessed silences of the old rite, a silence so lamentably lacking in the new, reminds us that devotion is more than words, but is the heart's offering. Newman asserts that the gentleman following the priest's words in his Missal is in no way superior to the old Neapolitan crone who chatters to her crucifix, or to the French peasant who said of the sacrament, 'I look at him and he looks at me'. It has been argued, as in Antony Archer's Newcastle-based *The two Catholic churches: a study in oppression*,[37] that with the advent of the wordy modern liturgy, the working class Catholicism of pre-Vatican II, founded on actions, not words, simply faded away.

Yet words are important. To know a prayer, a collect, a litany by heart, with its associations of times of joy and gladness, and to repeat it in moments of sorrow or weariness or stress, is to find the consolation of the faith when it is felt most needed. Indeed this is possibly especially the case for largely unlettered people whose culture is

34 Eamon Duffy, *The stripping of the altars: traditional religion in England, c.1400–c.1580* (London, 1992).
35 Mary Heimann, 'Catholic revivalism in worship and devotion' in Sheridan Gilley and Brian Stanley (eds), *The Cambridge history of Christianity: world Christianities, c.1815–c.1914* (8 vols, Cambridge, 2006), viii, p. 83.
36 Herbert Thurston SJ, 'Benediction of the Blessed Sacrament', *Report of the nineteenth Eucharistic Congress, held at Westminster from 9th to 13 September 1908* (London, 1909), pp 452–64.   **37** Antony Archer, *The two Catholic churches: a study in oppression* (London, 1986).

more oral than written, and who relate more easily to the simple repetitions of a litany and to the rhythmic pattern of versicle and response than to anything more challeng-ingly literary or intellectual. It may be otherwise on the higher slopes of mystical experience, but at a lower altitude, if there is nothing in the mind but a void, without familiar images or well-known forms of words, the person praying may well pray in vain.

This world of the Devotional Revolution now seems as lost as the city of Lyonesse beneath the sea, though it was flourishing in the lifetime of many still living. It still awaits its Eamon Duffy to bring it back to life.

3 The Redemptorists and the shaping of Irish popular devotion, 1851–1965

BRENDAN McCONVERY

In his poem, 'The Redemptorist', Austin Clarke (1896–1974) describes a confessor terrifying a working-class woman by his refusal to grant her absolution on the grounds of her failure to comply fully with the Church's teaching on contraception. It is a bitter and trenchant criticism of an authoritarian, narrow kind of Catholicism that is ultimately destructive of the human spirit. As the poem develops, the Redemptorist of its title subtly takes on the trappings of other religious orders prominent in Ireland – the Jesuit in his castle at Rathfarnham, the bearded Capuchin, the Passionist with a badge on his habit or the Franciscan in his church, 'Adam and Eve's' (Dublin). In contemporary Ireland, 'Redemptorist' has sometimes been used as a shorthand term for a negative and repressive form of Catholicism. By Irish standards, however, the Redemptorists are comparative new-comers on the Irish religious scene. Unlike the friars, who have been in Ireland since the Middle Ages, their foundations were comparatively few. As preachers of parish missions throughout the country, however, they have had access beyond their numbers to ordinary parochial life for more than a century and a half. This essay attempts to outline how the members of this particular religious community have contributed to the shaping of Irish popular religious culture from their arrival in Ireland in 1851 until the period immediately following the Second Vatican Council.

THE REDEMPTORISTS AND PARISH MISSIONS IN IRELAND

Paul Cullen (1803–78) returned to Ireland as Archbishop of Armagh in 1849 after an absence of almost thirty years with a reforming agenda that was unveiled at the Synod of Thurles of 1850. Emmet Larkin has described the transformation of post-Famine Catholicism initiated by Cullen's reform as a 'Devotional Revolution'.[1] One of the synod's decrees, 'On avoiding dangers to the faith', instructed bishops to organize parish missions by the members of the Congregation of St Vincent de Paul, the Society of Jesus and others as a means of instructing the people in the faith and 'driving away the danger of error'.[2]

Parish missions as a strategy of evangelization and religious renewal can be traced to the work of Vincent de Paul (1581–1660), who founded the Congregation of the

---

1 E. Larkin, 'The Devotional Revolution, 1850–1875' in Emmet Larkin, *The historical dimension of Irish Catholicism* (Dublin, 1984), pp 57–91, though the precision of the term has been questioned.   2 *Decreta Synodi Plenariae Episcoporum Hiberniae apud Thurles habita Anno MDCCCL* (Dublin, 1851).

Mission to promote the re-evangelization of rural France. A mission was an extended time, usually lasting between two and four weeks, of preaching and instruction in the parish. Its purpose was to re-present to the people the 'Great Truths of Salvation' and to encourage them, through a renewed administration of the sacraments, to take their places once more in the mainstream of church life. During the next two centuries, the mission movement spread rapidly in Europe, especially in France and Italy. Due to the religious conditions, parish missions in Ireland did not begin until shortly after Catholic Emancipation. The first mission that we can date was given in Athy in 1842 by a group of young priests who had formed themselves into a society modelled on that of Vincent de Paul and which would eventually be incorporated into his Congregation of the Mission in 1847.[3] Cullen's strategy of using missions as an agent in Catholic renewal was assisted by the arrival in Ireland of several religious congregations specifically devoted to this work, such as the Fathers of Charity (Rosminians) in 1848, the Passionists (1849), the Redemptorists (1851) and the Oblates of Mary Immaculate (1856). These congregations, which had been founded in the eighteenth or early nineteenth century, were, to a degree, in 'expansionist mode'. Political upheaval in Europe following the 'year of revolutions' of 1848 made it expedient for them to find other places if they were to survive. The Oxford Movement of the 1840s and the conversion of such notable figures to Catholicism as John Henry Newman appeared to herald 'a second spring' for the Catholic Church in Britain and Ireland and these religious wanted to be part of it.

The impact of parish missions on Church life in mid-nineteenth-century Ireland was due to the convergence of a number of factors. The social and personal upheaval of the Famine and its aftermath had created a sense of desperation, leading to an increasing dependence on the consolations of religion. Mission preaching, with its dual emphasis on the precariousness of mortal life and the prospect of ultimate salvation, provided a map in which the stark 'Great Truths' of Christianity – the importance of salvation of the immortal soul, the danger of eternal loss in Hell, the great mercy of God for the repentant sinner, no matter how lost they might imagine themselves to be – became a horizon of meaning that enabled people to leave the horrendous suffering of the famine years behind. The emphasis on the day-to-day living of the Christian Gospel (observance of the commandments, daily prayer, the exercise of practical neighbourliness and the importance of virtues like sobriety and family values) may have enabled people to begin to construct a better life for themselves where older traditions had broken down. Missions were also spiritual and social events out of the ordinary, capable of unleashing a spiritual energy that lifted the spirits of people who had every reason to feel abandoned by the earthly powers. In the more remote parts of the country, especially in the west and south, parish missions

---

3 For an account of early Vincentian Missions, see James Murphy, 'The role of Vincentian parish missions in the "Irish Counter-Reformation" of the mid-nineteenth century', *Irish Historical Studies*, 24:94 (1984), 152–71.

were regarded either as crusades of rescue or as pre-emptive strikes in areas targeted by the Evangelical Mission Societies.[4] The Vincentians entered the fray in places like Dingle and Doon, where the Missionary Societies had established thriving colonies of converts, while the Italian Rosminian, Fr Luigi Gentili, led an extensive mission campaign throughout the diocese of Tuam between the years 1848 and 1854.[5]

Four Redemptorists preached their first mission in Limerick in 1851. They were a mixed group, comprising an Austrian, a Russian convert from Orthodoxy, a Belgian and a Scottish convert from Anglicanism. The extensive programme of missions led by the members of their Congregation in the latter half of the nineteenth century has been studied extensively by John Sharpe.[6] The 'Mission Chronicle', compiled anonymously by a member of the community, gives relatively detailed information on each mission.[7] Accustomed to the more regular church life of the European mainland, the early Redemptorists were surprised by the low levels of religious practice they encountered in Ireland. The chronicler of the Mallow mission of 1854, for example, observed that 'a remarkable number of young men and young girls between 15 and 22 or 25 years of age had not made their first communion'.[8] That same year, more than 1,000 adults were confirmed at the end of the mission in Athenry, Co. Galway. The report of the Dundalk Mission (1859), which is also a balance-sheet of almost a decade of experience of mission preaching in Ireland, noted that

> *On every mission* [emphasis in the original] people are met with of 50, 60, 70 years of age who have never received a sacrament except baptism, and perhaps marriage, and who are in excellent dispositions, shedding abundant tears when they hear they are deemed worthy to receive our dear Lord in the holy sacrament of the Eucharist.[9]

The missioner's day was a busy one. It began early, in urban areas generally about 5.30am or earlier, with Mass and a short instruction lasting half an hour. Depending on the size of the parish, other Masses were celebrated in the course of the morning,

---

4 On the work of evangelical missionary societies in Ireland, see Desmond Bowen, *Souperism: myth or reality? a study in souperism* (Cork, 1970) and *The Protestant crusade in Ireland* (Dublin, 1978); also Miriam Moffitt, *The Society for Irish Church Missions to the Roman Catholics, 1849–50* (Manchester, 2010); for a regional study, see idem, *Soupers and jumpers: the Protestant missions in Connemara* (Dublin, 2008).   **5** *Missions in Ireland by the Fathers of Charity, 1848–54* (Dublin, 1855).   **6** John Sharpe, *Reapers of the harvest: the Redemptorists in Great Britain and Ireland, 1843–1898* (Dublin, 1989), p. 21. For twentieth-century missions, see Brendan McConvery, 'Some aspects of Redemptorist Missions in the new Irish state (1920–1937)', *Spicelegium Historicum Congregationis Ss. Redemptoris*, 47 (1999), 105–25 and idem, 'Hell-fire and poitín: Redemptorist Missions in the Irish Free State, 1922–36', *History Ireland*, 8 (2000), 18–22.   **7** The first volume of the mission chronicle, 'Domestic and Apostolic Labours, vol. 1 (1851–68)', is in the Redemptorist Provincial Archives, Dublin. Each community kept its own chronicle and these are held in the domestic archives of the respective foundations, especially Mount St Alphonsus, Limerick, Dundalk (1876–), Clonard Monastery, Belfast (1898–), Esker, Co. Galway (1903–) and Marianella, Dublin (1912–).   **8** 'Mission in Mallow' in 'Domestic and Apostolic Labours', vol. 1, p. 9.   **9** 'Mission of Dundalk', ibid., pp 73–7, here p. 76, no. 9.

sometimes with a repetition of the morning instruction. The purpose of the morning instruction was didactic, to emphasize some aspect of the Christian life; preparation for the 'mission confession' was of particular importance in these instructions, and aspects of it would be covered over several days. Although every word was carefully prepared, the instruction was delivered in a relatively informal manner.

The evening service began about 7.00pm with the recitation of the Rosary, accompanied by a meditation or short instruction on one or other of the 'mysteries'. The main sermon lasted about one hour and the service concluded with Benediction of the Blessed Sacrament. The singing of hymns punctuated the different parts of the service. The focus of the 'Great Sermons', particularly in the early part of the mission, was on the 'Great Truths' – Sin, Conversion, Death, Judgment. In contrast to the informality of the morning instruction, the 'Great Sermon' was delivered with a display of dramatic oratory, designed to move the hearers emotionally. An observer of a mission in Carndonagh, Co. Donegal, noted that

> Every sentence, every word, nay, every gesture seemed destined to produce the most amazing effect. The big gushing tear and the loud sigh were followed by a universal outburst of feeling, and the vast assemblage was soon buried in a flood of tears as if mourning the death of some dear departed friend.[10]

Apart from a break of a few hours in the afternoon for a meal, the missioners spent much of the day, as well as several hours after the evening sermon, hearing confessions. The mission confession was frequently a 'general confession' or the review of the penitent's life since childhood. These might be terrifying ordeals for the penitent, but their number, rather than the attendance at the sermon, was the touchstone of the success of the missioner's labours. The chronicler of the Dundalk mission (mentioned earlier) observed that many penitents spent several nights in the church or at least somewhere near it, waiting their turn for confession and sometimes fasting for two or three days in order to be able to take communion as soon as they could. Many had no shoes, yet 'in the depths of winter amid rain, hail and snow, they come before the aurora (dawn) and remain the whole day barefooted on the cold damp floors of the village churches. The floors are sometimes of stone flags, but more generally of earth or clay'.[11]

By the end of the nineteenth century, Cullen's programme for a revitalized type of Irish Catholicism had been well and truly put in place, if rates of sacramental practice and devotional life are any measure, and a significant role in the process had been played by the parish mission movement. The missions had not outlived their usefulness, however, and proved adaptable in meeting new spiritual challenges.

---

10 Sharpe, *Reapers of the harvest*, p. 158, citing a report in *The Tablet*, 26 June 1858. 11 'Mission of Dundalk', in 'Domestic and Apostolic Labours, vol. 1', p. 76, no. 6.

Despite the success of Fr Theobald Mathew's temperance crusades in the decade preceding the Great Famine, alcoholism remained an intractable social problem and finding measures to curtail the manufacture and use, especially of illicitly distilled spirits, tried the resources of church and state. The bishops of the Tuam province, for instance, launched such a temperance campaign in 1909. The main arm proposed for taking the word to the people was a campaign of three-day missions throughout the west. Although unconvinced of the efficacy of short missions devoted to a single topic, the Redemptorists nevertheless preached eighty-three 'temperance missions' in the region in the course of 1909–10. Somewhat more successful, perhaps, were the Redemptorists' own 'poitín missions' some decades later in the same region. They targeted the manufacture of the illicit spirit as one element within the general renewal in the parish. Where poitín-making was rife, the mission closed with a dramatic public burning of the equipment for its manufacture.[12] In the troubled years following the War of Independence and the Civil War, missions, as religious events inviting all members of a parish community to a renewed participation in its life, served as instruments of reconciliation in communities that had been deeply divided, as well as reinforcing the rather austere moral and social life of the new republic.[13]

REDEMPTORIST MISSIONS AND POPULAR DEVOTION

While the message of the mission preaching was stark, if dramatic, it would be wrong to consider it in an exclusively negative light. A distinctive feature of the Redemptorist mission method, as developed by its Italian founder Alphonsus Liguori, was its emphasis on the *vita divota* or 'the exercises of the devout life'. Alphonsus believed that the best way of securing the continuing fruits of the mission was by moving the heart to the practice of a daily routine of prayer and devotion. Each week of the mission had a number of special celebrations – a celebration in honour of the Blessed Sacrament, the performance of the Way of the Cross, consecration of the parish to Mary, and finally, the planting of a 'Mission Cross' as a perpetual reminder of the event, together with the renewal of baptismal vows. All of these were intended to foster a warm spirit of devotion through the use of light, colour and communal hymn-singing in contrast to the austere preaching of the 'Great Truths'. While such practices eventually became the common currency of Irish devotional life, they were relatively unknown, especially in rural areas where churches were often poor and lacking even in basic furnishings and liturgical equipment. In Enniskillen, Co. Fermanagh, for example,

> The church was low and the altar small, with a torn picture above the altar. The church was dirty, and one could see here and there cobwebs. Our first task was to clean out the cobwebs and sweep the church … We covered the torn picture

---

12 McConvery, 'Hell-fire and poitín', pp 20–4.   **13** McConvery, 'Aspects of Redemptorist Missions', pp 124–5.

and replaced it with a picture of the Mother of God we had brought with us for the devotions and put the crucifix we had brought on the altar. The Catholic people looked extremely miserable, even pitiable.[14]

The church in Doe, Co. Donegal, was still more wretched, lacking even a tabernacle, not to speak of a monstrance for giving benediction. The missioners' appeals to the emotions of the congregation were not always taken in good part by the local clergy. During the ceremony in honour of the Blessed Sacrament in Kilkenny Cathedral, for instance, the rather volatile Russian, Fr Vladimir Petcherine, invited the congregation to respond to his invitation to repentance by 'crying aloud for mercy'. So enthusiastic was the response that the bishop, who was presiding at the celebration, ordered proceedings to be stopped and demanded that the people leave the church immediately. In their rush to comply, they stampeded, overturning and damaging several of the new benches the bishop had recently installed at great expense.[15]

MISSIONS AND PROMOTION OF DEVOTIONAL OBJECTS

The promotion of popular devotion included the propagation of the rosary, use of scapulars and medals, as well as religious images for use in the home. In the account of the Dundalk mission mentioned above, the anonymous chronicler observed that

> the people generally are very poor, yet they purchase on every mission from the Hawkers who follow the missioners everywhere, one, two, or sometimes even three hundred pounds worth of pious books, scapulars, rosaries, crosses, medals etc.[16]

Religious goods stalls continued to be a feature, especially of rural missions, well into the twentieth century. In his novel *Tarry Flynn*, Patrick Kavanagh recreates the carnival atmosphere of the mission in the Monaghan of his youth, with gaily coloured rosaries and other objects displayed in stalls tended by 'fantastic dealing-women with fluent tongues and a sense of freedom unknown in Dargan. They were Bohemians who had an easy manner with God – like poets or actresses'.[17]

A Redemptorist with more than forty years' experience of parish missions describes the mission-stallholders and their work:

> The mission stallholders were private traders. Their family tradition goes back probably as long as the missions themselves. They made a living from the

---

14 From the translation of the Irish portions of the extensive diary of Joseph Prost, first superior of the Redemptorists in Ireland published as *A Redemptorist Missionary in Ireland: 1851–1854. Memoir by Joseph Prost CSsR*, ed. Emmet Larkin and Hermann Freudenberger (Cork, 1998), p. 54. **15** Account of Kilkenny mission in 'Domestic and Apostolic Labours, vol. 1', pp 50–7. **16** Account of Dundalk Mission, ibid., p. 76, no. 8. **17** Patrick Kavanagh, *Tarry Flynn* (London, 1948), p. 33.

work, which was not easy, and there was often great rivalry between the various stallholders. They often intermarried too. While they imported a variety of religious goods from abroad, they also spent a lot of the wintertime making rosary beads by hand and framing pictures etc. for the next season. There were stallholders all over the country, among the best known in Munster of my day [1960s to present] were the Murphys and the Gormans from Nenagh, the Coffeys from Little William St, Cork, the Wards in the west of Ireland and Francie Gallagher from Donegal and McNally from Castleblaney. The life was hard and they often had to stay in very poor digs while the missioners 'dined sumptuously every day'. At the beginning of the Mission seasons, they contacted the various religious orders for a list of their missions. Then they had to get permission and good will from the parish priest to erect their stall in fairly close proximity to the church – a matter of great rivalry in olden days, when there might be seven or eight mission stalls angling for space. Some stallholders were double jobbing in the sense that in the summer months they would run little sweet stalls at the seaside and at village fairs. With the passage of time, the cost of transport and digs, together with children not following in the family business, led to most of them going to the wall. The survivors, like Francie Gallagher, tended to have several stalls to cover missions that were in progress simultaneously. They would employ local people to run the stall and they would give them a salary or a percentage of the takings. This did away with one of the core values of the mission stall 'apostolate'. I use the word very deliberately because stallholders who were approachable often acted as 'confessors' for many of the people who were making the mission. Parishioners who shared some of their problems and were often scared of going to confession would be advised by them to go to such and such a missioner.[18]

The image of the Blessed Virgin most commonly propagated by the Redemptorists was that of Our Lady of Perpetual Help (formerly known as 'Perpetual Succour'). Probably of fourteenth- or fifteenth-century Cretan origin, this icon had been venerated in the Church of St Matthew in Rome until the church and convent were destroyed during the Napoleonic occupation. Brought to the safety of the Augustinian convent of St Maria in Posterula, it remained relatively unknown until 1866 when it was entrusted to the care of the Redemptorists, whose new Roman church of St Alfonso was close to the former site of the convent of St Matthew. The first copy was brought to Ireland the following year and exposed for veneration in the Redemptorist church in Limerick. In handing over the icon to the Redemptorists, Pope Pius IX had reputedly remarked 'make her known to the world'. The picture soon became the centre-piece of Redemptorist mission preaching on Mary. It made its way into churches and homes throughout Ireland, becoming one of the most familiar images of

18 Private communication of Fr John J. Ó Ríordáin CSsR to the author.

Mary. During the Second World War, Fr Matthew Meighan, an American Redemptorist military chaplain, introduced the weekly devotions of the 'Perpetual novena' in the Redemptorist church in Clonard, Belfast. 'Perpetual novenas' to Mary under various titles had achieved a remarkably popular following in the United States of America during the period of the great depression and had been adopted by the American Redemptorists in honour of Our Lady of Perpetual Help. From Belfast, the devotion spread first to other Redemptorist churches as well as many others.

The advent of 'evening Mass' after Vatican II led to a decline of popular non-liturgical devotions, including weekly novenas. By the 1970s, however, it had been transformed into an annual 'Solemn Novena', celebrated over nine continuous days. If parish missions have declined quite considerably in recent decades, the annual novena continues to attract considerable crowds several times daily during its celebration in Redemptorist churches and, notably, also in Galway Cathedral.

Following the canonization of the Redemptorist St Gerard Majella in 1903, the Redemptorists promoted devotion to him as patron of pregnant women and their babies, and especially on missions, as 'patron of a good confession'. Statues and pictures of St Gerard, along with prayer cards and novena booklets were commonly on sale in repositories and mission stalls. The extent of devotion to this eighteenth-century Italian saint can be gauged by the number of Irish people of an earlier generation who are called by one or other form of his name; for example, Gerard, Gerardine, Majella.[19]

PRINT CULTURE AND THE MISSIONS

In addition to being an important figure in the development of Catholic moral theology in the eighteenth century, Alphonsus Liguori was a writer of numerous popular devotional and ascetical works. His prayers for the exercise of the Way of the Cross, for instance, became the standard form of this devotion and were frequently reprinted in manuals of popular devotion, while his *Visits to the Blessed Sacrament* ran through many hundreds of editions in all the major languages. The appearance of his works in Ireland preceded the coming of the Redemptorists by some years. Several were translated by Nicholas Callan, Professor of Natural Philosophy at St Patrick's College, Maynooth, a priest-scientist and pioneer in the development of electricity.[20] Callan's editions in the 1840s were published anonymously under the imprint of James Duffy of Dublin as the work of 'a Catholic clergyman' and sold at a nominal cost. The first translation into Irish of a work of Alphonsus was by John McHale, Archbishop of Tuam, who translated the Way of the Cross in 1854.[21]

It was inevitable that the Redemptorists would propagate the writings of their

---

19 See Eamon Duffy, *Faith of our fathers: reflection on Catholic tradition* (London, 2004) on devotion to St Gerard in his home town of Dundalk, pp 11, 22.   **20** P.J. Corish, *Maynooth College, 1795–1995* (Dublin, 1995), p. 445.
21 *Toras na Croiche* (Dublin, 1873).

founder. The *Visits to the Blessed Sacrament* (first English translation published in Manchester in 1831) went through fifteen editions in Britain and Ireland in the course of the nineteenth century alone, including those edited by the Redemptorists Robert A. Coffin (London, 1855), John Magnier (Dublin, 1908) and John Baptist Coyle (Dublin, 1925).[22] The first version in Irish was published in 1906, followed by another in 1933. During his brief emotional flirtation with religion as recorded in *The portrait of the artist as a young man*, James Joyce records how he was enchanted by the romantic imagery of the book which he used for his daily devotions. Alphonsus' major work on the Blessed Virgin, *The glories of Mary*, appeared in several editions, beginning with that of R.A. Coffin in 1868: it too was translated into Irish by Conn Ó Mongain CSsR as *An mhaighdean ghlórmhar* (1936).

Like their founder, later generations of Redemptorists appreciated the importance of devotional literature for the consolidation of the work of the mission. The Austrian Redemptorists produced *Unterichts und Andachtsbuch* ('Book of instructions and devotions') in 1826. Translations were subsequently published in Belgium, Holland, France, North America (1851), Britain (1852) and Ireland (1857, 1891, 1916).[23] The 'Mission Book' was at once a book of instruction and a prayer book. In addition to daily prayers and devotions for confession and Holy Communion, the first part contained private devotions to be read during Mass, taken for the most part from the writings of Alphonsus. The second part was a treasury of less familiar prayers and litanies, including Alphonsus' devotions for the Way of the Cross. The instructions contained in the third part were a virtual summary of the Christian life – treating such subjects as general confession, the sacrament of marriage, advice on courtship, the duties of young Christians, how to assist the sick and the dying, and a summary of Alphonsus' classic teaching on prayer as the great means of salvation. The final part included Latin texts for Sung Mass, vespers and compline for Sunday and the more common Latin hymns and litanies.

While the first American edition was heavily dependent on the German, it included a selection of English hymns to be sung during missions. Catholic hymns in English were relatively scarce in the nineteenth century. One which first appeared here was 'Holy God, we praise thy name', a translation by Fr Clarence Walworth (1820–1900), of a German popular version of the *Te Deum* he had first heard sung by his Austrian fellow-novices while making his noviciate in Saint Trond in Belgium.[24] It remains one of the best-known Catholic hymns in English.

22 Statistics from Maurice de Meulemeester, *Bibliographie générale des Ecrivains Rédemptoristes*, i (Louvain, 1933), p. 223.   **23** The editions I have been able to consult include *The Mission Book: instructions and prayers to preserve the fruits of the mission*, drawn chiefly from the *Writings of St Alphonsus Maria de Liguori, new and revised edition* (Dublin, 1891); (new and rev. 12th ed., Dublin, 1916); *Missionsbuchlein fur Junglinge und Jungfrauen. Ein Unterrichs- und Andachtsbuch als bestandige Hausmission* (15th Auflage, Munich, 1909); *The new Mission Book of the Redemptorist Fathers* by Very Revd F. Girardey CSsR (St Louis, MI, 1911; repr. 1928); *Le Souvenir de la Mission ou le Salut Assuré aux âmes de bonnes volontés d'après St Alphonse à l'usage des personnes du monde qui veulent assuré leur salut*, ed. J.-M. Blancpied (Lyon and St-Etienne, 1913).   **24** Fr Walworth left the Redemptorists in 1858

The editor of the 1911 American edition describes its function succinctly:

> The New Mission Book is, in the first place, a Prayer Book. Secondly, it is
> Manual of Instruction. And finally, *it acts the part of a Missionary* [italics added].
> It continues the work of the Mission, calls to mind the truths preached therein
> and points out the means of perseverance. The Mission Book should be
> frequently read and seriously meditated. In this way, it will produce the fruits of
> salvation and encourage all to keep the resolutions made during the mission.[25]

It is difficult to say how widely the *Redemptorist Mission Book* was disseminated among
the laity in Ireland. Its cost and size probably restricted its popularity.

A more common substitute was the 'mission remembrance' distributed free to all
who took part. This was a simple prayer card, measuring about 12cm by 8cm, folded
in two. The front cover incorporated an image of the crucifixion, along with the date
and place of the mission. The contents were unchanging and contained a summary of
the message of the mission, as in the following example:

> Remember, dear Christian that you have but one soul to save, one God to love
> and serve, one eternity to expect. Death will come soon, judgment will follow,
> and then Heaven or Hell for ever! Therefore, O Child of Jesus and Mary, keep
> the good resolutions of the Mission. Avoid sin and all dangerous occasions of
> sin. Pray without ceasing. Go frequently to Confession and Holy Communion.
> Be faithful to the Christian practices which have been recommended to you
> during the Mission.[26]

There was also a short set of prayers for morning and evening use, including the
following: 'When in bed, fold your arms in the form of a cross and say: I must die –
I do not know when – nor how – nor where. But if I die in mortal sin – I am lost for
ever. O Jesus have mercy upon me.'[27] Although other prayer books edited by
Redemptorists imitated the mission book genre (for example, *Mission keepsake:
devotions and prayers taken chiefly from the writings of St Alphonsus*, compiled by Francis
McNamara CSsR, Dublin, 1932) or the still more modest *Redemptorist hymn book and
prayers* (Dublin, 1946), a mere thirty-six small pages in length, the last and most
successful examples of the type appeared in the 1950s.[28] They were the work of Fr Leo
O'Halloran, a native of Hospital, Co. Limerick, and a veteran of the Irish
Redemptorist mission in India and Ceylon (now Sri Lanka). The first in the series,
Prayer book for men, appeared in 1952, reaching its fortieth edition in 1959. The

along with Fr Isaac Hecker to form the community of the Paulist Fathers. **25** *New Redemptorist Mission Book*
(Baltimore, 1911), p. 2. **26** 'Remembrance of the Mission preached by Redemptorist Fathers at Ballinabrackey
Church, September 1888'. Box N: Early Home Missions. Redemptorist Provincial Archives, Dublin. **27** Ibid.
28 For example, *Manual of Our Lady of Perpetual Succour* (London, 1944).

following year saw the appearance of *Prayer book for boys*, which reached its nineteenth edition by 1959. Marginally less successful were the *Prayer book for girls* (1956) and one for women (1957).[29] The success of these books is probably due to their small size (8cm by 11.5cm), ideally suited for slipping into a handbag or inside pocket of a jacket.

In addition to the familiar assortment of common prayers, they contain much that might be termed instruction on the basics of the Catholic faith and the devotional life, adapted to the needs of the audience to which they were addressed. Each contains a short list of 'dos and 'donts' as well as brief sections on temptations, on the choice of a state of life, on habits etc. Much of the advice is, inevitably, of the 'single transferable sermon' variety. Women preparing for marriage are advised to be prudent in their choice and to look for 'a practising Catholic; sober; industrious; one who respects you and promises to be a devoted husband and a good father to your children',[30] while men are to look for 'a Catholic, a housekeeper, a homemaker; one who is as like to Mary as possible and to your own good mother – kind, considerate, helpful, that is, one who promises well to be a devoted wife and a good mother to your children'.[31] Boys (and girls) are reminded that:

> [...] regular company keeping is not lawful until 1. one is of marriageable age, 2. in a position to marry, 3. seriously contemplating marriage within a reasonable time. It is obvious, therefore, that company keeping is not allowed the school-going boy (or girl) for some time (years) until he has finished school.[32]

The longest section in each book is devoted to the preparation for confession, including a lengthy 'examination of conscience' appropriate to the audience to whom the book is addressed. Fr O'Halloran's prayer books paint a picture of the 'ideal Catholic' of the 1950s – prayerful, devout, sober, industrious, who sets a high premium on chastity and sexual restraint.

Liturgical change in the wake of the Second Vatican Council rang the death-knell for the prayer-book genre. Redemptorist mission print culture continues, but in a different way. Mission and novena prayer books, often brightly illustrated, continue to be produced by Redemptorist Communications, the Irish Redemptorist publishing house, with significant differences of style and content, but a detailed study of these is beyond the limits of this essay.

CONCLUSION

Assessing the Redemptorist contribution to the culture of Irish devotional life is complex. At a superficial level, it might be measured by counting the number of

---

29 They were published by Fallon of Dublin, with some British editions by Burns and Oates of London. **30** Leo O'Halloran, *Prayer book for women* (Dublin, 1957), p. 105. **31** Idem, *Prayer book for men* (Dublin, 1952), p. 74. **32** Idem, *Prayer book for boys* (Dublin, 1956), p. 107.

mission-crosses that survived the re-ordering and redecoration of churches or by observing the frequency with which one encounters images of the Mother of Perpetual Help in homes or elsewhere. Once popular devotional literature, such as the *Visits*, *The glories of Mary* or the *Way of the Cross* has had few readers for several decades now.

At a somewhat deeper level, one might ask how a century of exposure to the message of the mission shaped the deeper mindsets of the Irish Catholic persona. If they were not the only preachers of parish missions, by the mid-twentieth century the Redemptorists had become one of the major providers and, despite declining numbers and new commitments, continue to regard fidelity to the itinerant preaching apostolate as a badge of fidelity to a living tradition. At its best, Redemptorists' preference for 'ordinary folk' marked them out as the communicators of a certain kind of Catholic theology, not one remarkable for its inventiveness or for its appeal to the higher reaches of the imagination, it is true, but one which sought to offer 'sound doctrine' and to promote loyalty to the Church as an institution. The message may have been 'iron rations' and its moral underpinning often narrow, but theologically speaking, the nineteenth and early twentieth centuries were a period of theological poverty, caught between the Church's long-running battle with political liberalism on the one hand and a more short-lived theological struggle to enter the world of modernity on the other. I have tried to show in this essay how a certain kind of devotionalism sought to fill the void and to provide warmth or a sense of belonging in what was at times, to use a modern Irish cliché, 'a cold house'.

4 Modernity and Catholic Restoration: the cases of the Blessed Anna Maria Giannetti Taigi and the Blessed Elisabetta Canori Mora

SARAH FIONA MACLAREN

INTRODUCTION

On 30 May 1920 in the crowded square of St Peter's in Rome, Pope Benedict XV beatified a woman called Anna Maria Giannetti Taigi (1769–1837). On 24 April 1994, over seventy years later, Pope John Paul II beatified another Roman woman called Elisabetta Canori Mora (1774–1825). What is remarkable about the two episodes is that both of these *beatae* were ordinary wives and mothers of several children who put up with the burdens of everyday life. What was so extraordinary about these women that made them into 'saints' with established cults? They achieved sanctification by living the ordinary life of wife and mother in a spirit of Christian mission, showing how an ordinary housewife and mother can become a saint and positively affect society and the lives of those with whom she comes into contact.

This essay will show how Anna Maria Giannetti Taigi and Elisabetta Canori Mora are, like most Catholic saints, small tiles of a broader mosaic of sainthood. As social, cultural and historical studies have shown, saints belong to and reflect the societies which produce and honour them. Furthermore, the 'politics of sainthood' has revealed how saintly models have been devised according to the context and time in which they developed. Thus, the history of saints' cults casts light not only on changes in mentality and social structure, but also on the role the Church has played in making saints.

As we shall see, Anna Maria's and Elisabetta's model of sainthood was devised at one of the most difficult times for the Roman Catholic Church. This was between the French Revolution and the Restoration and continued throughout the nineteenth century when Italy underwent political unification causing the Church to lose its temporal power. Anna Maria and Elisabetta are connected to the Church's struggle with modernity and its attempt to regain its leadership after the devastating effects of the Enlightenment, secularization and rationalism. In a modern, disenchanted world, women become the most significant resource for the reconversion of society to Christianity.

MODELS AND THE 'POLITICS' OF SAINTHOOD: THE
SOCIAL STUDY OF SAINTS AND THEIR CULTS

Sainthood has always occupied a prominent role in Christianity and particularly in the
Roman Catholic Church. Linked to an exceptional religious experience, the saint is
the person who, both dead and alive, provides a point of contact between the natural
and supernatural worlds. Following the example of Jesus Christ, the saint has the
power to intercede between humanity and God, to secure help in all circumstances of
adversity, to prevent or cure sickness of all kinds, to mediate during life and at the hour
of death and to bring general good fortune.

Derived from the Greek *hagios* and the Latin *sanctus*, the term 'saint' was initially
applied in the Early Church to baptized church members and to the faithful departed.
In the most general sense, the saint is a friend of God whose virtue makes him the
object of divine consideration. More narrowly conceived, the saint also belongs to a
spiritual elite whose heroic virtue elevates him above other human beings. Finally, as
an individual exemplar, he is something different for different people at different
times: in late antiquity, he was a martyr or an ascetic; in medieval times, he was a
mystic or miracle worker; in modern times, he is a practitioner of charity.[1]

Within the traditions of social sciences and history, the study of sainthood and the
cults of saints have yielded significant fruits. Rather than focusing on theological
issues, these studies have shown how the saints and their cults reflect important
features of the societies in which they occur. These include not only modes of religious
perception and feeling but also social relationships and political structure.[2] Going
beyond Pitrim Sorokin's naïve vision of sainthood as a form of idealized altruism,[3] this
research has revealed that saints belong to and reflect the societies which produce and
honour them.[4] Hagiographical literature – the so-called 'Lives of the saints' – and

1 See H. Delehaye, *Sanctus: Essai sur le culte des saints dans l'antiquité* (Bruxelles, 1927). It must be admitted,
however, that these categories are not exclusively confined to particular periods; indeed, saints who have espoused
these qualities have been recognised throughout Christian history.   **2** For the social and historical study of saints
and their cults see E. Durkheim, *Les formes élementaires de la vie religieuse* (Paris, 1912); P. Delooz, *Sociologie et
canonisations* (Liège, 1969); M. De Certeau, *L'écriture de l'histoire* (Paris, 1975); M. Bloch, *Le rois thaumaturges:
etude sur le caractère surnaturel attribué à la puissance royale particulièrement en France et en Angleterre* (Paris, 1983);
P. Brown, *The cult of the saints* (Chicago, 1981); A. Vauchez, *La sainteté en Occident* (Rome, 1981); D. Weinstein
& R.M. Bell (eds), *Saints and society: the two worlds of west*. Pio di Pietrelcina (1887–1968), canonized in 2002 by
Pope John Paul II, is one of the latest cases. For many years the Vatican ostracized the Capuchin monk's 'sanctity',
but he managed to safeguard his saintly reputation thanks to a group of very well-connected and powerful patrons
who supported 'Padre Pio' throughout his life. Here again see Luzzatto, *Padre Pio: ern Christendom, 1000–1700*
(Chicago, 1982); S. Wilson (ed.), *Saints and their cults: studies in religious sociology, folklore and history* (Cambridge,
1983), contains a full annotated bibliography; A. Kleinberg, *Prophets in their own country: living saints and the
making of sainthood in the later Middle Ages* (Chicago, 1992); S. Boesch Gajano, *La santità* (Roma-Bari, 1999),
contains a full annotated bibliography; M. Caffiero, *Religione e modernità in Italia (secoli XVII-XIX)* (Pisa, 2000);
M. Gotor, *I beati dei papi: Santità, Inquisizione e obbedienza in età moderna* (Firenze, 2002); S. Luzzatto, *Padre
Pio: miracoli e politica nell'Italia del Novecento* (Torino, 2007).   **3** See P. Sorokin, *Altruistic love: a study of
American 'good neighbours' and Christian saints* (Boston, 1950).   **4** The Belgian sociologist Pierre Delooz's point
of departure is that 'to be a saint is to be a saint for other people'.

other material related to their cults thus provide us with the whole symbolic, aesthetic, social, cultural and political 'field' in which a saint's reputation was built up.[5] No matter how 'saintly' one may be and how many 'saintly' qualities one may possess, such as charisma, the ability to work miracles and heal the sick, heroic virtues, gifts of ubiquity and prophecy, these will not be enough for one to become a saint unless there is a group of patrons ready to recognize, invest in, negotiate and support the 'sanctity' of that particular person.[6] The whole process of canonization, which was finally established by the Congregation of Rites in Rome in 1587, is such an elaborate, expensive and slow bureaucratic procedure that only well-established pressure groups, and particularly the religious orders, manage to have saints recognized. Furthermore, the papacy and its bureaucracy have always powerfully influenced the selection of those who were ultimately canonized; that is, of those who were entitled to a public cult. Finally, these studies have also revealed how notions and types of sanctity have varied over the centuries. No one would expect early twenty-first-century believers or non-believers to have the same saints as the contemporaries of Francis of Assisi, or to regard them in the same way. The history of saints' cults is thus extremely complex and reflects the most profound changes in mentality and social structure.

Models of sainthood, however, are connected to the 'politics of sainthood'. In her magisterial works *La politica della santità. Nascita di un culto nell'età dei Lumi* (1996) and *Religione e modernità in Italia* (2000), the Italian historian Marina Caffiero argues that the Roman Catholic Church has over the centuries elaborated specific models of sainthood and cults according to the social, historical and political contexts in which it found itself. These were conceived to stand as paradigms of moral and religious behaviour for the Christian community, hence fulfilling a function of social and cultural control.

The models and cults would vary according to the purpose and the message the Church wished to enforce, such as promoting modernized forms of religiosity and spirituality more suitable to the times, or encouraging a specific type of moral behaviour. This was particularly the case when the Church felt threatened by adverse political and anti-clerical conditions. For instance, in Italy around the end of the fifteenth century and the first decades of the sixteenth century there was a proliferation of ladies – known as *sante vive* (living saints),[7] gifted with charismatic, visionary and prophetic powers, who gained high social status and political influence at the Italian courts. The propagandistic use of prophecies, which was generally encouraged during moments of crisis, was supported in order to legitimize and sacralize the political power of the princes. However, a few decades later, towards the end of the sixteenth century, due to the centralization of the Church after the Council of Trent, a new

---

5 On the notion of 'field', see P. Bourdieu, 'Genèse et structure du champ religieux', *Revue française de sociologie*, 12:3 (1971), 295–334.   **6** The case of St Pio of Pietrelcina has been noted above.   **7** See G. Zarri, *Le sante vive: profezie di corte e devozione femminile tra '400 e '500* (Torino, 1990).

model of sainthood was enforced, which substituted medieval prophetism and mysticism with heroic virtues and religious commitment.

Although new concepts of sainthood may also come from unofficial and lower groups, they need, however, to gain the Church's approval in order to be legitimized as a cult.[8] Therefore, the study of the 'politics of sainthood' and the cults connected to it reveals the theological, ideological, symbolic and cultural strategies adopted by the Church, and the processes which allowed it to modernize and keep up with the times; in other words, how it adjusted, overcame, resisted and adapted to political and social transformations.

Rome and the Papal States therefore deserve special attention. This is not only where ecclesiastical decisions and strategies were made, but also where the new models of sainthood and cults were devised, experimented and tested, before being institutionalized and finally applied elsewhere.

We shall now turn to a very particular model of sainthood devised in Rome over the last decades of the eighteenth century and the first part of the nineteenth century showing how the Church coped with one of the deepest crises of the modern era and how this model would have long-lasting effects throughout the twentieth century.

OVERCOMING MODERNITY: THE *CHRISTIANA RESTAURATIO* FROM THE ENLIGHTENMENT ONWARDS

Anna Maria Giannetti Taigi's and Elisabetta Canori Mora's model of sainthood seems most unusual. Neither was a nun; indeed both were wives and mothers. Although they were fervent Catholics and became lay tertiary Trinitarians in Rome, they pursued sanctity within their everyday life without neglecting their children and husbands. Their type of sainthood seems to have little in common with other great examples such as St Catherine of Siena, who dedicated her whole life to prayer and meditation. However, as we shall see, their model of sainthood was specifically devised by the Church to promote a new type of sanctity with which to face the deep political and spiritual crisis that shook this institution to the foundations.

The eighteenth century was a difficult time for Roman Catholicism. The Church lost its international political power due to the fact that the Papal States could no longer compete with the large European powers and the advent of enlightened monarchies undermined Rome's influence in their states. The Enlightenment accelerated the process of secularization of society, bringing about a modern mentality, and emphasizing the importance of science and of people using their own reason, rather than merely relying on traditional authorities including those of religion. The Church, to

---

8 Once again, the case of 'Padre Pio' is emblematic. Although, as mentioned earlier, he had an influential group of patrons, the Vatican officially recognized his 'sanctity' only after the advent of Pope John Paul II, who supported his canonization. Here again, see Luzzatto, *Padre Pio*.

some extent, lost the support of the well-off, learned and disenchanted elites. Moreover, economic transformation resulted in the introduction of novel systems of production and capitalism, and the advent of a diffident and anti-clerical bourgeoisie.

The second half of the eighteenth century, however, brought even harsher surprises, such as the suppression of the Society of Jesus in 1773, the French Revolution that put an end to the *ancien régime*, and the rise of Napoleon Bonaparte who threw Europe into turmoil until he was defeated at Waterloo in 1815. These and many other events had devastating effects on the Church. The Roman Republic was proclaimed in 1798, putting an end to the pope's temporal power. Pope Pius VI was imprisoned and taken to France, and riots broke out among the lower classes in Rome caused by famine and the economic crisis of the Papal States.

How did the Church cope with the eighteenth-century process of modernization? How did it deal with the loss of political power, the processes of secularization, disen-chantment?[9] Did it withdraw from the world, adopting a negative, passive and defensive attitude towards the overall process of modernization? Or rather, did it assume an active role, enabling it to adapt the processes of the modern world to its own advantage?

While eighteenth-century Europe was drifting further and further away from Roman Catholicism, because it was lagging behind the modernization and advancement of society, the Church was working frenetically to lay the foundations for modernizing its entire institution.[10] The outcome of this process was a 'modern' form of intransigent and reactionary Catholicism, which would be consolidated throughout the nineteenth century when the Church tried to regain its ancient prestige. As the deep eighteenth-century crisis raged on, in Rome there were numerous groups and people involved in setting up the strategies which would allow the Church not only to defend itself from the crisis, but also to plan its so-called 'Catholic Restoration' – *Christiana Restauratio* – of society, which would take place in the following century.[11] The process, which has been called 'conservative innovation' or 'anti-modern modernization', shows that whenever the Church has been induced to react against the effects of modernization, it ends up absorbing and using 'modern' processes in order to re-establish its traditional order.[12]

During the Enlightenment, when 'the crisis of the European conscience' took place,[13] bringing about a modern mentality, the Church and papacy managed to turn the threat into success and to use it to bring society back under its control. In order

---

9 According to Max Weber, secularization and disenchantment (*Entzauberung der Welte*) are the essential features of modernity.   **10** See M. Caffiero, *La politica della santità: nascita di un culto nell'età moderna* (Roma-Bari, 1996). Here again, see Caffiero, *Religione e modernità in Italia*.   **11** Here again, see Caffiero, *La politica della santità*, pp 8–11; Caffiero, *Religione e modernità in Italia*, pp 11–22. See also further on the case of Benoît-Joseph Labre.   **12** Here again, see Caffiero, *Religione e modernità in Italia*, pp 11–15. For 'conservative innovation' see W. Reinhard, 'Gegenreformation als Modernisierung? Prolegomena zu einer Theorie des konfessionellen Zeitalters', *Archiv fur Reformationgeschichte*, 68 (1977), 226–52.   **13** See P. Hazard, *La crise de la conscience européene (1680–1715)* (Paris, 1935).

to do so, the Church made use of a renewed model of medieval Christianity, and its mythical past and 'purity'. This became the platform on which it could confront modernity and establish an intransigent institution.[14] Many of the meanings and strategies developed around this mythical medieval past would turn into the main features of nineteenth-century Catholic intransigence and restoration, such as the controversy over a modern rational culture, the legitimacy of novel forms of social control, and the recognition of the pope's supreme authority culminating in the doctrine of papal infallibility (1870). These strategies also included the reintroduction of traditional medieval political models, the launch of 'female Catholicism', the re-establishment of counter-reformed collective devotional instruments, the political use of miracles, visions and prophecies, and the re-launch of anti-Semitism and missionary work.

As has been shown regarding movements of religious restoration and modern proto-fundamentalist movements,[15] with which the *Christiana Restauratio* has many features in common, a crisis is tackled by setting up a complicated system of defence and, at the same time, introducing some of the 'modern' features which threaten to destabilize its order. Rather than assuming a merely passive and defensive attitude, they actually take on an active role by 'inventing' new symbols, rites and liturgies or giving a modern touch to old elements. This, therefore, seems to confirm the thesis according to which the ideological and political constructions of the movements of religious restoration, even though they employ anti-modern orientations and symbols, end up using features and strategies typical of the modernity they are trying to fight against and outlast.

THE 'POLITICS' OF FEMALE MODELS OF SAINTHOOD

Anna Maria Giannetti was born on 29 May 1769 in Siena, in the heart of Tuscany. Owing to financial difficulties, her family moved to Rome when she was only six years old, hoping to find a better future in the city. The family was so poor, however, that all three of them had to travel on foot. In Rome they settled in the Monti *rione*, one of the old quarters in the centre close to the Colosseum, and inhabited by the lower classes. She was sent to the school of the *Maestre Pie* (the Pious Teachers) – to which we shall return – where she was taught to read, sew and embroider. Then she went to work as a maid in order to help her family and on 7 January 1789 she married Domenico Taigi, who came from a modest background and was a servant in the aristo-cratic Pamphili family. Domenico was a rough man with a bad temper and his

---

14 On the medieval models and in particular the case of St Benoît-Joseph Labre here again, see Caffiero, *La politica della santità*. During the Renaissance and the Baroque one of the Church's main models was 'magnifi-cence'; see S.F. Maclaren, *La magnificenza e il suo doppio: il pensiero estetico di Giovanni Battista Piranesi* (Milano, 2005). **15** S.N. Eisenstadt, *Fondamentalismo e modernità. Eterodossie, utopismo, giacobinismo nella costruzione dei movimenti fondamentalisti* (Roma-Bari, 1994). Here again, see Caffiero, *La politica della santità*, p. 10.

character would always put a strain on the couple's relationship. The hagiographers wrote that the first years of Anna Maria's marriage were happy; she was a pretty young woman who was quite frivolous, liked nice clothes and enjoying herself.[16] However, she decided to modify her attitude after a chance encounter with a priest in St Peter's Square, who was taken aback by her frivolity. From then onwards, Anna Maria's life would be filled with mystical and religious experience. She became a fervent church-goer, prayed continuously, did penances, mortified herself and performed works of charity. In 1808 she took vows and became a lay tertiary Trinitarian without relinquishing her duties as a wife and mother.

Anna Maria had to combine her spiritual and ascetic drive with her everyday life. As a wife and mother of seven children (three of whom died when still very young) she had several duties, such as looking after her family, doing the household chores and working in order to earn some extra income. She also had to put up with her husband's moods and aggressions. Furthermore, she raised her children during the turbulent years from the French Revolution to the Restoration that shook the Papal States. Anna Maria embraced the role of the perfect wife and mother. She was sweet, patient and ready to sacrifice herself, doing her utmost to please everyone and to make sure that her family life would be peaceful (see plate 1).

Anna Maria, however, would not only be remembered as an ordinary woman, a hardworking and pious housewife who put up with her husband and reared her children. In Rome – and particularly among the clergy and reactionary circles – she started gaining a 'saintly' reputation due to the prophecies and allegories that she kept delivering regarding the future of the Church, the popes and even of the Catholic religion. Anna Maria claimed to be accompanied by a 'sun', a supernatural light, a sign of God's presence, on account of which she was able to look into the hearts and souls of people, see things occurring far away from Rome and predict events that would happen in the future. She foresaw the fire of St Paul's Basilica (1823), the deaths of Tsar Alexander I (1825), of popes Pius VI (1799), Pius VII (1823) and Leo XII (1829), the election of Pope Pius IX (1846), the many struggles the Church would have to cope with throughout the nineteenth century and how the 'final triumphs would strongly re-establish ecclesiastical teaching on society'.[17] Priests, cardinals, royalty and aristocracy constantly consulted her visions and prophecies. Her mystical experiences were taken into such consideration that the priest Fr Raffaele Natale, a prominent personality within the Roman clergy, moved into her house in 1817 to write her spiritual diary.[18] After her death her husband converted and lived until he was over 90.

16 See F. De Palma, 'Il modello laicale di Anna Maria Taigi' in E. Fattorini (ed.), *Santi, culti, simboli nell'età della secolarizzazione (1815–1915)* (Torino, 1997), pp 529–46. 17 See M. Caffiero, 'Dall'esplosione mistica tardo-barocco all'apostolato sociale' in L. Scaraffia and G. Zarri, (eds), *Donne e fede: Santità e vita religiosa in Italia* (Roma-Bari, 1994), pp 327–73. Here, see p. 362. 18 Anna Maria could read only; she could not write. Father Raffaele continued living with the Taigi family even after Anna Maria died, until his death in 1871 at the age of ninety-one.

A quite similar story is told of Elisabetta Canori. She was born into a wealthy family in Rome on 21 November 1774. Her mother was an aristocrat and her father a well-off landowner. She was educated at home and then sent to a school run by the Augustinian nuns. When she was old enough, her family introduced her into the fashionable society of the capital. Elisabetta was known for her beauty, elegance and refined manners and at the age of 22 she was married to the young and promising lawyer Cristoforo Mora on 10 January 1796. She had four daughters (although only two survived), but the marriage, against all expectations, was far from a happy one; indeed, owing to Cristoforo's expensive lifestyle and infidelity, it turned out to be disastrous. The worsening of the new family's economic situation and Cristoforo's continual betrayals did not bend Elisabetta. She was deeply convinced of the sanctity of matrimony and she was dutifully faithful and dedicated to her husband, looking after him when he was seriously ill, putting up with the scandals of his infidelity, taking care of the home and her daughters, selling her personal belongings when her husband got into debt and acting as the sole breadwinner in her family. Elisabetta's only comfort was her religion, her prayers and her charitable work. She too became a lay tertiary Trinitarian in 1807, a year before Anna Maria (see plate 2).

Elisabetta's religious devotion was based on the conviction that her personal suffering and the misunderstandings she had to live with were similar to those of Jesus Christ. She therefore decided to offer all her sufferings and her whole life for the peace and sanctity of the Church, her husband's conversion and for all sinners. Like Anna Maria, Elisabetta had extraordinary prophetic and visionary powers. She too could see through hearts, foresee souls being freed in Purgatory (above all Pope Pius VI) and predict that heresy would fall on the Church. She also foresaw the return of Pius VII from imprisonment by Napoleon, the restoration of the Society of Jesus and the final triumph of the faith. She died in Rome on 5 February 1825. After her death, her husband repented of his behaviour and became a Trinitarian priest in 1834. He retired to a monastery in Sezze, near Rome, where he died in 1845. Her youngest daughter Maria Lucina, who had always been as devoted as Elisabetta, joined the order of the Trinitarians and became a nun. She would have a prominent role in advocating her mother's sanctity. She looked after Elisabetta's spiritual diary and wrote a *Memoire* of her mother's life. Both Maria Lucina and Cristoforo were witnesses during the initial proceedings for her beatification.

As we have seen, these two women shared many things in common. Although they came from different social backgrounds, their model of sainthood seems to have been shaped in the same way. They are perfect mothers and wives, put up with their husbands' bad behaviour, work to look after their families and are actively involved in charity work. Their spiritual life is alike too. They are extremely religious, consider themselves servants of God, bring their children up as good practising Catholics, attend mass every day, become lay tertiary Trinitarians, have an active role in the religious Trinitarian community of San Carlino at the Quattro Fontane in Rome and die in *fama sanctitatis* (with a reputation for sanctity). Both of them are mystics, prophetesses, healers and miracle workers. They possess heroic virtues and predict the restoration of the Church after various downfalls. And, last, but not least, both their husbands repent and become fervent Catholics after their wives' deaths.

The establishment of their respective cults follows a similar path, their reputation for sanctity being officially recognized by the Church while they are still alive. Their prophecies are listened to and their healing capacities are invoked by all sorts of people, both rich and poor. Drawings and death masks are made at their deaths and their corpses are exposed for public devotion. They are both granted public and solemn funerals and the ordinary trials of beatification are presented to the Congregation of Rites soon after their deaths. They are both buried in two churches in Rome administered by the Trinitarians, where their cults have been set up. Anna Maria is in a chapel of the basilica of St Crisogono in Trastevere (see plate 3), whereas Elisabetta is in the church of St Carlino alle Quattro Fontane (see figure 4.1). Pope Benedict XV beatified Anna Maria in 1920 and Pope John Paul II did the same for Elisabetta in 1994.

Anna Maria's and Elisabetta's model of sainthood and their cults are connected to the Church's struggle with modernity. In fact, they belong to and reflect the process by which the Catholic Church tried to regain its ancient prestige in society after all the eighteenth-century calamities caused by modernization, secularization, the French Revolution and the Roman Republic. The Church needed to reconvert society to Christianity and realized that women could play an important role in doing so. Due to the secularization of society and the lack of religious vocation among the wealthy, well-educated, but disenchanted classes, the Church realized that it would have to turn to other sections of the population in order to re-establish its former hegemony. Having lost its traditional network of support, the Church realized that the *Christiana Restauratio* could proceed by drawing on the lower classes and women. Thus, ordinary lay women like Anna Maria and Elisabetta became one of the means by which the Church could regain its leadership. They were perfect Christian wives and mothers, whose exemplary conduct would set a paradigm for all women and, by extension, for their children, husbands and all society. Encouraging wifehood and motherhood as a female model of Christian perfection thus provided a form of social and religious control and also gave every ordinary woman the opportunity to pursue a saintly life. This strategy would allow the Church to restore its supremacy, but in the meantime it gave women unprecedented freedom of action and emancipation in a society they were expected to help reconvert to Christianity.

'CATHOLICISME AU FÉMININ': MODERN MODELS OF FEMALE SAINTHOOD

Although Anna Maria and Elisabetta represent a modern model of sainthood, they also reflect the ambiguous attitude the Church has had towards modernity and

4.1 Elisabetta Canori Mora. Buried in the church of San Carlino
alle Quattro Fontane, Rome (photograph by the author).

concerning the role assigned to women within religious life and institutions. From the
end of the seventeenth century onwards, the role and position of women in Christian
society became more and more relevant, opening up all sorts of opportunities previously unavailable to them. Called *catholicisme au féminin* in France and
femminilizzazione religiosa in Italy[19] this type of 'female Catholicism' refers to the
phenomenon whereby women from all backgrounds were allowed to carry out various
kinds of socially useful activities on behalf of the Church in order to reconvert society
to Christianity. Starting off in the rural areas of Italy at the end of the seventeenth
century and restricted to providing poor girls with a very basic education, throughout
the following two centuries it gradually extended to a vast range of activities, such as
charitable work, looking after the sick and elderly, taking care of the poor and orphans,
and working as missionaries. Compared to many previous models of female
sainthood, which were based on a contemplative religious life led entirely behind the
walls of convents, this modern type was a sort of 'lay sanctity', which encouraged all
sorts of women – and not only nuns – to go out into the world and play an active
Christian role within their families and society.

As noted above, this new phase in Catholicism was brought about at a time when
secularization and disenchantment towards religion had caused the elites and the men
to turn away from the Church. Therefore, women and the lower classes became the
only platform available on which the Church might curb the effects of modernity and
organize the strategies for the *Christiana Restauratio*. 'Female Catholicism', however,
represents a paradoxical and ambivalent phenomenon. On one hand, it upsets the
tenets of the counter-reformed Church because it gives women a 'modern' and

19 For France, see C. Langlois, *Le catholicisme au féminin: les congrégations françaises à supérieure générale au XIXe*
siècle (Paris, 1984). For Italy here, see again Caffiero, *Religione e modernità in Italia*, pp 111–89.

emancipated role in society, whereas on the other it allows the millennial institution to reintroduce intransigent and reactionary features. Although the ultimate outcome would be the solemnization of the Church's traditional hegemony and the setting up of an intransigent institution based on a renewal of medieval Christianity which was fully achieved during the nineteenth century, the strategy of involving women in this process granted unprecedented and 'modern' opportunities to this section of the population.

The first area touched by the process of modernization and reconversion was education. In the last decades of the seventeenth century, in northern Latium, in the heart of the Papal States, many schools were opened up by the lay *Maestre Pie* (Pious Teachers) Venerini and Filippini, so called by the names of their foundresses. The institutes represented an important novelty in Italy. Rosa Venerini (1656–1728), a middle-class woman from Viterbo, established a female congregation to teach girls with the support of Cardinal Marcantonio Barbarigo, bishop of Montefiascone and Corneto (today Tarquinia). The schools were free and aimed at poor or abandoned girls living in rural areas, offering them an alternative to working in the fields, which could compromise their reputations. The first school was opened in Viterbo in 1685 and was followed by many others all over the region. Venerini's friend and rival, Lucia Filippini (1672–1732), was an aristocrat born in Tarquinia. Having worked with Venerini and run her schools for several years, Filippini decided to establish her own. What separated the two women were their religious inclinations. Venerini was closer to the Jesuits, whose pedagogical principles she adopted, whereas Filippini was under the spiritual direction of the *Pii Operai* (Pious Workers), who advocated an active devotional practice, based on asceticism and penance.

Regardless of these differences, the two types of institutes established by these women can undoubtedly be considered cutting-edge for their times. Firstly, the *Maestre* belonged to a secular congregation. They were lay teachers who did not need to become either nuns or tertiaries. Although they had habits and rules, they were not required to live in a convent or take formal vows. The vows they took were informal and temporary, leaving the *Maestre* free to retire from the congregations whenever they wished. Secondly, the schools were run by two or three *Maestre* who worked all over Latium and Rome. The *Maestre* were therefore expected to teach in several schools in rural and urban areas, granting them the freedom to move about on their own, which was most unusual for women at that time. Thirdly, they were social pioneers. Their duty was to give their pupils such a thorough Catholic education that once the latter got married they would bring up their own children as model Christians and possibly re-convert their husbands. Lastly, anybody could become a *Maestra* regardless of her social background or income. In fact, in contrast with the rules of the convents, a woman who wanted to be a *Maestra* did not need a dowry. What's more, many girls who attended the schools became teachers when they grew up, thus promoting unprecedented social mobility.

Thanks to her well-connected patrons and to the *Pii Operai*, Lucia Filippini managed to open a school in Rome before her rival Rosa Venerini. Lucia was such a capable businesswoman that she was able to convince the pope to support her congregation. She depended directly on the pope and the Papal Almonry, allowing her to bypass the local ecclesiastical authorities. As already noted, the Filippini congregation demanded intensive spiritual and devotional activities, encouraging its pupils to embrace these practices. Besides giving the girls a strict Catholic education, the *Maestre Pie* Filippini taught them to read, sew and embroider. Whereas Rosa Venerini gradually started accepting slightly better off and middle-class girls, Lucia Filippini insisted on taking poor pupils only.[20] Filippini's first school in Rome was opened in the Monti quarter with the *Pii Operai*'s support. This is where Anna Maria Taigi lived and she attended the Filippini school, where she distinguished herself for her religious devotion.

One episode is worth mentioning briefly, however, in order to grasp the capillary action of the Church and the *Maestre Pie*, and how women and the lower classes were essential to re-launch religious supremacy in a modernizing society. It concerns the canonization of the Frenchman Benoît-Joseph Labre, who died in the Monti neighbourhood in Rome during Holy Week of 1783 at the age of thirty-five. Labre was a tramp who went on pilgrimages to the major shrines dedicated to the Virgin Mary in Europe. After being refused by many religious orders, he settled in Rome, in the densely populated Monti, where he could be seen praying devoutly and incessantly. He was a solitary man who lived off alms he did not ask for. Infected with parasites, he slept under the arches of the nearby Colosseum or in one of the dormitories provided for the poor. Immediately after his death, however, the news spread that a 'saint' had died, causing episodes of excited collective enthusiasm. The crowds were so insistent on having a glance at the 'saintly' corpse that the burial had to be put off for several days. And when the funeral did take place, it was necessary to call the army to keep the crowds at bay and stop them from stealing relics belonging to Labre.

What is most impressive, however, is the fact that against all principles of canon law, Labre's canonization started immediately. In 1792 he was declared Venerable. The trial for his beatification took place between 1792 and 1796, breaking all the laws according to which it was necessary to wait fifty years after the person's death. Although the second phase was stopped due to the political upheavals that hit Rome, Labre's beatification proceeded after the Restoration. He was beatified in 1860 and finally canonized in 1881. Needless to say, the dates of Labre's solemnization coincide with critical moments for the Church and the Pontifical State (see plate 4).

Labre's saintly career has been accurately reconstructed by Marina Caffiero in her book *La politica della santità: nascita di un culto nell'età dei Lumi* (1996), highlighting

---

20 It is no coincidence that Elisabetta Canori Mora sent her two daughters to the Venerini rather than the Filippini school. It was probably due to Elisabetta's aristocratic background. Unlike Anna Maria Taigi, Elisabetta and her daughters could both read and write.

the political milieu of the Church. For our purposes it is sufficient to mention just a few aspects that provide further insights into the politics of a 'lay' and 'female' sainthood proposed by Roman Catholicism and strictly connected to Anna Maria Taigi's case. Firstly, at a time of political and economic crisis, famine and revolt of the lower classes, the Church presented a model of sainthood drawing on the medieval notion of poverty. As poverty was becoming a terrible and revolutionary force, the Church changed it into a 'saintly' virtue, showing that it was not disgraceful to be poor. It could control the lower classes and the turmoil they were causing by offering them a saint they could identify with, showing them that they too stood a chance of attaining sainthood.

Secondly, Labre's sainthood was modelled with particular attention to women, gaining him the reputation of being a 'woman's saint'.[21] The *Maestre Pie* Filippini were Labre's patrons. They witnessed his saintly virtues during the trials of beatification and fuelled his cult by turning their pupils into devoted followers. Labre became the 'male' version of a 'lay and female' sainthood, embodying the model of virtue and behaviour for women. The Christian values the *Maestre Pie* Filippini instilled in their girls were humility, modesty, obedience, prayer, chastity, charity, mortification of the body and self-sacrifice. These were the same values ascribed to Labre. It is no wonder that the virtues of sacrifice, suffering and charity would characterize the female and maternal ideal of the nineteenth century. This model was closely connected to the image of the Virgin and was supported by Labre's example, who was also devoted to her.

Thanks to women and devotion to the Virgin, Labre became the saint of the Christian family and of women as mediators of reconversion. Women were considered the best way to restore Christian values as, thanks to their natural gifts, they had an irresistible appeal to the younger generations, and were the most suitable people to save both the family and society. Anna Maria Taigi's model of sainthood is the female version of that of Labre. She must have seen Labre in the *rione* Monti where she grew up. She attended the *Maestre Pie* Filippini school, where Labre was venerated. She was fourteen when he died and what an impression his funeral must have made on the poor, humble and almost illiterate girl. Anna Maria must have thought that even a penniless and uneducated girl like her stood a chance to stand out in her society and attain the success of sainthood.

However, once the Church had achieved its purpose and regained its hegemony, it changed its course. It gradually put a stop to emancipating activities and started reintroducing traditional ideals of womanhood. A woman's primary aim was to be a model Christian mother and wife, obey her husband and raise her children as good Catholics. If, on the contrary, she were involved in apostolic activities, she would now be under the supervision of male ecclesiastics. Even the lay congregations of the

---

21 See M. Caffiero, 'Un santo per le donne: Benedetto Labre e la femminilizzazione del Cattolicesimo tra Settecento e Ottocento', *Memoria: Rivista di storia delle donne*, 30:3 (1990), 89–106.

Maestre Pie Filippini and Venerini underwent a similar transformation during the nineteenth century. Having been secular organizations, they were turned into religious orders and their teachers were now required to become nuns.[22]

The Church's reactionary programme is also confirmed by the new models it was trying to impose on society. Once again, Anna Maria Taigi is a fruitful example. As already noted, she gained her *fama sanctitatis* not only because she embodied the perfect, humble mother and wife, but also because she made prophecies regarding the Church's future. In his work *Il modello laicale di Anna Maria Taigi* (1997), Francesco de Palma analyzes the deep transformations her hagiographies underwent and how they were paradigmatic of the evolution of the models of female sainthood over the nineteenth and twentieth centuries.[23]

The first hagiographies highlight, rather than Anna Maria's motherly virtues, her 'prophetic' and 'political' ones. She predicts the attacks on the Church and the pope, but she foresees their future resurrection, the restoration of order and morality and the return of all the enemies under obedience to the faith. What emerges in the early hagiographies is the model of the *femina virilis* or *femme forte* ready to offer herself as a victim to stop divine justice in order to save sinners and restore the Church.[24] Anna Maria's image, in these first reconstructions, has hardly anything to do with the model of 'female and lay' sainthood, which will later emerge. Her apocalyptic approach to the dangers of modernization and its consequences regarding the loss of faith were favourably met by prominent clergymen and royal personalities. This will be further reinforced in the decades following her death on 9 June 1837. The Roman clergy and aristocracy will not waste time in establishing and spreading the veneration of this humble mother, who witnessed and guaranteed divine protection at such a dramatic moment for the Church. It is no coincidence that most of the people granted graces by the future blessed lady during the nineteenth century are clergymen and nuns.[25] Furthermore, a picture showing Anna Maria praying next to Pope Pius IX was distributed in Rome just before the battle of Mentana in 1867. Thus, during the mid-nineteenth century, Anna Maria belongs to the 'strong' model of sainthood, quintessentially Roman, pro-papal and political. Anna Maria is the one who talks to the powerful and the learned, who with manly courage puts aside her female weakness to stop the evil 'plague of laicism' from spreading.

From the end of the nineteenth century, however, when the scar of Porta Pia starts healing and the Church sets out to re-establish its control within the recently unified

---

22 At the beginning of the twentieth century, the Pontifical Institute of the Religious Teachers Filippini (*Maestre Pie Filippini*) sent a group of nuns to the USA to lead pioneering work in americanizing the children of Italian immigrants. See E. Vezzosi, 'Mediatrici etniche e cittadine: le Maestre Pie Filippini negli Stati Uniti' in E. Fattorini (ed.), *Santi, culti, simboli nell'età della secolarizzazione (1815–1915)* (Torino, 1997), pp 495–514. **23** Here again, see De Palma, 'Il modello laicale di Anna Maria Taigi'. **24** Another model of *femme forte* is Marie de l'Incarnation, superbly retrieved by N. Zemon Davis, *Women on the margins: three seventeenth-century lives* (Cambridge, MA, 1995). **25** Here again, see De Palma, 'Il modello laicale di Anna Maria Taigi', pp 530–3.

Italian state, a new image of Anna Maria emerges.[26] Embracing the models presented
by the French hagiographers, the Church gradually discards the 'strong' and 'manly'
features of Anna Maria, and highlights her 'weak', soft, spiritual, female and motherly
virtues. Anna Maria's political profile is pushed more and more to the margins to make
way for her feminine aspects. Anna Maria is no longer the saint of the popes, the
cardinals and the princes, but rather the model for young women on the verge of
marrying. Anna Maria is invoked as the woman who did not take marriage lightly,
who obeyed and respected her husband, who kept family peace thanks to her
prudence, who humbly submitted to the will of her companion appointed by God,
who with love and sacrifice brought up her children as good Catholics, who worked
and kept the family, and who put up with all sorts of misfortunes. Anna Maria thus
turns into the model Christian wife and a paradigm for society. The late nineteenth-
century hagiographers of both Anna Maria and Elisabetta invite every woman to be
aware of her ascetic, apologetic and apostolic role. The aim is to convince women that
rather than annul themselves in wifehood and motherhood, they can actually become
the primary form of conversion of their dearest, and reconvert family after family and
even the whole world.

It is no wonder that Anna Maria's case is striking. For centuries, conjugal status had
been considered an insuperable obstacle to canonization. The only concession made
was to chaste widows who had decided to retreat to the convents and take formal
vows. Why, then, all of a sudden, is it enough to be a good wife and mother to become
a saint? At a time when modernization was also changing women's roles, making them
work and behave like men, the Church started emphasizing that the model to follow
was wifehood and motherhood. Thus, the humble Roman woman becomes a
paradigm for modern Christian women involved in the burdens of everyday family
life. Anna Maria is the 'saint of the hearth', the 'saint in the family and for the family',
'for her spouse and children', 'amongst the joys and anguishes of marriage', 'never
neglecting the duties of matrimony and of motherhood', 'who tried to make her
husband as happy as possible' 'keeping him away from bad company and bad habits'.[27]
Anna Maria and Elisabetta are the proof that a woman can become a saint *thanks to*,
and not *in spite of*, her family life.

26 On 20 September 1870, the bersaglieri soldiers opened a breach in Porta Pia in Rome, completing the unification of Italy and the ending of the Papal States. **27** The quotes are taken from the twentieth-century
hagiographers Paolo Valle and Cardinal Carlo Salotti. Here again, see De Palma, 'Il modello laicale di Anna Maria
Taigi', pp 541–2.

5 The visual rhetoric of medals representing nineteenth-century Marian apparitions

ELI HELDAAS SELAND

The nineteenth century saw the rise and development of numerous popular pilgrimages and devotions related to the Virgin Mary, and for this reason it is often referred to as the Marian age in literature concerning the modern history of Catholicism.[1] Visions and apparitions[2] were reported throughout Europe, many of which inspired local and regional cults of considerable volume and impact,[3] but few were formally recognized by the Church.[4] Four took place in France within a period of fifty years: Paris (1830), La Salette (1846), Lourdes (1858) and Pontmain (1871).[5] Among them, Bernadette Soubirous' visions in Lourdes stand out as the most famous, engendering an enormous activity – both devotional, such as pilgrimage, and practical – for example, the provision of infrastructure and the production and retail of pious objects. Therefore, the phenomenon of 'Lourdes' occupies a unique position in the history of modern piety. In the history of religious images, the Miraculous Medal, struck and distributed worldwide in an astonishing number over a very short period of time, has played a role of perhaps equal importance. It was issued following a series of apparitions of the Virgin Mary to Catherine Labouré in Paris in 1830.

This essay is concerned with the representation of visions and visionaries as seen in some select devotional medals: the Miraculous Medal and typical Lourdes medals.[6] The medals are perceived as primarily visual, devotional objects, and pictorial analyses

---

1 The first to use it was perhaps Louis Veuillot, the ultramontanist editor of the newspaper *L'Univers*, who proposed to call the nineteenth century the 'Siècle de Marie'. Quoted in N. Perry & L. Echeverría, *Under the heel of Mary* (London, 1988), p. 71. More recent examples include B.C. Pope, 'Immaculate and powerful: the Marian revival in the nineteenth century' in C.W. Atkinson et al. (eds), *Immaculate and powerful* (London, 1987), pp 173–200 at p. 173; V. Turner & E. Turner, *Image and pilgrimage in Christian culture: anthropological perspectives* (New York, 1995), p. 208; B. Calamari & S. Di Pasqua, *Visions of Mary* (New York, 2004), p. 15.   2 According to Victor Turner, the word 'apparition' 'refers to a supernatural vision that is bodily, or visible. The generic term "vision" includes not only apparitions but also "imaginative visions", usually produced in the imagination during sleep. There is also a category of "intellectual visions", in which the mind perceives a spiritual truth, without any sensory image'; Turner & Turner, *Image and pilgrimage*, p. 173.   3 For example, Périgord 1814, Valence 1848–9, Ceretto 1853, Mettenbuch 1877 – all mentioned in D. Blackbourn, *Marpingen: apparitions of the Virgin Mary in nineteenth-century Germany* (New York, 1993), pp 7–8; Dolina 1849, Saint-Bauzille-de-la-Sylve 1873, Pellevoisin 1876 are mentioned by M.L. Nolan & S. Nolan, *Christian pilgrimage in modern Western Europe* (Chapel Hill, NC, 1989), p. 286.   4 On the attitude of the Church towards the apparitions, see T.A. Kselman, *Miracles and prophecies in nineteenth-century France* (New Brunswick, NJ, 1983), ch. 6.   5 Ecclesiastically approved apparitions have undoubtedly had a more universal appeal, and they have been better documented. Many other cults have had a considerable impact, too, however, and are a part of the grand picture.   6 There exist millions of Lourdes medals and the production and sale of these objects is not controlled by the Church. A comprehensive study is neither possible nor necessary. The motifs which will be discussed here recur so often they may safely be treated as 'typical'.

of the motifs, seen in the light of central texts concerning the material, form the basis for the essay. In the age of mass production, these items have been distributed in huge numbers, and therefore they represent a considerable communicative potential. In my forthcoming doctoral dissertation, I investigate this potential and what has been made of it by asking *what* is communicated, *how* and *under which conditions* it is communicated and *why*. The aim of this essay is to indicate the fruitfulness of a new approach to the material, as there are demonstrably many questions to which the existing research has not provided satisfying answers. One of the shortcomings of earlier studies is a seeming lack of interest in the function of devotional medals, which I believe must be taken into account when interpreting the motifs. This essay pays some attention to the question, and argues that the function of devotional medals is above all rhetoric, as a consequence of their position in Catholic visual and devotional tradition.

THE MIRACULOUS MEDAL

A young novice, Catherine Labouré, had a series of visions in the mother house of the Vincentian Daughters of Charity at Rue du Bac in Paris in 1830. In two of these visions, the Virgin instructed her to see to it that a medal was made, after a model which she then showed her. She promised to bestow her graces upon those wearing it around the neck, and particularly those of great faith.[7] The novice dutifully conveyed this message to her confessor Fr Aladel, who at first did not believe her, but who eventually obtained the necessary permission from the archbishop, Msgr Quélen, and effectuated the production of a medal, starting in the summer of 1832. The medal was sold and distributed via various channels, by the Daughters of Charity and many others, and its success was immense. The engraver who was first given the commission for the medals, Vachette, reported in a letter to Aladel in 1837 that he himself had been responsible for the production of more than two million specimens since 1832; 1,972,844 in copper; 74,203 in silver; 191 in gold. He further described the activities of his colleagues in France and abroad, and estimated that the total number of medals sold across Europe at that time must exceed twenty million.[8] The medal's legend was found in many languages, and the medal was distributed worldwide as early as the first decade of its existence.[9]

The name 'Miraculous Medal' was not used from the very beginning; in early written sources the medal is called the 'Medal of the Virgin of the Rays',[10] the 'Medal

7 'toutes les personnes qui la porteron[t] recevron[t] de Grande[s] Grâce[s] en la portans au cou, les Grâses ceron[t] abondante[s] pour les personnes qui la porteron[t] avec Confiance': Catherine Labouré's own account, cited from R. Laurentin & P. Roche, *Catherine Labouré et la médaille miraculeuse: documents authentiques, 1830–1876* (Paris, 1976), p. 295. **8** Laurentin & Roche, *Catherine Labouré*, pp 276–7. **9** M. Ajmar & C. Sheffield, 'The Miraculous Medal: an Immaculate Conception or not', *The Medal*, 24 (1994), 37–50 at 41; J. Cribb, 'Medaglie cristiane e croci usate in Cina', *Medaglia*, 15 (1978), 21–39. **10** 'La médaille de la Vierge aux rayons' in Laurentin & Roche, *Catherine Labouré*, pp 183–4.

of the Most Holy Virgin'[11] and the 'Medal of the Immaculate Conception'.[12] In 1834, Aladel published the first version of a pamphlet (anonymously), the title of which may be translated as *Historical note on the origin and the effects of a new medal in honour of the Immaculate Conception of the most holy Virgin Mary, generally known by the name of Miraculous medal.*[13] The volume of the pamphlet, which was published in eight editions between 1834 and 1842, increased with the number of miraculous healings and conversions reported and believed to have been caused by the medal. It was these incidents that gave the medal its current name – *The Miraculous Medal* – now commonly applied to all medals that share certain features.

The medal (see plate 5) is normally, but not necessarily, oval, like the first ones. On the obverse is depicted the Virgin Mary, standing on a globe, with a serpent beneath her foot. Her hands are outstretched on either side of her body, the palms visible. One normally (and in Vachette's version) sees rays emanating from her hands. Below the globe on which she stands, the year 1830 often appears, and the legend *Oh Mary, conceived without sin, pray for us who have recourse to thee* encircles her. On the reverse the central motif is a capital 'M'. A crossbar cuts through the 'M', and upon it stands a cross. Below the 'M' are two small hearts; the left one has thorns bound around it and the right one is pierced by a sword. Flames normally rise from the hearts, and sometimes a little cross rises from the flames above the left one. Twelve stars encircle the motif.

I will concentrate on the obverse in this analysis. Let it be said briefly that the reverse is sometimes referred to as the sorrowful side.[14] The Cross refers, of course, to the Passion of Christ. It is interlaced with the letter 'M' – the initial of Mary – and thus the link between the two is emphasized visually. The crossbar that unites them may be seen to symbolize an altar, the place where the Passion is remembered through the Eucharist. The two hearts represent the hearts of Jesus and Mary; their love and suffering. The twelve stars are interpreted somewhat differently in the literature. An obvious reference from scripture is Revelation 12:1: 'A woman clothed with the sun, and the moon under her feet, and upon her head a crown of twelve stars.' This corresponds to the representation of the Virgin Mary as the Immaculate Conception on the obverse. The number twelve, however, often refers to the twelve apostles. The twelve tribes of Israel may also be read into it; which would support an interpretation of the motif as the community of the Church. I will go no further into the iconographical or theological details of the reverse here, but let Calamari and Di Pasqua summarize:

11 'La médaille de la très sainte Vierge' in Laurentin & Roche, *Catherine Labouré*, p. 186. **12** 'Médaille de l'Immaculée Conception' in Laurentin & Roche, *Catherine Labouré*, p. 195. The Immaculate Conception is a dogma of the Catholic Church as of 1854, which states that the Virgin Mary 'in the first instance of her conception, by a singular privilege and grace granted by God, in view of the merits of Jesus Christ the Saviour of the human race, was preserved exempt from all stain of original sin': http://www.newadvent.org/cathen/ 07674d.htm, accessed 27 Aug. 2008. **13** *Notice historique sur l'origine et les effets d'une nouvelle médaille en l'honneur de l'Immaculée Conception de la très Sainte Vierge Marie, généralement connue sous le nom de Médaille miraculeuse:* Laurentin & Roche, *Catherine Labouré*, p. 208. **14** http://www.chapellenotredamede- lamedaillemiraculeuse.com/EN/D3.asp, accessed 28 July 2008.

'in the Miraculous Medal lie the symbols of Mary's role in salvation from Genesis to Apocalypse.'[15]

The Miraculous Medal is recognized worldwide today, but it was new in 1832, and the process of establishing an iconography for what is now venerated as Our Lady of the Miraculous Medal was not straightforward. The iconography of the obverse is based on and closely related to the *immaculata* type, which was developed in the seventeenth and eighteenth centuries.[16] Key elements for the type are found in Revelation 12:1, which is quoted above, and Genesis 3:15: 'and I will put enmity between thee and the woman, and thy seed and her seed; it shall bruise thy head, and thou shalt bruise his heel'. Elements derived from this tradition include the Virgin depicted alone, without the child, standing on a globe, treading on a serpent. The globe in traditional *immaculata* representations is often, but not always a crescent moon (an ancient symbol of chastity). Here, if we follow the testimony of the visionary, the globe must – as we shall soon see – be interpreted differently, but its visual correspondence with the tradition for *immaculata* representations is so strong it nevertheless leads to recognition of the motif as an *immaculata*. In the original medal, twelve stars figure on the reverse, but not on the obverse.[17] In many later representations, medals, prints and statues, the Virgin is depicted with a halo made up of twelve stars, an element derived from the *immaculata* type and probably also inspired by the tradition of poetry and hymnody (for example, Ave Maris Stella). Later producers have gone further than the makers of the original medal in adapting it to the conventional *immaculata* type; or, perhaps more precisely: the identification is more outspoken. The reference to the Immaculate Conception is nevertheless unquestionable, above all in the legend: 'Oh Mary, *conceived without sin*, pray for us who have recourse to thee'.

There are chiefly two elements that deviate from the traditional *immaculata* iconography. The first is the pose of the Virgin. Her hands do not meet in front of her chest in the conventional gesture indicating prayer or piety; they are stretched out on either side of her body. The second unconventional element is the rays that emanate from her hands. Besides, the meaning of the globe upon which she treads is altered, or extended.

According to her own words, Catherine Labouré saw the Virgin holding a round object representing the globe[18] – in one account she says it was surmounted by a cross[19]

15 Calamari & Di Pasqua, *Visions of Mary*, p. 61. **16** The type was codified by the Spanish painter Francis Pacheco in his *Art of painting* from 1649: see J. Hall, *Hall's dictionary of signs and symbols in art* (London, 1992), pp 326–7. It was particularly popular in Spain: see S.L. Stratton, *The Immaculate Conception in Spanish art* (Cambridge, 1994). **17** The stars are not mentioned by Labouré herself, but may be seen in an early drawing believed to be based on her description. Reproduced in Laurentin & Roche, *Catherine Labouré*, p. 301 and Ajmar & Sheffield, 'The Miraculous Medal', 42. Dirvin claims that 'Catherine transmitted the details of the serpent and the stars to her director, at least by word of mouth, is morally certain, for she approved the Medal which bore both details from the first.' J. Dirvin, *Saint Catherine Laboure of the Miraculous Medal*, http://www.ewtn.com/library/MARY/CATLABOU.HTM, accessed 18 Aug. 2008, p. 51. **18** 'les *M*ains *Æ*levée[s] a la [h]auteur de l['][e]stomac d'une manièr[e] très aysée, tenan*s* dans *C*es *M*ains une bou*l*le qui représent*o*it le *G*lobe' in Laurentin & Roche, *Catherine Labouré*, p. 293. **19** 'Le Globe surmont*e* d'une petite croix' in Laurentin & Roche,

– in both hands. She also says that beautiful rings with gems appeared on the Virgin's fingers, and from these gems emanated rays of light, which were gradually extended so that eventually they made it impossible to see the gems.[20] She heard a voice telling her that the globe represented the world, particularly France, and each person in particular.[21] The rays were symbols of the graces which the Virgin would grant to those who asked for them.[22]

It seems sensible to see the medal as a compromise; it is neither precisely what the visionary reported to have seen, nor a purely conventional type. Traces of controversy regarding just the globe and the rays can be seen in historical facts and in the literature on the apparitions. Several commentators have raised the question whether there is a conflict between the visionary's own account and that of her confessor.[23] Eriksen and Stensvold, in a book on the cult of Mary in modern Catholicism from 2002,[24] Ajmar and Sheffield, in their article on the Miraculous Medal from 1994, and Laurentin and Roche, in their book on the same subject from 1976, all discuss the relationship between the report of the visionary and the medal. The centre of attention is the globe that the Virgin, according to Labouré, held in her hands.[25] The lack of just this element in the medal seems to have troubled the visionary herself, and in 1876 a statue of the Virgin holding a globe in her hands was made by Froc-Robert following Labouré's instructions. The Congregation of Rites prohibited this statue to be placed in the chapel at Rue du Bac, and it is therefore kept in the house of Catherine Labouré's own order, the Filles de la Charité at Reuilly.[26] Today there is a statue of the Virgin holding a globe in the Chapel of Our Lady of the Miraculous Medal. It was sculpted by Real del Sarte and placed there for the centenary in 1930.[27]

In 1878, a revised edition with commentary of Aladel's *Notice historique …* (see

---

Catherine Labouré, p. 351.   **20** 'des ann[e]aux à *c*es doi[gt]s *R*eve*t*ue de pierr[er]ie[s] plus belles les une[s] que les autres, les une[s] plus Gros[s]es et les autres plus petites, qui *J*ai*t*o*i*s des *R*ayons plus b[e]aux les un[s] que les autres, Ces *R*ayons sor*t*o*i*s des pierres les plus *G*rosses de plus *G*ros *R*ayons, toujour[s] en ses largissant et les peti[t]es plus peti[t]es et toujour[s] en *E*largissan*s* en bas ce qui *R*emplissoit tout le bas, *j*e ne *V*oye*n*s plus ces pier*d*[s]; …' in Laurentin & Roche, *Catherine Labouré*, p. 293.   **21** 'Comme je co*m*templais ce b[e]aux tableaux une voix *c*e fit entendre au fon[d] du cœur qui me dit ces parol*l*es. Cet[te] boul*l*e que vous voyez *R*ep*r*esente le Monde entier particulièremant la *f*rance et *C*haque personne*s* en particulier' in Laurentin & Roche, *Catherine Labouré*, p. 294. This is the reason why we can sometimes see 'FRANCE' written on the globe on which the Virgin stands.   **22** 'C'est le sï*m*bo*l*le des *G*ra*c*e[s] que je *R*ep*e*nd[s] sur les personnes qui me les demende[nt]' in Laurentin & Roche, *Catherine Labouré*, p. 294.   **23** The discussion up to 1976 is referred to by Laurentin & Roche, *Catherine Labouré*, pp 74–85.   **24** A. Eriksen & A. Stensvold, *Maria-kult og helgendyrkelse i moderne katolisisme* (Oslo, 2002), pp 125–7.   **25** The globe has associations with *Salvator mundi* iconography, and may therefore have been seen as unsuitable in terms of doctrine. It is also problematic that in Labouré's account the Virgin holds the globe in her hands, the same hands which carry the rings from which the rays representing the graces of the Virgin emanate. As the globe is said to represent the world, France and each person, it ought to be the *receiver*, not the *source* of the rays, as it may appear when held in the hands. Laurentin & Roche, *Catherine Labouré*, pp 74–85; Ajmar & Sheffield, 'The Miraculous Medal', 43–5.   **26** Laurentin & Roche, *Catherine Labouré*, p. 83.   **27** In 1933, the body of Catherine Labouré was exhumed, and afterwards it was moved to the Chapel of the Miraculous Medal. It now rests beneath the Altar of the Virgin of the Globe, so-called after the statue by Real del Sarte upon it. http://www.chapellenotredamedelamedaillemiraculeuse.com/EN/B3.asp, accessed 28 July 2008.

above, note 13) was issued under the name *La Medaille Miraculeuse: origine, histoire, diffusion, résultats*. This was to a large extent the work of M. Jules Chevalier, though it is Aladel's name that appears on the cover.[28] This book is the first to identify the – until then – anonymous visionary from Rue du Bac as Catherine Labouré (who died in 1876) and the first biography of her life. Chevalier apparently felt a need to reconcile the alleged discrepancy between the report of the visionary and the expression on the medal and to stress Aladel's truthfulness to Labouré's vision. He underlines the fact that the apparition – according to Labouré's own account – evolved through different phases, and claims that the motif on the medal is exactly correspondent to the last phase of the apparition.[29] Two engravings in the book illustrate two distinct stages of the apparition (fig. 5.1).[30]

So, does the Miraculous Medal depict the vision of Catherine Labouré or not? Does it portray one specific moment or perhaps a more general 'idea' that can be extracted from her accounts? The thoughts of those responsible have not been recorded in any sources, so we have to look to the images themselves and to tradition for answers. There can be little doubt that in composing the medal, Vachette, the engraver, in agreement with Aladel, made a conscious selection of elements to include. There is, however, nothing unusual or controversial about that. The engraver has to make formal considerations, and in the case of medals the small format is always a challenge. To the representatives of the Church, the message conveyed by the image would be most important; their interest was above all to make the most of the rhetorical potential which the material of Catherine Labouré's vision represented. A personal experience like a vision must be transferred or translated into a form which can be meaningful to others. If it is to be shared, and to become a common point of reference within the Church, the image must be articulated in a form, or a language that can be understood by all.[31] To be able to perform this act of translation, one must begin by interpreting the material – one must see it *as* something. Catherine Labouré's vision was – not unreasonably – seen as an *immaculata*, and therefore the *immaculata* scheme was used as the basis for the new type, with the alterations described above. A plausible reason for this is the concern that a motif closer to the description of the visionary might not so easily have been understood. The rays streaming from the hands of the

---

28 Laurentin & Roche, *Catherine Labouré*, pp 28–30. I have consulted a revised and extended edition from 1881, which I refer to in the following as Aladel, *La Médaille Miraculeuse*. **29** 'Ainsi l'on peut pense et dire que l'apparition décrite par soeur Catherine et celle rapportée par M. Aladel concordent parfaitement ensemble.' Aladel, *La Médaille Miraculeuse*, p. 78. **30** The first is signed PAN (N inverted), and the other is signed R. SELLIER and PANNEMAKER (Ns inverted). No date is given for the engravings, but they appear to be made for the book. According to Laurentin and Roche, the first image is corrected after the first edition of the book: 'le rayonnement a été rendu plus discret, à la suite de vives réactions': Laurentin & Roche, *Catherine Labouré*, p. 81. They further illustrate the different versions, and underline that the relationship between the images and the text of Chevalier present a problem which should be studied in further detail. **31** Today, the internet and film are popular media, much used to encourage devotion to, for example, Our Lady of the Miraculous Medal. See http://www.youtube.com/watch?v=C2pF5XhNSJk, accessed 28 Aug. 2008.

5.1 Engravings from the 1881 edition of Chevalier's book: the two phases of the apparition.

Virgin, representing her grace, are visually striking and intuitively understandable; they are therefore rhetorically efficient.

Many writers have noted the value and the adaptability of the Miraculous Medal and of the visions of Catherine Labouré to those eager to propagate the dogma of the Immaculate Conception.[32] The hermeneutic horizon of Fr Aladel and Msgr Quélen was of course decisive to the reception and interpretation of the visions, and they were no doubt more liable to seeing the apparition as the Immaculate Conception than other historical actors would be. Victor Turner points out that 'the Church obviously has a strong interest in strengthening and periodically revivifying faith in its basic doctrines and tenets'.[33] In early nineteenth-century France, it was above all faith in and devotion to Mary that it wished to revivify, and, in retrospect, we see that the Miraculous Medal was a factor that contributed to this development.

The role and function of visions, in the tradition of the Church, is not primarily to provide new knowledge, but to deepen the understanding of the eternal truths, by articulating or demonstrating different aspects in new contexts: 'Visions cannot add to, or even embellish, the deposit of faith; if genuine, and not spurious or of diabolic origin, they can only enhance devotion to, and perhaps understanding of, the truths therein contained'.[34] To do so, however, visions, just like material images, must be, and always have been, subject to interpretation. The representation of visions in material images is *one* articulation of such an interpretation. It is possible that the typical nineteenth-century visionaries, mostly children from rural areas, have enjoyed a lower status than clerical and learned visionaries from earlier centuries. Some interpreters, to a certain extent backed up by popular opinion, have suggested that the visionaries and their testimonies have not been taken seriously enough, and that they have experienced a form of power abuse on part of the Church.[35] One must be aware, however, that the visionary has never had 'copyright' to his or her own visions. Others may, and should, contribute to the interpretation of visions, if they are to fulfil any function beyond being a private experience of an individual.

The Miraculous Medal is in one sense atypical as an image based on an apparition in that there is no trace upon it of the visionary; only the year 1830 refers to the event that was the 'cause' of the medal. Based upon what we have said above about adapting visions to traditional forms, it seems unlikely that respect for the authority of the apparition as reported by the visionary would have prevented those responsible for designing the medal from including the visionary, *had they had a reason to do so*. There is a long tradition of representing the visionary and the vision together, as we shall see

---

32 The Immaculate Conception was proclaimed a dogma by Pius IX in 1854. Ajmar and Sheffield, for instance, argue convincingly that the Miraculous Medal functioned as a means to propagate and prepare the ground for the dogma. This point was, however, made already by Chevalier in Aladel, *La Médaille Miraculeuse*, pp 60f.
33 Turner & Turner, *Image and pilgrimage*, p. 210.   34 Ibid.   35 See for instance Eriksen & Stensvold, *Maria-kult*, pp 125–7. David Blackbourn gives a more balanced picture in *Marpingen*, p. 37. Émile Zola also discusses the role of Bernadette in his novel *Lourdes* from 1894.

below. The story about the apparition needs a visionary – therefore 'a sister' appears in the narrative and illustrations in the *Notice Historique* and some other early images, but her identity was not revealed until after her death. Catherine Labouré did not even appear before the commission whose task it was to investigate her visions; she spoke only to her confessor Aladel.[36] I will not speculate about the reasons for the long-lasting anonymity, but note the effects of it: the focus, that is, people's attention and devotion, were directed at the object of the vision – Our Lady of the Miraculous Medal, which has a close affinity to the Immaculate Conception. The presence of the Holy Virgin on Earth and not least her will and power to intercede and effect miracles, which was demonstrated by the 'workings' of the Miraculous Medal, became the key issue; not the visionary or the circumstances of the apparitions (see plate 6).

After her death, Catherine Labouré's portrait started appearing in popular images, often alongside the medal, and more attention was directed at her person. In 1933, her body was exhumed and moved to the chapel at Rue du Bac. She was beatified that year and canonized in 1947. Many books have been written about Catherine Labouré and the chapel at Rue du Bac is visited by many pilgrims. Still, the cult of the Miraculous Medal is above all a generalized devotion and 'such devotions attempt to purify and render more virtuous, life in a familiar, structured place, rather than to seek initiatory renovation through a journey to a far shrine'.[37]

LOURDES MEDALS

The variations in the images concerning the Miraculous Medal are few and the literature about it fairly discrete. The writings about, the images representing and all the material traces of Lourdes, on the other hand, are so many and so varied that our approach to this material must necessarily be different. The differences regarding the apparitions in Paris and Lourdes – the historical circumstances, the respective roles of the visionaries, the development of the cults and the interpretations of the messages – are notable and interesting. However, the two events are also closely related; in time and space and with regard to content and subject.

Lourdes is among the largest pilgrimage sites of the world; about six million visitors go there each year,[38] and the numbers were already high in the nineteenth century.[39] The pilgrims come to see the place where the Virgin appeared to the young girl Bernadette Soubirous eighteen times, between 11 February and 16 July in 1858. On one occasion (25 March), the Virgin identified herself thus: 'I am the Immaculate Conception'. Though popular among all sorts of pilgrims, Lourdes has above all been a place where sick people have come in the hope of being cured of diseases – drinking

36 Laurentin & Roche, *Catherine Labouré*, p. 235; Dirvin, *Saint Catherine Labouré*, p. 62; Kselman, *Miracles and prophecies*, p. 154.   37 Turner & Turner, *Image and pilgrimage*, p. 213.   38 http://www.lourdes-france.org/, accessed 18 Aug. 2008.   39 Kselman, *Miracles and prophecies*, p. 165.

and bathing in water from the source revealed to Bernadette in her ninth vision, and praying at the grotto where all the apparitions took place.

Pilgrimage commenced spontaneously as early as 1858 and soon became well organized events.[40] A railway line to Lourdes was opened in 1866. Hospitals and hotels were built to accommodate the pilgrims, as was practically a whole new town, which could cater for their various needs. Facilities to bathe in the holy water and a medical office where alleged healings were investigated were established early. The first chapel to be built was blessed and opened in 1866, with Bernadette Soubirous present.[41] It is today the crypt of the larger Basilica of the Immaculate Conception, which was finished in 1872.[42] The Rosary Basilica was finished by 1889 and consecrated in 1901.[43] National pilgrimages were organized from 1873 and several organizations were formed, with the intent of helping people reach Lourdes, for example by collecting money to finance their journeys, actually accompanying the sick on the way there, etc. Volunteers and clergy worked side by side in this place, which was in many ways a traditional shrine, but at the same time had features in common with early tourist destinations.[44] The use of the printed press for advertising and the railway for transport, and the mass production of religious souvenirs are examples of distinctly modern features without which it is hard to imagine such a development.[45]

Pilgrims and tourists take home souvenirs. Such souvenirs serve different functions, depending on the attitude and needs of the owner. For a pious Catholic, a souvenir from Lourdes may become an instrument of devotion. Some medals from Lourdes are treated like relics; they may contain Lourdes water, or they may have touched the rock of the grotto and/or been blessed by a cleric on the spot. As most shrines, certainly in modern times, and probably at all times, Lourdes has, from the very beginning, hosted a number of retailers of religious goods, such as medals (see plate 7).

We shall take a closer look at some elements that recur in an overwhelming number

40 Bishop Laurence bought the territory of the grotto in 1861. In 1866, the missionary order the Missionaries of the Immaculate Conception, commonly known as the Grotto Fathers, were given ecclesiastical jurisdiction over all matters at the site. At first they were responsible for organizing pilgrimages too, but that was later taken over by the Augustinian Fathers of the Assumption: S. Kaufmann, 'Selling Lourdes: pilgrimage, tourism and the mass marketing of the sacred in nineteenth-century France' in S. Baranowski and E. Furlough (eds), *Being elsewhere: tourism, consumer culture, and identity in modern Europe and North America* (Ann Arbor, MI, 2001), pp 63–88 at p. 66. See also R. Harris, *Lourdes: body and spirit in the secular age* (New York, 1999).   **41** http://www.lourdes-france.org/index.php?goto_centre=ru&contexte=en&id=436, accessed 18 Aug. 2008; Harris, *Lourdes*, p. 136.   **42** http://www.lourdes-france.org/index.php?goto_centre=ru&contexte=en&id=435, accessed 18 Aug. 2008.   **43** http://www.lourdes-france.org/index.php?goto_centre=ru&contexte=en&id=438, accessed 18 Aug. 2008.   **44** Suzanne Kaufmann claims that 'Catholic pilgrimage in western Europe was altered by the very development that created modern tourism during the second half of the nineteenth century' and 'the rise of consumer culture during this period transformed the act of pilgrimage into an early form of tourism characterized by inexpensive church-organized voyages and the buying and selling of mass-produced sacred goods': Kaufmann, 'Selling Lourdes', p. 64.   **45** This view is held particularly high in S. Kaufmann, *Consuming visions: mass culture and the Lourdes shrine* (Ithaca, NY, 2005). This book is dedicated to establishing Lourdes as a distinctly modern shrine, and polemicizes against Kselman's *Miracles and prophecies* and Harris' *Lourdes*, which both see historicist, medievalizing ideas as constitutive in the formation of the Lourdes shrine and cult. The discussion will be thoroughly treated in my dissertation.

of images,[46] and which therefore can be said to constitute a standard repertoire of iconographic markers of Lourdes.[47] The 'classical' Lourdes medals have a representation of Bernadette Soubirous praying before the Virgin, who appears in the grotto, on one side.[48] In polychrome images, prints and sculpture, the Virgin is always dressed in white robes with a blue sash, and there are normally roses (which should be yellow or golden according to Soubirous' description, but are often red or pink) at her feet. Medals are normally monochrome, and because of the small size not all details are discernible.[49] The Virgin is, however, normally depicted with hands joined in front of her chest, as in prayer, and with a rosary hanging over her right arm. Sometimes the words 'I am the Immaculate Conception' accompany her picture, for instance in the form of a halo around her head. On the other side of the medal is often an image of the Virgin (for example, as the type Our Lady of Lourdes, to which I will return, or the Immaculate Conception), sometimes a portrait of Bernadette Soubirous,[50] an image of the Basilica of the Immaculate Conception and the Rosary Basilica at Lourdes, or a text like 'Souvenir from Lourdes' or 'I have prayed for you at Lourdes' (see plate 8).

The most direct, literal understanding of the most common motif – Bernadette praying before the Virgin in the grotto – is as a representation of the event which is the reason and basis for all that has happened at Lourdes, and the place where it all happened. The narrative form of the representation gives the image the appearance of depicting one particular instant. As we know, however, Bernadette Soubirous had several visions, over a period of months. There exist depictions of the singular apparitions, discernible by details in the iconography for those with a detailed knowledge of the particularities, for example, in the stained glass windows in the Basilica of the Immaculate Conception and in the *gemmaux* in the Basilica of St Pius X in Lourdes. Some medals may of course be based on such images and refer to one specific apparition, for example, the sixteenth, where the Virgin identified herself as 'The Immaculate Conception'. In general, however, I do not think one can expect the average user of a Lourdes Medal to be able to discern the individual apparitions, and therefore it is more reasonable to interpret the motif as a synthesis of all the apparitions – or rather of the idea 'Our Lady of Lourdes appearing to Bernadette Soubirous'.

As was the case with the Miraculous Medal, and as is indeed the case with all religious images, to apprehend their full meaning, we must investigate beyond that which is immediately seen. Let us now take a look at the three key elements in the images: Bernadette Soubirous, the Virgin Mary and the physical surroundings.

---

46 It is often hard to date these images; they are mass-produced products of a visual culture in which artistic individuality and progress are irrelevant. Therefore we risk some chronological inaccuracies in treating many images together, but due to the conservatism and uniformity of the culture, that need not be a problem. **47** These elements do not appear in *all* images or medals – they are *typical* and *common*, not *necessary* or *obligatory*. **48** In duplicate Lourdes grottos, which exist in thousands across the world, a statue of Bernadette Soubirous praying is also normally included. **49** Because of the popularity of the motif, one can assume many beholders were able to 'fill in' the missing details themselves – a point which will be elaborated in the course of the argument. **50** These are presumably all post 1933, when Bernadette Soubirous was canonized.

THE VISIONARY

First of all, we notice that the motif presents not only the vision of Bernadette, that is, what she saw, but also *her seeing* the Virgin. A whole scene, set in a physical space, is represented. In this, the Lourdes medals differ from the Miraculous Medal. Devotional medals from older shrines typically portray a (miraculous) image or a celestial being, normally codified in a 'type', that is, the object of pilgrimage and of devotion. The Miraculous Medal stands in this tradition, and the medal itself, which is of course understood to represent what the visionary saw, even though it has been subject to some interpretation, becomes the miraculous image. The Lourdes medals, however, relate to a different pictorial tradition, that of representing *visionaries and their visions* together.

Bernadette is always portrayed kneeling, humbly, sometimes praying the rosary, and sometimes holding a candle. It is a central aspect of the tale of Lourdes that Bernadette did not know or understand what she was witnessing – yet she behaved 'correctly' because of her good nature and pious attitude. Facing a being that she could not identify, but intuitively took to be celestial, she knelt down and started praying. In doing this, Bernadette Soubirous is an example to all. The representation of that which really happened is at the same time a model for all devotion to Our Lady of Lourdes.

In the universe of Catholic piety, the saints play the role of mediator between man and God, and in the history of images we find many genres and pictorial traditions that articulate this relation in different ways (Sacra Conversazione, Saints' Lives etc.). In donor images, not saints but donors mediate between the viewer and the portrayed deity.[51] Visionaries are often portrayed along with the representation of their vision (see plate 9). Their presence aids the identification of the motif as just *their* vision, and in some cases serves as a reminder that the gift of a vision is obtainable, in the sense that visions are part of the living tradition of the Church, not something belonging exclusively to the past. The truth keeps unfolding in time, in history, and theoretically, anyone may experience it.[52] Visions are often experienced after intense meditations and prayers, and they are often understood as happening to someone who has reached an elevated level of consciousness through a spiritual effort. Historically, they are probably relatively more common within monastic communities and among mystics who actively seek them. However, this is not necessarily so, and many of the most famous nineteenth-century Marian apparitions took place in very different milieux and under different circumstances. The apparitions in La Salette in 1846, Lourdes in 1858 and Pontmain in 1871, as well as those in Fatima in 1917, all took place outdoors, in rural environments, and were experienced by children. Including the visionaries in

---

51 A donor image is an image in which the person(s) who has paid for it with the intention of donating it, normally to a church or a chapel, is included in the image. The donor is often depicted somewhat 'off-centre' of the motif, but integrated in the composition.   **52** N. Frye, *The great code: the Bible and literature* (New York, 1982), p. 136.

1 Portrait of Anna Maria Giannetti Taigi in the church of San Crisogono, Rome (photograph by Sarah Fiona Maclaren).

2 Portrait of Elisabetta Canori Mora in the church of San Carlino alle Quattro Fontane, Rome (photograph by Sarah Fiona Maclaren).

3 Anna Maria Giannetti Taigi. Buried in the church of San Crisogono, Rome
(photograph by Sarah Fiona Maclaren).

4 Benoît-Joseph Labre. Buried in the church of the Madonna dei Monti, Rome
(photograph by Sarah Fiona Maclaren).

5 The Miraculous Medal, twenty-first century, aluminium. Bergen Museum,
Collection of Coins and Medals (photograph by Svein Skare).

6 Catherine Labouré and the Miraculous Medal. Twentieth-century devotional card.

7 Lourdes Medal by Penin of Lyon. Nineteenth century, silver. This is a more elaborate version than most popular medals with the same motif. Bergen Museum, Collection of Coins and Medals (photograph by Svein Skare).

8 Lourdes Medal, integrated in wallet-size laminated card, with images of St Bernadette, the vision, the basilicas and the sculpture presently in the grotto, 2008. Bergen Museum, Collection of Coins and Medals (photographs by Svein Skare).

9 The vision of King Heraclius, from the frontal of Nedstryn church in Nordfjord, Norway, fourteenth century, painted panel. Bergen Museum (photograph by Svein Skare).

10 D. Georgantas, 'Platytera', wall painting in the Church of St John,
Markopoulo, Attika, 1910–20 (photograph by Georgios Kordis).

11 Bronze medal, 1852, by a French medallist, A. Lecomte. The medal commemorates the reintroduction in Lille of public processions with the most Holy Sacrament (photograph by Henrik von Aachen).

12 The reverse of a zinc medal by August Neuss (active c.1840–70) commemorating the national effort to finish the cathedral of Cologne. The inscription on both obverse and reverse reads: 'Cologne of old once founded this wonderful house of God/1248, but Germany has now come together and finishes it with the help of God/1842' (photograph by Henrik von Aachen).

13 Frontispiece and title page of the *Manuel de la Passion de Notre Seigneur Jésus Christ, suivi de quelques pratiques de piété en l'honneur de Jésus souffrant* by the Flemish Jesuit Fr Victor de Buck, published by Ch. Beyaert-Storie in Bruges, 1885. The book design copies the character of late gothic Books of Hours (photograph by Henrik von Aachen).

14 Cerro de los Angeles, the monument to the Sacred Heart of Jesus destroyed during the civil war; contemporary state (photograph by Ewa Klekot).

15 Cerro de los Angeles, monument to the Sacred Heart of Jesus constructed after the civil war (photograph by Ewa Klekot).

16 Cerro de los Angeles, statue of the post-war monument with the inscription
Reino en España (I rule in Spain) (photograph by Ewa Klekot).

17 Contemporary sticker by *Comunión Tradicionalista Carlista*; the
motto says *Reynaré en España* (I will rule in Spain) (private collection).

18 Material religion in a Catholic home in Northern Ireland (photograph by E. Frances King).

19 Material religion in a Protestant home in Northern Ireland (photograph by E. Frances King).

20 Personal devotional leaflets in Northern Ireland (photograph by E. Frances King).

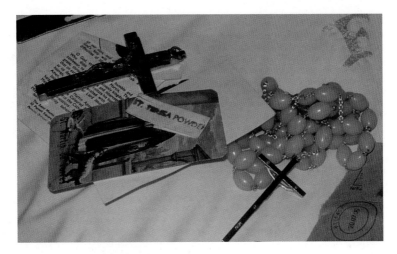

21 Religious items in a bedroom in Northern Ireland (photograph by E. Frances King).

22 Royal memorabilia in Northern Ireland (photograph by E. Frances King).

images is a way of stressing the point that the Virgin sees and cares about everybody, not only the very learned or spiritually 'advanced'. It may even suggest that she prefers to turn to these country children, presumably 'innocent' in the sense of unspoilt by the rationalism and individualism which to an increasing extent pervaded society, and to which the Church was strongly and openly opposed.

Many Christians, and (potential) users of medals, to whom the Church wanted to communicate something, could identify themselves with Bernadette Soubirous. A poor but pious, almost illiterate country girl of ill health, she also easily aroused sympathy. And the pilgrims who were in time particularly attracted to Lourdes – the *malades* – probably found hope and consolation in Bernadette's own story. The Virgin, in one of the first apparitions, said she could not promise to make her happy in this life, but in the next. Bernadette Soubirous, to whom the source of the water which is believed to have cured so many was revealed, was never cured of her own illness. She died at the age of thirty-five, having endured severe suffering and physical pain in her short life. Knowing that she shared their destiny may be a comfort to those who are *not* cured at Lourdes, and may make their sufferings easier to bear.

Including Bernadette Soubirous in the pictures then, is a way of appealing to a wide audience, and also a way to encourage them to join in the devotion to the Virgin Mary. Depicted in front of the grotto, kneeling and praying, she is an example to pilgrims to Lourdes, and to those addressing Our Lady of Lourdes elsewhere. An encounter between a visionary and a heavenly person is often understood to take place, in the words of Barbara Nolan, 'between time and eternity'.[53] The representation on the medal can help the pious to spiritually transcend time and space, and experience a sense of community with Bernadette Soubirous, with all the other pilgrims and faithful who turn to Our Lady of Lourdes, and with all those whom she protects and bestows her grace upon.

In the first years after the apparitions, whereas the cults of the Immaculate Conception and of 'Notre Dame de Lourdes' were eagerly promoted, it may seem as though Bernadette's person was seen almost as a threat, by the authorities of the shrine, due to 'the perpetual possibility that her presence would divert attention away from the sanctuary, the Grotto and the Virgin herself'.[54] Ruth Harris notes that 'she remains omnipresent in the story, but astonishingly absent from the place'.[55] Suzanne Kaufmann points to the fact that only after the departure of Soubirous could the shrine be developed as the grotto fathers wanted.[56] Bernadette Soubirous is a necessary element in the story of Lourdes; without her, the story loses much of its

---

53 B. Nolan, *The gothic visionary perspective* (Princeton, NJ, 1977), p. 39. The state described thus, is sometimes referred to as *aevum,* and Nolan, writing about medieval visions specifies three possible uses of that term: 'Finally, and most important for us, *aevum* is used to describe the durative state of the human soul when, drawn out of the pure succession of events in earthly time, it is raised up to the realization of its own wholeness and perfection by coming into contact with the divine presence.' **54** Harris, *Lourdes*, p. 137. **55** Ibid. **56** Kaufmann, *Consuming visions*, pp 21–2.

poignancy and appeal; therefore she is present in all these images, even though she is not the object of the cult.

THE VIRGIN

Portraying Bernadette was not too difficult; she lived in Lourdes until 1866 and was painted and photographed on several occasions. The representation of the Virgin is a little different. An unmistakeable type needed to be established, based on a visual interpretation of Bernadette's testimony. She had to describe what she had seen on numerous occasions, and comment on several images presented to her as grounds for comparison.[57] Her descriptions of *aquéro*[58] are fairly coherent, but not entirely. The question of whether she looked like the Miraculous Medal was brought up by several interrogators. It was interesting because such a link might help establish a connection between the two apparitions. Soubirous did not always give the same answer, and Laurentin, who sums up the discussion of different contributors, can only conclude that 'Our Lady of Lourdes *sometimes* had a pose which reminded of the Miraculous Medal, but without the rays'.[59] The 'normal' pose, which characterizes the type Our Lady of Lourdes, is with joined hands, as in prayer. This is the pose of the 'authorized' depictions of Our Lady of Lourdes from the early history of the shrine: Fabisch's sculpture in the grotto, Cabuchet's sculpture in the Upper Basilica and Raffl's sculpture in the Rosary Square[60] – which together constitutes the type.

THE PLACE

The type 'Our Lady of Lourdes' is recognizable without reference to a place, yet the grotto and the landmarks of Lourdes figure in millions of popular images. The Basilica of the Immaculate Conception and the Basilica of the Rosary at Lourdes are included in the background of many representations of Bernadette praying before the Virgin in the grotto, and on the reverse of medals. The basilicas were, of course, not there when Bernadette had her visions, but were built later, as a consequence of the visions and events that later occurred at the site. Their presence not only underlines that a chronological development must be interpreted in the images; it has several further implications.

---

57 It is an interesting, though hardly surprising, fact that Bernadette was not satisfied with any of the images shown to her – no one seemed to capture her experience of the Virgin. R. Laurentin, *Lourdes histoire authentique*, 3 vols (Paris, 2002), iii, pp 184ff.   **58** The word used by Bernadette for what she saw. She herself never identified the Virgin and when she repeated the words of the object of her vision, identifying itself as the Immaculate Conception, many assume that Bernadette did not understand what that meant, as she was probably not familiar with the idea. Alan Neame challenges this view in *The happening at Lourdes or the sociology of the grotto* (London, 1968), pp 62–6.   **59** 'Notre-Dame de Lourdes eut *parfois* un geste qui ressamblait à celui de la médaille miraculeuse, sans les rayons' in Laurentin, *Lourdes histoire authentique*, p. 186.   **60** The grotto statue was consecrated in 1864. The two other Madonnas were both crowned in 1876.

In the thirteenth apparition, the Virgin requested that a chapel be built at the site, and that people come there in procession. The basilicas are the manifest answer to that request, and including them in the representations brings a dialogic aspect to the images.

The role of the geographical place 'Lourdes' in the visual culture to which the medals and images belong, is complicated. The apparitions at Lourdes are closely attached to just that particular place, but at the same time the whole myth can be transferred to other places. The holy is, in Catholic tradition, not fixed in space or time. It can be de-localized; water from Lourdes is assumed to be 'efficient' anywhere, and it can be reproduced; 'Duplicate shrines became sacred because they participated in the story of Lourdes'.[61] There exist numerous Lourdes grottoes across the Catholic world, where one can experience the spirit of Lourdes and direct one's prayer and devotion to Our Lady of Lourdes.[62] Thomas Kselman describes devotions dedicated to Our Lady of Lourdes as the most prominent of the generalized devotions developed in the nineteenth century.[63] Still – the actual place of Lourdes *is* special, even though the duplicate grottos are perceived practically as authentic, and the basilicas, which are unique to Lourdes, help identify that place.

According to Ursula Hagen, who has written a thesis on pilgrims' medals in the Rhineland, it became increasingly common to include depictions of shrines and places of pilgrimage in such medals in the nineteenth century, eventually at the expense of other motifs.[64] She points to how increased stress on the earthly reality may, in its extreme consequence, lead to a total profanization of the medals; previously religious objects become souvenirs of geographical, political or social places, rather than distinctly religious ones. Whether this may be said to be the case with Lourdes medals will depend on the attitude and the intention of the person using the medal.

THE FUNCTION OF THE IMAGES

From these fairly specific analyses of some selected motifs, I would like to turn now to more general reflections on the function of medals. Historically, religious medals have had didactic, commemorative, social and devotional functions.[65] They have identified

61 C. McDannell, *Material Christianity: religion and popular culture in America* (New Haven, CT, 1995), p. 155. **62** According to a decree of 5 December 2007, Benedict XVI agreed to grant Plenary Indulgence for the occasion of the 150th anniversary of the apparition of the Blessed Virgin Mary at Lourdes 'to the Christian faithful who, from 8 December 2007 until 8 December 2008, devoutly and in accordance with the established conditions, visit the Grotto of Massabielle, as well as those who, from 2–11 February 2008 visit a blessed image of the Blessed Virgin Mary of Lourdes solemnly displayed for public veneration, in any church, oratory, grotto or suitable place.' http://www.vatican.va/roman_curia/tribunals/apost_penit/documents/rc_trib_appen_doc_20071121_- decreto-lourdes_en.html, accessed 10 May 2010. **63** Kselman, *Miracles and prophecies*, p. 35. **64** U. Hagen, *Die Wallfahrtsmedaillen des Rheinlandes in Geschichte und Volksleben* (Köln, 1973), p. 26. **65** See E.H. Seland, '19th-century devotional medals' in H. Laugerud and L.K. Skinnebach (eds), *Instruments of devotion: the practices and objects of religious piety from the late Middle Ages to the 20th century* (Aarhus, 2007), pp 157–72. The topic is discussed in my doctoral dissertation.

members of societies and confraternities and united the pious in the common showing forth of a shared guiding star; they have been souvenirs from pilgrimages, and gifts to people whom pilgrims and Catholics in general have wished well. They have been carried as tokens of love and highly cherished. They have to some extent taught children and adults about the Virgin Mary and other holy persons, but probably more importantly, they have *inspired* them to devotion and faith, aided them in and directed their prayers, articulating their hopes of healing and salvation. The Miraculous Medal has been reported to work miracles, such as sudden conversions and instantaneous healing of diseases and presumably incurable conditions. According to the teaching of the Catholic Church, however, a medal as such cannot work miracles;[66] only God, in this case through the intercession of the Virgin Mary, can do so.

It is common for medals to be blessed by clergymen using an appropriate formula, and thus they obtain the status of sacramentals. Sacramentals are defined by the Second Vatican Council as 'sacred signs that bear a resemblance to the sacraments; they signify effects, particularly of a spiritual kind, which are obtained through the Church's intercession'.[67] Sometimes, medals also have indulgences attached to them. Medals can be, then, not only instruments of devotion, but instruments of Divine mercy administered by the Church. If medals must be blessed to 'work' anyway, to paraphrase David Freedberg, could not any stone or piece of metal be blessed; need they have images on them? Does it matter how they look?[68] Of course this question is purely rhetorical, and Freedberg answers affirmatively that the shaping of the image must be of some importance when small reproductions can transmit the religious power of archetypal images;[69] it cannot all amount to consecration or power derived from contact[70] – which is nevertheless relevant, as part of existing practices.

In the case of Catholic devotional medals, an important point in support of the assertion that it matters how they look is that the blessing is a *general* quality invested in the medal by someone authorized to do so. It is the motif on the medal that *articulates* and *specifies* the general blessing. The tradition of Catholicism contains innumerable objects, texts and practices, the function of which is just to show forth, or remind of, or provide an occasion to reflect upon, certain aspects of the comprehensive and eternal Truth. The concrete articulations of discrete phenomena provide an access to their common cause and first mover, that is, God. Thus, the abstract is grasped through the concrete; the whole is grasped through its parts.

---

66 See, for example, L. Ott, *Fundamentals of Catholic Dogma* (St Louis, MO, 1964), p. 349.   **67** Here cited from J.M. Miller, CSB, 'Sacramentals in Catholic theology' in A. Ball, *The how-to book of sacramentals* (Huntington, IN, 2005), pp 9–19 at pp 11–12.   **68** This question is posed in David Freedberg's influential work *The power of images: studies in the history and theory of response* (Chicago, 1991), p. 112.   **69** In our case, apparitions take the place of archetypal images, and as we have seen, the adaptation of apparitions involves an act of interpretation which can be complex and controversial. I do not see, however, that this transformation is essentially different to that which Freedberg discusses, from archetype to reproduction, so his discussion is of interest to us.   **70** Freedberg, *The power of images*. The discussion fills much of chapters 5 and 6; see particularly pp 124 and 135.

Furthermore, medals are images like any other images in the Catholic tradition, with complex roles. The veneration of images has played an important part in pious life throughout the history of the Church, even though there have been times when it has been controversial. It is not the image as such that is venerated, but that which the image represents, the prototype of which the image is a sign; holy persons, and ultimately God. As stated by the Council of Trent (1545–63):

> The honour which is shown them is referred to the prototypes which they represent, so that by means of the images which we kiss and before which we uncover the head and prostrate ourselves, we adore Christ and venerate the saints whose likeness they bear.[71]

This was no new idea, simply a confirmation of the teaching and tradition of the Catholic Church, which had been brought to the fore in answer to the iconoclasm of the Reformation. The Seventh Ecumenical Council at Nicaea in 787 also confronted iconoclasm, and sought to put an end to the conflicts that had raged in Byzantium by encouraging the continuation of the tradition of making

> pictorial representations, agreeable to the history of the preaching of the Gospel, a tradition useful in many respects, but especially in this, that so the incarnation of the Word of God is shown forth as real and not merely phantastic.[72]

The general didactic function of images has long been recognized and appreciated. Pope Gregory I's letters to Serenus of Marseilles of July 599 and October 600 have for some time been regarded as *the* classical articulation of medieval image-doctrine, and are the source of the notion of images as the 'Bible of the illiterate'. Several authors have shown this to be an insufficient interpretation of Gregory's words.[73] In the thirteenth century, the didactic function of images was specified further, for example, by Thomas Aquinas, and by Johannes Balbus, both of whom name three ways in which the Church may use images didactically: to instruct the simple people; to imprint the examples of holy persons in their memories by letting them see images of them before their eyes every day; and to arouse and strengthen pious sentiments that are more likely to be affected by what is seen than by what is heard.[74] The Council of Trent also underlined the didactic value of the images:

---

71 http://www.ewtn.com/library/councils/trent25.htm#2, accessed 6 Aug. 2008. **72** http://www.newadvent. org/fathers/3819.htm, accessed 6 Aug. 2008. **73** See L.G. Duggan, 'Was art really the book of the illiterate?', *Word and Image*, 5:3 (1989), 227–51 and C.M. Chazelle, 'Pictures, books and the illiterate: Pope Gregory I's letters to Serenus of Marseille', *Word and Image*, 6:2 (1990), 138–53. **74** H. Laugerud, 'Det hagioskopiske blikk. Bilder, syn og erkjennelse i høy- og senmiddelalder (The hagioscopic gaze: images, sight and knowledge in the high- and late Middle Ages)' (PhD, U Bergen, 2005), pp 62–3.

Moreover, let the bishops diligently teach that by means of the stories of the mysteries of our redemption portrayed in paintings and other representations, the people are instructed and confirmed in the articles of faith, which ought to be borne in mind and constantly reflected upon; also that great profit is derived from all holy images, not only because the people are thereby reminded of the benefits and gifts bestowed on them by Christ, but also because through the saints the miracles of God and salutary examples are set before the eyes of the faithful, so that they may give God thanks for those things, may fashion their own life and conduct in imitation of the saints and be moved to adore and love God and cultivate piety.[75]

The medals belong to the same tradition, and obviously it matters what is depicted: it matters what the images 'teach', what the faithful have presented to them, what is imprinted in their memories. It matters because they are to be moved to follow the example of Christ and the saints in their own lives.

To a pious user of a devotional medal, it is primarily the image, and sometimes the accompanying words that direct his or her thoughts and emotions – in this case, to the Virgin, represented as the Immaculate Conception. Marina Warner claims that 'only Catholics with a decided theological bent grasp the exemption from original sin defined by the dogma'.[76] Beholders without such competence have also, however, recognized the particular types which she is *simultaneously* represented as; the concrete manifestations of the theoretical concept, that is, Our Lady of Lourdes and Our Lady of the Miraculous Medal, to whom they have in turn directed their devotions, prayers and hopes.[77]

RHETORIC AND MEMORY

For an image like those on devotional medals to 'work', it is crucial that the beholder interprets it correctly, that is, *recognizes the motif.* Therefore, the most important quality of a devotional image is not artistic, nor didactic; it is rhetorical. Depending on the attitude of the beholder, the role of the image may be to instruct or remind her or him of that which is depicted, to reinforce the message it stands for, and/or to persuade her or him of its truth, strength and relevance. Last, but not least, the image should move the beholder to certain actions or practices – specifically devotional or more generally Christian, hence 'good'.

75 http://www.ewtn.com/library/councils/trent25.htm#2, accessed 6 Aug. 2008.   **76** M. Warner, *Alone of all her sex: the myth and the cult of the Virgin Mary* (London, 1976), p. 238.   **77** Devlin recounts an anecdote from F. Boulard's *Premiers itinéraires en sociologie religieuse* (Paris, 1966) from Brittany around 1890, which shows that the faithful were sometimes very specific in terms of who they turned to: 'a preacher ... insisted that no matter where one worshipped, one still honoured the same Virgin. At the exit, an old lady was heard remarking to another: "Did you hear that old fool maintaining there's only one Our Lady everywhere? As if everyone didn't know that the daughter is here and the mother at Revecourt"' in J. Devlin, *The superstitious mind: French peasants and the supernatural in the nineteenth century* (New Haven, CT, 1987), p. 7.

These functions of images are derived from classical rhetoric. One must take care not to reduce the vast tradition of rhetoric to a narrow theory of eloquence or a receipt of persuasion; it concerns many aspects of human communication, in a wide sense. Rhetoric may also be visual, and Aristotle's key terms defining different means of appeal – ethos, logos and pathos – and Cicero's tasks of the orator (*officia oratoris*), often listed as *docere, delectare, movere*[78] – that is teach, please, move – are highly useful tools when analyzing images.[79]

In order to fulfil these functions, images must meet some criteria, which cannot be universally articulated, but which are specific to the singular communicative situation. The devotional medals we have discussed are characterized by a visual rhetoric that is particular to them. This rhetoric is closely connected to the function of the images, which again depends on how people relate to the images: what they expect from them, what they find in them and how they treat them.

The motifs analyzed here are characterized by a simplicity and uniformity typical of the visual culture to which the medals belong. This culture may be seen as more or less contrary to that of 'high art'. This does not make the popular images inferior; they simply operate differently, in another rhetorical situation. Their rather simple and unoriginal appearance may be seen as a consequence of mass production. Nevertheless, the medals possess a clarity that may be appreciated as a virtue. Their motifs are recognized by their intended audience, rarely confused, which is a good fundament for rhetorical efficiency. This can be seen in relation to the insight identified by Mary Carruthers in medieval monastic culture, where images and rhetorical mnemotechnical craft go hand in hand: 'crowding' was a well-recognized principle of 'forgetting'. Too many images overlapping each other in a given location, 'images that are too much alike will confuse and even cancel one another out'.[80] Therefore, the types must be simple, yet distinct. Repetition is good, variation potentially hazardous. This in part explains the necessity obviously felt by Church authorities to modify Catherine Labouré's vision so radically before issuing the medal that later became 'the Miraculous Medal'.

To understand how the medals can communicate and have a specific rhetoric, we have to take into account the importance of memory. Memory is a central aspect of all rhetoric. It is one of the five parts of rhetoric (or activities of the orator) often listed as *inventio, dispositio, elocutio, memoria* and *actio*.[81] *Memoria* is often translated as 'memorizing' – learning by heart, but memory is also a creative category, which contributes to actively constituting knowledge as much as passively storing it.[82]

78 M.T. Cicero, *On the ideal orator* (New York, 2001), pp 10, 29; G.A. Kennedy, *Classical rhetoric and its Christian and secular tradition from ancient to modern times* (Chapel Hill, NC, 1980), p. 100; Ø. Andersen, *I retorikkens hage* (Oslo, 1995), pp 42–3.   **79** A thorough and interesting text about visual rhetoric in history, theory and practice is J. Kjeldsen, *Visuel retorik* (PhD, U Bergen, 2002). An electronic version can be found at http://hdl.handle.net/1956/2643, accessed 21 Dec. 2010.   **80** M. Carruthers, *The craft of thought: meditation, rhetoric, and the making of images, 400–1200* (Cambridge, 1998), p. 55.   **81** Cicero, *On the ideal orator*, pp 29 ff; Andersen, *I retorikkens hage*, p. 43.   **82** See Carruthers' *The craft of thought* on the importance of memory in the

A classical mnemotechnique, the invention of which is attributed to Simonides of Ceos,[83] is to compose mental maps, or physical, spatial entities such as architectonic structures, furnished rooms etc., which one in turn 'fills' with the material to be remembered. The iconography of Lourdes medals, with the visionary and her vision situated in a clearly defined space may perhaps be seen as an example of this represented visually. Our Lady of Lourdes has an individual iconography, and the type as such is independent of the place where she appeared, but in popular images she is very often depicted in the grotto. This fact not only identifies the motif and fixes it in geographical space; it also provides a mental space that the beholder may fill with his or her memories, of the story they have heard and/or of the place they have visited. The image cannot represent, or tell the whole narrative; but it can trigger the memory of the beholder – who must of course be familiar with the story in order to make use of the image. The image can be seen as a form of synecdoche; that which is represented stands for more, and as is normally the case with such tropes it requires a common, often tacit knowledge, to grasp the meaning in its full extent.

Another reason why memory is such a central category is of course that the whole tradition of the Church can be said to consist in anamnesis – recalling. What is recalled and re-enacted is above all the Life and Passion of Christ. The articulations of these memories constitute the liturgical year, the elements of the mass, the sacraments etc. In addition, the tradition of piety consists in remembering, addressing and imitating not only Christ himself, but also important events and holy persons. The primary function of the devotional medals is therefore to remind the faithful of the Virgin Mary, of the Immaculate Conception and of the continuing interest and love she demonstrates through her apparitions to different visionaries and through the miraculous cures she is believed to effectuate.

All images can facilitate and participate in anamnesis, but medals are perhaps particularly well suited to doing so. Being medals, they have something in common – what we might with Wittgenstein call a family resemblance with other medals.[84] The members of this family have differing features and functions, but one connotation that clings to them all is that of commemoration. Devotional medals commemorate, for example, Marian apparitions as other contemporary medals commemorate events of private, public or political character. The relationship between the family members has the effect of emphasizing that which they have in common – and just those features stand out as characteristic of the singular exemplars, despite their individual variations. Being part of the medal family, the devotional examples have their commemorative function emphasized.

The other reason for which medals are particularly well suited to work as memory triggers is more phenomenological: medals are made to be carried with you; you can

medieval monastic world. **83** By Cicero, in *De Oratore*, by Quentilian in *Institutio Oratoria* and in the anonymous *Ad C. Herennium libri IV.* F.A. Yates, *The art of memory* (London, 2007), p. 18. **84** L. Wittgeinstein, *Philosophical investigations* (Oxford, 2001), p. 27 §67.

look at them anytime. You can also experience their other physical characteristics, and thus be reminded to pray, to live well and to do the right things.

CONCLUSION

The Miraculous Medal and medals from Lourdes are essentially different in that the former is perceived as an *apparition in itself*, whereas the latter are typically representations of an *apparition taking place*. They both have dialogic aspects to them; the Miraculous Medal in the prayer inscribed on it and the Lourdes medals in the references to the churches that have been built, and the cult that has been established, in answer to the request from the Holy Virgin. Both of them simultaneously remind the beholder of historical events, and encourage piety.

Being images, they belong to a visual tradition, and their communicative function and rhetoric efficacy are funded in that tradition. Since they are not just images, but also devotional objects, they must be understood against the background of devotional instruments – which is linked, but not identical, to the visual tradition. Being medals, they have the qualities and the connotations of this third category attached to them as well, and therefore they are complex objects of study.

In this essay, I have discussed some pictorial elements from the medals, trying to relate them to the existing literature, but at the same time broadening the perspective somewhat, by addressing topics that have not been much discussed in the context of devotional medals heretofore. First and foremost, I have stressed the importance of seeing the medals in the larger context of tradition. I have also pointed to the primary function of the medals as rhetorical, and discussed some of the consequences such an understanding must have on our interpretation of the motifs.

PART II

Devotions and the arts

6 *Regnavit a ligno Deus*: tradition and modernity in Liszt's *Via Crucis*

PETER DE MEY & DAVID J. BURN

THE DIALOGUE BETWEEN MUSIC AND THEOLOGY

Before proceeding with a musico-theological analysis of Franz Liszt's *Via Crucis*, some remarks are in order on the interdisciplinary conversation between theology and music against the background of recent research on this subject.

For musicologists, it is essential to ask such questions as: What text material did the composer use when writing sacred compositions?; How was this text interpreted at that time?; How did the composition function in the liturgy?; What do texts that the composer did not borrow from liturgical tradition tell us about the composer's theological views?; Did the composer employ pre-existent melodies with liturgical or theological associations?; How might these associations relate to the larger message of the composition?

Systematic theology, too, is substantially enriched by contemplating sacred art as an expression of religious experience. When is a theologian's interest in a composition aroused? There are many possible answers to this. Otto Hermann Pesch is only interested in compositions that proceed from a statement of faith.[1] It is not that he wishes to pass judgment on the personal faith of the musician – only God can do that – but for him it is possible, all the same, to objectively describe the witness to faith behind certain compositions.

Francis Watson's interest, on the other hand, is not limited to Church-commissioned music or to that which has its place in the liturgy. For him, all music that has a consoling function forms an interesting analogy with the comfort that is offered in the Christian faith without necessarily having the comfort of that faith as content.[2] Watson sees it as the task of the theologian to explain the relation between the vague and partial consolation offered by certain compositions and the consolation that faith offers. It is his conviction that this relation, even though it is now less expressly recognized than in the past, is still 'at certain points an essential one and not merely accidental'.[3]

With regard to the *Via Crucis*, the reader will discover that the notion of 'sacred music' is enlarged. Liszt's *Via Crucis* was too advanced for his time to be able to

---

1 Otto Hermann Pesch, 'Musik als Glaubenszeugnis: Anmerkungen zu Bach, Beethoven, Bruckner, Strawinsky und anderen' in Michael Kessler (ed.), *Fides quaerens intellectum: Beiträge zur Fundamentaltheologie. Festschrift Max Seckler* (Tübingen, 1992), pp 467–94 at p. 468.   2 Francis Watson, 'Theology and music', *Scottish Journal of Theology*, 51 (1998), 435–63 at 451.   3 Ibid., 460.

function as part of the liturgy. Yet Liszt considered it as a faithful resonance of his own religious feelings when reflecting on Christ's passion. In this sense, both the criteria put forward by Pesch and those of Watson are partially applicable to Liszt's master-piece.

BIOGRAPHICAL BACKGROUND

Biographers usually divide the musical career of the Hungarian Catholic composer Franz Liszt (1811–86) into three stages.[4] In the first stage of his career, Liszt travelled throughout Europe as a virtuoso pianist, performing both his and others' music. In 1847, during what would turn out to be his last concert tour in Russia as a soloist, he fell in love with Princess Carolyne Sayn-Wittgenstein (1819–87). The second stage in Liszt's career began when the latter left her husband to live with him in Weimar. During this second stage (1847–61), Liszt's main musical activity consisted of composing symphonic music. At the same time, under the influence of his partner, he also composed a number of successful sacred works. Among these, particular mention should be made of the so-called *Gran* Mass, which he composed in 1855 for the inaugu-ration of the basilica of Esztergom, near Budapest.

In 1858, growing dissatisfaction with the city's provincialism led Liszt to abandon his position as orchestral director at the Weimar court. A new turning point in Liszt's life came in 1861, when he followed Princess Carolyne to Rome, where she tried in vain to get her first marriage annulled in order to marry the composer.[5] For Liszt himself, Rome provided an opportunity to rediscover the religious vocation of his youth. He decided to become 'l'abbé Liszt' by taking lower orders (which did not include vows of chastity, poverty and obedience). In his youth he had been inspired by Claude Henri de Saint-Simon (1760–1825) and became a good friend of Félicité Robert de Lamennais (1782–1854). As an old man, however, he accepted the decisions of the Holy See wholeheartedly, including those concerning papal infallibility.[6]

It was during this final part of his life that Liszt wrote his most important religious works: an oratorio on the life of St Elisabeth of Hungary (1862), the *Missa choralis* (1865), the oratorio *Christus* (1866) and the *Requiem* (1869). Between 1871 and the year of his death, he spent the summer in Weimar, the winter in Rome and the spring in

4 The following biographical section draws especially on Alan Walker, *Franz Liszt*, iii, *The final years, 1861–86* (London, 1996).   **5** Walker suggests that Princess Carolyne perhaps agreed with her family's wish to keep their possessions intact and thus abandoned seeking an official divorce. See Walker, *Franz Liszt*, iii, pp 21–34. **6** Walker, *Franz Liszt*, iii, p. 335. Compare the following extracts from his letters, as found in Ernst Günther Heinemann, *Franz Liszts Auseinandersetuzung mit der geistlichen Musik. Zum Konflikt von Kunst und Engagement* (München, 1978), p. 61: 'The first duties of Catholics are obedience and submission, while at the same time being patient and loving in Our Lord Jesus Christ, who was obedient unto his death at the cross!' and 'The whole of the Catholic Church is united in the almost reverential cult of the Pope who has proclaimed the dogma of the Immaculate Conception of the Holy Virgin and that of of the dogmatic infallibility of the supreme Pontiff, vicar of Jesus Christ and legitimate successor of Saint Peter'. Note: All translations from French and German are made by the authors. In agreement with the editors we have decided to render the quotations in English only.

Pest. It was also during this time that Pope Pius IX (1846–78) showed an interest in Liszt's work on several occasions.[7] At the pope's request, Liszt participated in a charity concert for the 'Peter's Pence' during Holy Week in 1864. In the summer of the same year, Liszt was invited to give a concert in Castel Gandolfo, and one year later he took part in the festivities surrounding the twentieth anniversary of Pius' pontificate. For the latter occasion, Liszt composed a papal hymn on the words of Matthew 16:18 and John 21:16–17. Under the title 'The founding of the Church', this work later took a central place in his oratorio *Christus*.[8] When Pius died, Liszt described him as 'a saint'. All this makes Liszt sound like a conservative. Yet he sided with the liberals on a number of fundamental issues, including the separation of church and state. Liszt was probably, as Alan Walker states, 'the only musician of his time to have been received not by one Vicar of Christ, but by two', since the next pontiff, Leo XIII (1878–1903), granted him a private audience on All Saints' Day, 1 November 1878.[9]

The work under examination in the rest of this essay, *Via Crucis*, also dates from Liszt's final period. The composer worked on it in September and October 1878 while he was staying in the Villa d'Este in Tivoli. Alan Walker, who pays ample attention to the religious aspects of Liszt's work in his biography, indicates that the *Via Crucis* was an expression of the composer's deep sadness over the death of a soul-mate, Baron Antal Augusz. Liszt himself wrote: 'The loss of Augusz touches me most painfully. Since the first performance of the "*Gran*" Mass, more than twenty years ago, we have been one in heart. He also confirmed me in my wish to settle myself in Budapest'.[10] Princess Carolyne was responsible for the selection of the texts. The score was finished in February 1879, when Liszt was staying in Budapest.

THE DEVOTION TO THE STATIONS OF THE CROSS
AS BACKGROUND TO THE *VIA CRUCIS*

Liszt's own introduction to the *Via Crucis* observes a direct connection between the spiritual exercise of the Way of the Cross and mourning rituals:

> The devotion to the Stations of the Cross, called *Via Crucis* – on the strength of numerous acquiesences relevant for the souls of the dead by the Sovereign Pontifices – has spread through all countries, and even become very popular in some of them. In some churches we find paintings showing the Stations of the Cross, and members of the congregation used to say their respective prayers

7 See Pauline Pocknell, 'Liszt and Pius IX: the politico-religious connection' in Michael Saffle and Rossana Dalmonte (eds), *Liszt and the birth of Modern Europe: music as a mirror of religious, political, cultural and aesthetic transformations*, Analecta Lisztiana III (Hillsdale, NY, 2003), pp 61–104.   **8** In contrast to Liszt, Princess Carolyne was much more critical of the Church. In 1870, she began to work on a book series entitled *Causes intérieures de la faiblesse extérieure de l'Eglise* – a work which eventually ran to twenty-four volumes and which she managed to complete just before her death in 1887.   **9** See Walker, *Franz Liszt*, iii, p. 384.   **10** Ibid., pp 380–1.

before each of the pictures hanging on the wall. Sometimes these prayers are said by single persons, sometimes by little groups, in which case the words of the prayers are divided among themselves. (…) An organ cannot be used in the first, above-mentioned case, nor when the Stations of the Cross are represented out of doors, as for instance at S. Pietro in Montorio at Rome. It is easy to grasp that the most solemn, most touching devotion took place on a Good Friday at the Colosseum, at the very place where the martyrs had shed their blood. (…) Maybe one day a very big harmonium could be carried there so that the sound of the organ should support the singing. I should be indeed happy, if some day my music could be played there, even though it is only a pale reflection of the emotions that overwhelmed me when I, kneeling with the pious procession, knelt and repeated several times: 'O! Crux Ave! Spes unica!'

The introduction to the *Via Crucis* was not the first time that the composer described the powerful emotions that the cross inspired within him. In the testament that the composer wrote in Weimar on the feast of the Exaltation of the Holy Cross (14 September) 1860, he confessed that his true vocation was 'the foolishness and the exaltation of the Cross', that 'the divine light of the Cross has never entirely been withdrawn from me' and that he would die 'with my soul attached to the cross'.[11] He continued:

I wrote this testament on 14 September, when the Church celebrates the exaltation of the Holy Cross. The name of this feast also expresses the passionate and mysterious sentiment which has pierced my whole existence like a holy wound. Yes, the crucified Lord, the foolishness and the exaltation of the Cross, this has been my true vocation.

I sensed this in the deepest corner of my heart from the age of seventeen, when I asked with tears and supplications that I be permitted to enter the seminary of Paris, and when I hoped that I would be given the chance to live the life of the saints and perhaps to die the death of the martyrs. Unfortunately this has not been the case! – But since then, the divine light of the cross has never completely abandoned me, despite the numerous mistakes and errors which I have committed and which I sincerely repent. Sometimes it has even flooded my entire soul with its glory! I thank God for this and I will die with my soul attached to the cross, our redemption, our supreme beatitude; and in order to testify to my faith I long to receive the holy sacraments of the Catholic and Roman Church prior to dying, and so doing, obtain the remission and absolution of all my sins. Amen![12]

---

11 Jean Sichler, 'La *Via Crucis* de Franz Liszt', *Transversalités*, 69 (1999), 61–7 at 67.   **12** Ibid., 68.

The inclusion in Liszt's personal library of three copies of the *Paroissien romain* – a prayer book for Roman Catholics published in 1860 in Paris – constitutes a further witness to Liszt's devotion to the Way of the Cross. The strong emphasis on human sinfulness in the texts of the meditations contained in this book, however, and the arrival of gratitude for salvation only in the final station, seem at odds with the vision that Liszt expressed in his music.[13] Since devotion to the Cross was clearly central to Liszt's beliefs, it seems appropriate to briefly survey the devotion's historical development.[14]

In the first millennium, the tradition of re-enacting Jesus' path to Golgotha in a spiritual manner was still unknown. At that time, emphasis lay less on the exemplary value of the Son of God's suffering according to his human nature, but rather on the Son's triumph over the powers of death. The first images of Jesus crucified were of a king who rules from the cross. Very early, however, Christians developed the practice of making pilgrimages to holy places. An influential writer of mystical literature, focusing on Jesus' suffering as an example for the believer, was St Bernard (1090–1153). The devotion to the Cross, however, was especially propagated by St Francis (1181/2–1226) and his order, which disseminated the adoration of the suffering Lord. In the wake of the crusades, the Franciscans received permission to take care of the holy places in Jerusalem.

In the fifteenth century, other exercises of devotion to the passion of Christ came into existence: the recollection of Jesus' sevenfold stumbling (which would later become his threefold stumbling), of his painful footsteps on the way to Golgotha, and of the stops he made during his final journey. This last form of meditating on the Way of the Cross developed in the Low Countries. This spiritual exercise is thus a typical expression of Western devotion, rather than one with an origin in Jerusalem. One of the first books dedicated to it appeared in 1584, under the title *Jerusalem sicut Christi tempore floruit*. The author was Adrichomius, rector of the St Barbara convent in

---

13 The point is illustrated by the following representative extracts from the 'Exercice du chemin de la croix' (*Le paroissien romain* (Paris, 1860), pp 82–6): '… I beg you to withdraw the sentence of death which I have deserved because of my sins' (Station I); 'Consider, my soul, how Jesus bent down under the Cross, which your numerous sins made so heavy for him' (Station II); 'Divine Saviour, my failures are the cause of your falling. Grant me the grace not to renew your pain by falling back in sin' (Station III); 'Jesus, Mary, elicit in me an enduring sorrow about my sins' (Station 4); 'Lord, it is to me that you owe the Cross, because I have sinned. Grant that at least I accompany you, by carrying the cross of adversity out of love for Thee' (Station V). The same vein continues up to Station XIII: 'Holy Virgin, obtain for me the grace no longer to make Jesus die by being guilty of new sins'. Thankfulness is only evident in the last Station: 'My Redeemer, I thank you for all that Thou hast suffered in order to save me: I beg you to make me worthy to receive, in the Holy Communion, the body which you have surrendered for me, and establish forever your habitation in my soul'. 14 See, among others, Marco Talarico, *Der Kreuzweg Jesu in historischer Authentizität und katholischer Frömmigkeit*, Ästhetik – Theologie – Liturgik, 25 (Münster, 2004); P. Amédée [Teetaert] de Zedelgem OFM, 'Aperçu historique sur la devotion au chemin de la croix', *Collectanea Franciscana*, 19 (1949), 45–142 and the recent translation of this work: *Saggio storico sulla devozione alla Via Crucis: evocazione e rappresentazione degli episodi e dei luoghi della Passione di Cristo: saggi intro-duttivi*, ed. A. Barbero & P. Magro (Ponzano: Regio Piemonte, Parco naturale e area attrezzata del Sacro Monte di Crea, 2004).

Delft. The devotion received its final shape in Spain in the seventeenth century.[15] The first Italian 'Way of the Cross' was erected in Florence in 1628. The great promoter of the devotion to the Way of the Cross in that country was the Franciscan friar St Leonardo da Porto Maurizio (1676–1751). During his lifetime, he erected Ways of the Cross in 567 places. With the permission of Pope Benedict XIV, he also established a Way of the Cross at the Roman Colosseum. He published a book on the theory and practice of the Way of the Cross, which was translated into many languages and which was available in almost every diocese.[16] Leonardo also obtained papal indulgences for believers who practised the Way of the Cross. In the eighteenth century, the exercise was also encouraged by St Alphonsus de Liguori (1696–1787), especially in his *Esercizio della via crucis*.[17] It was during this period that the singing of two strophes of an appropriate song during the procession from station to station became a standard prescription. At the same time, it also became normal to sing selected strophes of the sequence *Stabat Mater* and of the hymn *Vexilla Regis* on the way back to the church.[18] It was probably this practice that inspired Liszt to integrate both pieces into his own *Via Crucis*.

The principal goal of partaking in the devotion of the Stations of the Cross was that of becoming conscious of one's complicity in Jesus' death, which was regarded as the result of human sinfulness. Saint Leonardo pointed to precisely these aspects in all his meditations on the Stations of the Cross.[19] Similarly, the spiritual exercises of Alphonsus de Liguori ask the devotees to pray as follows: 'I love Thee with my whole heart; I repent of having offended Thee. Never permit me to offend Thee again. Grant that I may love Thee always, and then do with me what Thou wilt'. The emphasis on repentance, however, was transformed, in the nineteenth century, into the joy of redemption. It was for this reason that an addition before each Station was made of the prayer: 'We adore you, O Christ, and we bless you, because by your holy Cross you have redeemed the world'.

Among Liszt's contemporaries, one of the most important contributors to the Way of the Cross was John Henry Newman (1801–90). In his meditations of 1860, Newman restored the focus on human co-responsibility for Jesus' death, as the following representative extracts demonstrate: 'Jesus is condemned to death. His death-warrant is

15 In 1991, Pope John Paul II decided to reform the Way of the Cross by removing the Stations with a legendary basis and replacing them with biblical scenes. The threefold stumbling of Jesus, the encounter with his mother, and the encounter with Saint Veronica now no longer form part of the official version of the Way of the Cross. See Talarico, *Der Kreuzweg Jesu*, pp 70–1.   **16** For a French edition, see S. Léonard de Saint-Maurice, *Via crucis ou Méthode pratique du chemin de la croix* (Tournai, 1852).   **17** The text is available in Latin and English translation at http://www.preces-latinae.org/thesaurus/Filius/ExercitumVC.html.   **18** Magda Marx-Weber, 'Die musik zur Kreuzwegandacht von Casciolini bis Liszt', *Kirchenmusikalisches Jahrbuch*, 73 (1989), 51–70 at 52 indicates that the most popular strophe of the *Stabat Mater* was the eleventh: 'Sancta Mater istud agas / Crucifixi fige plagas / Cordi meo valide'.   **19** See, for example, the following from his first set of meditations: 'Ah! It is too much not to deplore the insensibility of my heart and make me detest all my sins' (Station I); 'It is up to me, Lord Jesus, and not to you, to bear this cross, so crushing and so painful, because it is my great sins which made it' (Station II); 'Oh ! What shameful downfalls do I not have to reproach to myself with!' (Station III).

signed, and who signed it but I, when I committed my first mortal sins?' (Station I); 'Recollect, that heavy Cross is the weight of our sins' (Station II); 'Jesus, the strong and mighty Lord, has found for the moment our sins stronger than Himself' (Station III); 'He was now carrying the load of the world's sins' (Station IV); 'He falls because I have fallen' (Station VII); 'Oh, withdraw not from me. I am in a very bad way. I have so much evil in me' (Station VIII); 'Even when I am cleansed from my mortal sins, what disease and corruption is seen even in my venial sins' (Station X).[20] The meditation on Jesus' death should lead the believer to express his firm resolve to avoid all future sins: 'The salvation of my soul shall be my first concern. With the aid of His grace I will create in me a deep hatred and sorrow for my past sins. I will try hard to detest sin, as much as I have ever loved it.' The last station creates an occasion for Newman to reflect on the death of the Christian. All elements of Roman Catholic eschatology – in a nineteenth-century setting – are summarized here, and would be fully unfolded five years later in Newman's masterpiece *The dream of Gerontius*.[21] Here, Newman assumes a 'brief interval between death and the general resurrection', knows about 'the pains of Purgatory'. He recalls the importance of maintaining a communion between the human community and the departed, especially in the form of celebrating masses for them. Newman also pays much attention to the role of the guardian angels in this work.

THE *VIA CRUCIS* AGAINST THE BACKGROUND OF NINETEENTH-CENTURY PLANS TO REFORM CATHOLIC CHURCH MUSIC

Liszt certainly had great sympathy for the efforts of the Cecilian movement, founded in 1868 by Franz Xaver Witt (1834–88), to stimulate Catholic church music by 'the simplification of choral polyphony and of instrumental accompaniments in religious services'.[22] Within the movement, a pivotal model was provided by the works of Giovanni Pierluigi da Palestrina (1525–94), who was then considered to be the saviour of church music.[23] At the same time, the church began the task of rediscovering the Gregorian tradition. Some of Liszt's religious compositions, such as his settings of *Tantum ergo* and *O salutaris hostia*, appeared in the journals of the Cecilian movement. Others, such as settings of the *Ave Maria* and the *Pater Noster*, were published by Friedrich Pustet of Regensburg, who was closely connected with the *Cäcilienverein*.

---

20 The text is available at http://landru.i-link-2.net/shnyves/Newman.longer.stations.html.   **21** For a recent edition, see John Henry Newman, *The dream of Gerontius* (Oxford, 2001). A part of the poem's success must be attributed to Edward Elgar's oratorio with the same title, from 1900. See Geoffrey Hodgkins (ed.), *The best of me: a Gerontius centenary companion* (Richmansworth, 1999); John Allison, *Edward Elgar: sacred music* (Bridgend, 1994); Percy M. Young, *Elgar, Newman and the dream of Gerontius: in the tradition of English Catholicism* (Aldershot, 1995).   **22** Michael Saffle, 'Liszt and Cecilianism: the evidence of documents and scores' in Hubert Unverricht (ed.), *Der Caecilianismus: Anfänge – Grundlagen – Wirkungen* (Eichstätter Abhandlungen zur Musikwissenschaft, 5) (Tützing, 1988), pp 203–213 at p. 209.   **23** See James Garratt, *Palestrina and the German romantic imagination: interpreting historicism in nineteenth-century Music* (Cambridge, 2002).

Both the *Missa choralis* and the *Ave maris stella* were included in the catalogue of the *Allgemeiner Cäcilienverein*, which was edited in Regensburg by another of the movement's protagonists, Franz Haberl (1840–1910).[24] Liszt's *Missa choralis*, however, was removed from the catalogue in 1890, as the composer's progressive harmonic language and his efforts to integrate traditional Church hymns into modern compositions ultimately brought his works into conflict with the society's rigid views on church music.[25] It was to Pustet that Liszt offered his *Via Crucis*, along with *Septem Sacramenta* and *Rosario*. The composer was prepared to hand the works over for free, but his offer was nonetheless refused. As a result, the *Via Crucis* was never performed during Liszt's lifetime. The first performance took place in 1929; and it was only in 1936 that the piece was published, in his collected works. In the same year in which the *Via Crucis* was finished, Liszt reworked some of its material as part of his collection of *Deutsche Kirchenlieder und liturgische Gesängen*.[26]

Liszt first reflected on Catholic church music in his 1834 essay *Über die zukünftige Kirchenmusik*.[27] Although the contrast between Liszt and the Cecilian movement should not be exaggerated, his views did differ from theirs in important ways.[28] In a letter which he wrote in 1860, Liszt suggested banning all instruments except the organ in churches, and restricting the use of the organ to that of sustaining and strengthening the human voice.[29] Contrary to the Cecilians, however, he was highly interested in hymns and other church songs. He deplored the Catholic tradition's lack of hymn books equivalent to the Protestant *Choral-Bücher*. He was thus at times obliged to co-opt Protestant examples in his religious works, as was the case with the two chorales in the *Via Crucis*, as we will see. Well-known Catholic songs could also sometimes provide inspiration, such as 'Erde, singe, daß es klinge', which served as the basis for the *Gloria* of the *Missa Choralis*.

Liszt's idiosyncratic approach to church music resulted in the neglect of his works during his lifetime. This is clear from his attempt to publish the *Via Crucis*, and seems

---

24 Saffle, 'Liszt and Cecilianism', pp 209–10, without specifying the version of the *Ave Maria* and the *Pater Noster*. **25** Compare Heinemann, *Franz Liszts Auseinandersetuzung mit der geistlichen Musik*, p. 95: 'On the other hand in a number of sacred compositions from the seventies and eighties decisive musical primitivism is pursued that refrains entirely from mediating the various stylistic levels into a new synthesis, as is required by the neo-classicistic principle, and aims at a rigorous musical simplicity'. **26** The collection, which contains, among other pieces, *O Traurigkeit*, *O Haupt voll Blut und Wunden* and *Vexilla Regis*, was published in the 7th volume of the 1907–36 edition of Liszt's *Musikalische Werke*. **27** Important excerpts from this essay are available in Hans-Joachim Bauer, 'Franz Liszts Reformen zur Kirchenmusik', *Kirchenmusikalisches Jahrbuch*, 73 (1989), 63–70. Among other things, Liszt stated that 'We no longer know what Church music is all about, and how could it be different.' **28** Compare H.-J. Olszewsky, 'Liszt, Franz Ritter von', *Biographisch-Bibliographisches Kirchenlexikon*, 5 (1993), 127–34 at 129. The Church music of Liszt seems to represent the final stage of the development. Since it is conceived as the continuation of Haydn, Mozart and Beethoven, it stands in opposition to the development of official Church music, which Cecilianism sought to connect to previous times. Liszt's effort on the other hand, was aimed at transposing symphonic form into church music. See also Heinemann, *Franz Liszts Auseinandersetuzung mit der geistlichen Musik*, pp 74–8. **29** Liszt, *Briefe*, ed. La Mara, 8 vols (Leipzig, 1893–1904), vol. 5, pp 34f. Cf. Heinemann, *Franz Liszts Auseinandersetuzung mit der geistlichen Musik*, pp 76–7.

to have genuinely troubled the composer. After negative reactions to the revised edition of his *Des Bohémiens et de leur musique en Hongrie*, published in 1881, he wrote in a letter to Ölön Mihalovich:

> Everyone is against me. Catholics because they find my church music profane, Protestants because to them my music is Catholic, Freemasons because they think my music is too clerical; to conservatives I am revolutionary, to the 'futurists' an old Jacobin. As for the Italians, in spite of Sgambati, if they support Garibaldi they detest me as a hypocrite, if they are on the side of the Vatican I am accused of bringing the Venusberg into the Church. To Bayreuth I am not a composer but a publicity agent. The Germans reject my music as French, the French as German; to the Austrians I write Gypsy music, to the Hungarians foreign music. And the Jews loathe me, my music and myself, for no reason at all.[30]

More recent commentators have begun a significant reassessment of Liszt's contribution to the renewal of Catholic church music through both the quantity and quality of his sacred works.[31]

OLD AND NEW IN THE *VIA CRUCIS*

Liszt composed his *Via Crucis* for four-part choir, soloists (mezzo-soprano, baritone, bass, solo SATB quartet, and solo pair of sopranos and alto), and keyboard accompaniment, which may be played on the organ, harmonium or piano. He also arranged the work for piano solo or organ solo. The following discussion treats the original choral version, focusing on the separate roles of the various performers, and paying special attention to the way in which Liszt combines traditional and progressive elements.[32] The unusual ways in which the musical forces and material are treated make the genre of the work puzzling. Ernst Günther Heinemann is of the opinion that Liszt conceived his *Via Crucis* both as a representation of Christ's own passion and as accompanying music for devotional exercises.[33] On the other hand, the combination

30 Walker, *Franz Liszt*, iii, p 411 and n. 22. It is now known that the controversial chapter concerning the Israelites in *Des Bohémiens et de leur musique en Hongrie*, which contained a number of anti-Semitic statements, had been revised by Princess Carolyne. See Walker, *Franz Liszt*, iii, p. 405.   **31** See, for example, Roland Moser, 'Unitonie – Pluritonie – Omnitonie: Zur harmonischen Gedankenwelt in der Via crucis von Franz Liszt', *Basler Jahrbuch für historische Musikpraxis*, 21 (1997), 129–42 at 133. 'Liszt had conceived the *Via crucis* in 1873 and finished the composition between 1876 and 1879. Together with *Septem Sacramenta*, it constitutes the final major contribution to his project of renewing Catholic Church music, which he had pursued with an indefatigable intensity for more than thirty years. The fruit of these efforts consists not only of two evening-long oratorios, but above all of five masses, six psalms and more than fifty works in several parts, most of which were conceived for liturgical use.   **32** For another recent analysis of the *Via Crucis*, see Philippe Charru & Véronique Fabre, *Voici l'homme. Au croisement du 'Miserere' de Georges Rouault et de la 'Via Crucis' de Franz Liszt*. Editions Facultés Jésuïtes de Paris (Paris, 2006).   **33** Heinemann, *Franz Liszts Auseinandersetzung mit der geistlichen Musik*, p. 97:

of (albeit short) recitatives with hymns and other material lends the work some affinity with passion-oratorios. Magda Marx-Weber observed the same connection on the basis of the use of biblical text citations, although she ultimately considered the work to be a series of meditations.[34]

THE CHOIR

The *Via Crucis* consists of fifteen musical sections: an introduction, then a section devoted to each of the fourteen Stations of the Cross in turn.[35] The choir plays a role in eight of the composition's fifteen parts.

The introduction to the work consists of a choral setting of the first, third and sixth strophes of the hymn *Vexilla Regis*. This hymn, ascribed to Venantius Fortunatus, bishop of Poitiers, was first sung in 569, when a piece of the Holy Cross was carried in procession from Tours to the monastery of Sainte-Croix at Poitiers. Apart from its role in other commemorations of the passion, the hymn had its major liturgical place in the Good Friday liturgy, when it was sung during the procession in which the Holy Sacrament was carried to the altar where the consecrated bread was kept. Liszt used not only the words of the hymn, but also its traditional Gregorian melody. The *Via Crucis* begins with a short instrumental introduction (in bare octaves) based on the first three pitches of the chant, after which the choir sing the melody complete, and in unison, for the first two of their strophes. The fluid metre derives from the accentuation of the text, rather than the written barlines. For the four phrases of each strophe, the accompaniment alternates between bare octaves in parallel with the choir and purely consonant homophony with a strongly modal colouring (see figure 6.1).

Liszt apparently wanted to begin the piece with a clear assertion of its connection with the timeless traditions of the church. The opening collective expression of *Vexilla Regis* sets the tone for the whole piece. As will be seen below, Liszt decided to use *Vexilla Regis* not only to begin the work, but also to end it. Furthermore, material motivically related to the opening three pitches of the hymn (F-G-B flat) also appears at key moments within the work. The result is that it is not repentance, but the victory of the cross, that runs throughout the work as a connecting thread.

The choir next appears in Station III. This station, along with Stations VII and IX, portray Jesus' threefold stumbling. The opening words, 'Jesus cadit', are sung in

'The music of the *Via Crucis* is at the same time a representation of the way of the cross of Christ (the path Christ himself walked and its representation in the visual arts) and a procession'. **34** Marx-Weber, 'Die Musik zur Kreuzwegandacht von Casciolini bis Liszt', p. 56: 'The biblical citations, such as "Crucifige" and "Consummatum est", are elements from Passion settings. However, it is not correct to characterise Liszt's *Via Crucis* as a Passion oratorio. (…) The structure of the work – fourteen stations and a choral introduction – as well as the shortness of the composition unambiguously point in the direction of a meditation'. The most popular eighteenth- and nineteenth-century meditations on the Stations of the Cross, moreover, also contain references to Jesus' last words. Compare Saint Alphonsus: 'But Jesus said to them: "Weep not for Me, but for your children"' and Saint Léonard: 'O heaven! With what cry did he withhold the *consummatum est*'! **35** For an overview of the entire work, see the Appendix.

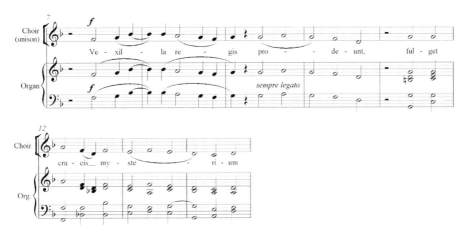

6.1 Introduction: *Vexilla Regis*, beginning of first strophe.

octaves and unisons by the male voices of the choir. The meaning of the text is vividly portrayed by the dramatic drop of a diminished 7th in the tenor, and the savage rhythmic contrast between the strong placing of the syllables on the first beat of the bar and the confinement of the accompaniment chords to the weaker second beats. In the accompaniment, Liszt applied the technique of the pedal point: a held bass F sharp, over which a rising then falling chromatic line creates a strangely non-functional harmonic progression (see figure 6.2).

The Station closes with a setting of the first verse of the *Stabat mater dolorosa* for three female soloists (see below). The related Stations VII and IX use music that is nearly identical to that of Station III. Station VII is the same as Station III except for a single harmony in the third bar of the accompaniment. Station IX differs in its opening pitch, and, as discussed below, in its treatment of the *Stabat mater dolorosa* section. Mounting tension across the three stations is created by the use of successive rising transposition: first up a semitone in Station VII, then up a further minor third in Station IX, bringing the opening to the extreme limit of tenor range. The interval structure of the transposition traces the outline of the *Vexilla Regis* motif across the work on a large scale (compare the pitch on which the tenor begins in each of the Stations: E flat, E natural and G).

Station VI consists of a four-part harmonization of *O Haupt voll Blut und Wunden*. The text of this chorale in fact goes back to another hymn by Venantius Fortunatus, *Salve caput cruentatum*. Liszt's setting is in direct imitation of Bach's treatments of the same chorale in the *St Matthew Passion*. The homage is left in no doubt through the occurrence of Bach's name in musical notes (B flat, A, C, B natural)[36] in the instrumental introduction, preceded by two variants of the *Vexilla Regis* motif (F-C-B, and

---

36 B natural is 'H' in German.

6.2 Station III: beginning, with pedal-point harmony.

F-A-B).[37] The sequential interval-structure of the motif (twofold falling semitone-and-rising third) allows Liszt to fluidly extend the motif, with the addition of chromatic notes (figure 6.3). Liszt's lifelong adoration of Bach extended so far as his choosing Thüringen as a place of residence. He and other nineteenth-century composers became ever more intimately acquainted with Bach's music thanks to the Bach-Gesamtausgabe, begun in 1850. For Liszt, Bach provided solace when overcoming the most tragic events in his life, such as when his son Daniel died in 1859, and he wrote his variations on themes from Bach's cantata *Weinen, Klagen, Sorgen, Zagen*.[38] Liszt's placing of the chorale in the *Via Crucis* contrasts interestingly with that found in Bach's *St Matthew Passion*. In the latter, the chorale reflects on the soldiers' cruel game of afflicting Jesus' head with a crown of thorns. In the *Via Crucis*, the piece meditates on Veronica's efforts to alleviate Jesus' suffering by cleaning his head with a sudarium.

In the shortest piece of the work, Station XI, the male voices of the choir repeatedly exclaim the single word 'crucifige' in unison. The treatment is similar to that found with the words 'Jesus cadit' in Stations III, VII and IX. Also like the latter Stations is Liszt's use of a pedal-point: in this case a G sharp, over which increasingly dissonant

37 Liszt had famously used the musical motif derived from Bach's name his *Praeludium und Fuge über den Namen B-A-C-H*, for organ (1st version 1855; 2nd version 1870).   **38** For more information on the significance of Bach for Liszt, see Michael Heinemann, 'Bach: Liszt', in Michael Heinemann, Hans-Joachim Hinrichsen & Joachim Lüdtke (eds), *Bach und die Nachwelt, 2, 1850–1900* (Laaber, 1999), pp 127–62.

6.3 Station VI: beginning with B-A-C-H motif.

harmonies are placed.[39] An aggressive climax is reached with a D-minor triad, a tritone removed from the pedal-note pitch (b. 10), followed by a dramatic silence. The Station closes in utter contrast, with a seven-note ascending melody in plain octaves, *piano*, for accompaniment alone. A connection may be heard between the first three notes of this melody and the opening of *Vexilla Regis*. The continuation can be seen to use the pitches of an ascending 'Hungarian' scale (a harmonic minor scale with a raised fourth). This was undoubtedly Liszt's way of illustrating the *exaltatio crucis*.

At the end of Station XII, the longest piece of the work, Liszt inserted a second chorale, *O Traurigkeit, O Herzeleid*. He probably knew Bach's setting of the same melody and words (BWV 404), yet, while maintaining the four-part homophony characteristic of chorales, Liszt chose this time to apply audaciously chromatic harmonies that are obviously typical of his own time (see figure 6.4).

39 Cf. Moser, 'Unitonie – Pluritonie – Omnitonie', p. 134.

6.4 Station XII: chorale.

The chorale-harmonization proper runs from the choir-entry in b. 77 to b. 95. The continuation appears initially to be a repeat of the same chorale strophe. After the opening phrase, however, the remainder of the station becomes caught in a litany-like repetition of the chorale's first four words, set to increasingly distorted chromatic lines. The station closes instrumentally, with an unharmonized recollection of the chorale's initial phrase, finally reaching an unstable first-inversion triad via chromatic contrary motion. The effect is of powerfully concentrated grief over Jesus' death on the cross.

The last station forms a complement to the work's opening section. As the *Via Crucis* began with *Vexilla Regis*, so it ends, with Station XIV setting a textual variant of the hymn's sixth strophe: 'Ave crux, spes unica, mundi salus et gloria, auge piis justitiam reisque dona veniam!' As before, the traditional plainchant melody is used in exactly the same rhythm as in the introduction. In contrast to the introduction, however, each phrase is now treated in dialogue, first stated by a mezzo-soprano soloist, then repeated by a choir consisting of sopranos, tenors and divided basses. The strictly consonant modality of the introduction is also abandoned, in favour of a more clearly focused tonal treatment (due, among other things, to the use of raised leading notes). After a very slow and sombre instrumental interlude, Liszt closes the work homophonically, with the full choir repeating words 'ave crux'. The music dissolves into octave and unison phrases with long rests between. The final word is given to the accompaniment, asserting the salvific nature of the cross with one last recollection of the opening of *Vexilla Regis*.

THE VOCAL SOLOISTS

Soloists feature in nine of the work's fifteen sections. Two approaches to the use of soloists may be distinguished in the *Via Crucis*: on the one hand, the use of solo ensembles; and, on the other, the use of individual voices.

Liszt sometimes uses solo duos, trios or quartets in the meditative sections of his work. In the introduction, the third strophe of *Vexilla Regis* is scored for four soloists (soprano, alto, tenor and bass). Liszt chooses this point, with its significant opening words, 'O crux ave!' to abandon the vocal unison of the previous sections, and to break into harmony between the voices for the first time. The text receives additional emphasis and prolongation by its drawn-out setting in imitation. The modal and consonant harmonies of the preceding section are preserved throughout the first half of the first hymn phrase. The second half of the phrase, 'spes unica', is both texturally and harmonically contrasting, through its homophony, and strongly directed tonal progression – the first in the whole piece. A similar opposition operates between the second line of the text ('hoc passionis tempore') and the rest of the strophe. The setting of the latter enacts an enharmonic transition from G-flat major to F-sharp minor (see figure 6.5; compare with figure 6.1).[40]

The Gregorian *Vexilla* melody is used in the soprano voice up to 'spes unica'. For 'hoc passionis', however, Liszt does not continue as expected but returns to the melody's opening material. The result is to emphasize the primacy of this motif as a signifier of salvation through the cross. The introductory section closes with octaves and a modal cadence, thus establishing a dynamic opposition between old and new harmonic practices that will colour the rest of the work.

In the Stations commemorating Jesus' threefold stumbling (Stations III, VII and IX), Liszt entrusted the depiction of the event itself to the lower voices of the choir, as already discussed. This is followed by a meditative setting of the opening verse of the *Stabat mater dolorosa*, for female soloists, without accompaniment.[41] The first line is sung by two sopranos. For the remaining lines, they are joined by an alto. Liszt had already set both the *Stabat mater speciosa* and the *Stabat mater dolorosa* in his oratorio *Christus*.[42] In Liszt's time, both versions of the *Stabat Mater* were ascribed to the Franciscan friar Jacopone da Todi (1230–1306). It may have been Liszt's Franciscan sympathies that led him to integrate them both into his oratorio and the *Via Crucis*. In Station III and its repeat in Station VII, Liszt preserved the Gregorian *Stabat Mater* melody intact in the first soprano. The second soprano follows in parallel thirds below. As Zsuzsanna Domokos has recently and convincingly argued, Liszt's use of such parallel melody-lines may have been inspired by the Sistine Chapel's practice of 'contrapunto alla mente', in which singers decorated plainchant with improvised

---

40 Although he does not presume that Liszt has studied François Joseph Fétis's *Traité complet de la théorie et de la pratique de l'harmonie contenant la doctrine de la science et de l'art* (1844), Roland Moser believes that this and similar passages in the *Via Crucis* apply what Fétis called 'l'ordre pluritonique'. See Moser, 'Unitonie – Pluritonie – Omnitonie', p. 135.   41 One wonders whether this separation between male and female singers was inspired by the liturgical prescription to keep the sexes apart in processions. Compare St Léonard de Saint-Maurice, *Via crucis*, p. 13: 'During all Sundays and official feast days, or at least on one Sunday each month, after vespers, a procession will be organised under the guidance of one or more priests, taking care to observe a perfect separation between the two sexes'.   42 See Günther Massenkeil, 'Das weihnachtliche Stabat Mater in dem Oratorium "Christus" von Franz Liszt' in M. Dobberstein (ed.), *Artes liberales: Karlheinz Schlager zum 60. Geburtstag*. Eichstätter Abhandlungen zur Musikwissenschaft, 13 (Eichstätt, 1998), pp 283–9.

6.5 Introduction: *Vexilla Regis*, third strophe.

countermelodies.[43] When the alto joins the two sopranos at 'juxta crucem lacrymosa dum pendebat filius', the harmony is dramatically coloured by an augmented triad. The end of the section is also unusual. Of all of the Stations, these two give the impression of offering the strongest closing cadence. Yet, in place of the expected root-position triad, Liszt chose an unstable first-inversion sonority, whose irresolution seems to mirror Jesus' hanging from the cross, or the never-ending sadness of Mary (see figure 6.6).

Like its companion Stations, Station IX, portraying Jesus falling for the third time, also closes with *Stabat mater dolorosa*. Its version, however, is not an exact copy of the two earlier instances. The voice disposition is initially inverted, so that the two sopranos are now spaced a sixth apart. The upper soprano transforms the chant melody from major to minor mode, while the lower soprano adds affective chromaticism. The previously tentative attempt at a closing cadence is now fully undermined. The overwhelming emotion is all the more touching for the relatively restrained means by which it is expressed.

The same three female soloists used in Stations III, VII and IX also appear in Station XII. There, they echo the words 'consummatum est', initially sung by the baritone solo (see below). Parallel thirds are again used, creating a textural relationship between this point and the words of the *Stabat mater dolorosa*.[44]

43 Zsuzsanna Domokos, 'The performance practice of the Cappella Sistina as reflected in Liszt's church music', *Studia Musicologica Academiae Scientarum Hungaricae*, 41 (2000), 389–406 esp. 398.   **44** Moser, 'Unitonie – Pluritonie – Omnitonie', p. 138.

6.6 Station III: 'Stabat mater' section.

The second type of solo intervention uses individual voices alone. For these, Princess Carolyne selected exclamations by Pilate and Jesus from the passion narratives of all four gospels. The first such moment is Pilate's statement in Station I, 'Innocens ego sum a sanguine justi hujus' (Matt 27:24). Sung by a bass, the sentiment is captured by the lilting rhythm, simple diatonicism of the melody, and the striking absence of accompaniment (this last feature characterizes almost every subsequent similar intervention as well). Jesus speaks for the first time in Station II, with the non-biblical 'Ave crux!'. His words, both here and later, are sung by a baritone (this voice-type was also used for Jesus in Liszt's oratorio *Christus*). The opening motivic pattern, setting the word 'Ave', may be derived from the opening notes of *Vexilla Regis* (chromatically modified from F-G-B flat to F sharp-G-B natural). Jesus then repeats the word 'Ave', with a melody that will play an important recollective role later in the work (it appears in the instrumental connecting material between the 'Jesus cadit' and 'Stabat mater' sections of Stations III, VII and XI and in the instrumental introduction to the last Station). In Station VIII, Jesus addresses the women of Jerusalem with the words 'Nolite flere super me, sed super vos ipsas flete et super filios vestros' (Lk 23:28). Jesus' final appearance is in Station XII, with his last words, 'Eli, Eli, lama Sabacthani?' (Matt 27:46), 'In manus tuas commendo spiritum meum' (Lk 23:46) and 'Consummatum est' (Jn 19:30). For 'Eli, Eli, lama Sabacthani?', Liszt employed the so-called 'Hungarian' or 'Gypsy' scale.[45] Jesus is accompanied instrumentally for the first time at the end of his final statement, 'Consummatum est', with one of the few plain and stable tonal cadences in the work. A brief instrumental interlude, based on the

---

45 Hamburger, 'Program and Hungarian idiom in the sacred music of Liszt', p. 251.

opening phrase of *Vexilla Regis*, follows. In the final station, a mezzo-soprano reflects on the salvific value of the cross in dialogue with the choir, as outlined above.

THE ORGAN, PIANO OR HARMONIUM ACCOMPANIMENT

The role of the instrumental accompaniment in the *Via Crucis* cannot be underestimated. The instrument plays a substantial part in characterizing the atmosphere of each Station, as suggested by the fact that Liszt deemed it possible to perform the piece on the organ or piano alone (with relatively little necessary alteration to its part). Four Stations (Stations IV, V, X and XIII) are entirely instrumental.

The introduction and Stations I, II, VI, VIII and XIV begin with instrumental solo sections of reasonable length. In the introduction, the first instrumental passage states motivic material, from the opening notes of the following hymn *Vexilla Regis*, that allows the Way of the Cross as a whole to be interpreted in salvific terms. The instrumental interlude between the first and second strophes isolates the same motivic material, again in plain octaves, as at the beginning of the work. The motif returns at the beginning of Station XIV, with imitation identical to that found at the beginning of the third hymn strophe in the introduction, and coupled with material from Jesus' solo exclamation in Station II. The other instrumental openings usually present individual material capturing the mood of the scene. In Station II, the melody-line twice buckles chromatically under the weight of the cross before finally managing, in b. 8, to rise a semitone above the pitch on which it began. In Station VIII, the weeping of the women of Jerusalem is represented in long descending chromatic lines, repeated in rising sequential patterns. The accompanying instrument also begins the three Stations in which Jesus falls (Stations III, VII and IX), and Station XI, though in these instances, the introduction is short. In Stations III and VII, the opening melodic pattern is a variant of the three-note *Vexilla* motif (now a rising semitone followed by a rising minor third). In Station XI in particular, the entry of the lower voices after a single instrumental chord seems designed to capture the crowd's impetuous resolve to crucify Jesus. The only station in which it is the voice, rather than the accompaniment, that begins is Station XII, with its opening vocal solo exclamation, 'Eli, Eli, lama Sabacthani?'

The accompanying instrument alone also ends six of the Stations (II, VI, VIII, XI, XII and XIV). The music that ends Station II, a drudging march-like ostinato, depicts Jesus' laboured steps on his way to Calvary. The same music recurs at the end of the purely instrumental Station V, and finally, in a rhythm twice as slow, in Station XIV (bb 59–60), to indicate that the procession has ended. Station VIII ends with an *allegro marziale* section, whose brass-fanfare figures and diatonicism contrast strikingly with the plangent chromaticism of the preceding section. The section is clearly influenced by Liszt's symphonic music, but can be interpreted in context as portraying Jesus' willingness to confront his fate on Golgotha with renewed energy after his meeting with the women of Jerusalem.

The longest Station, Station XII, offers the most elaborate interplay between vocal and instrumental expression, through instrumental interludes between each of Jesus' last words from the cross. The chromatically descending parallel augmented triads that follow 'Eli, eli, lama Sabacthani?' give way to clearly tonal material following 'In manus tuas commendo spiritum meum'. The uppermost melodic line is based on the *Vexilla Regis* motif (G sharp-A-C sharp, b. 13ff). A dramatic pedal-point crescendo precedes the touchingly simple treatment of 'Consummatum est'.

Of the entirely instrumental Stations, Station IV, describing how the suffering Jesus meets his mother on the way to Golgotha, and Station XIII, in which Jesus is taken from the cross, form a unity through the use of shared material. In theological terms, the two stations are also linked: Station XIII was sometimes entitled 'Jesus in the arms of his mother'.[46] Station IV consists of a long introduction (bb 1–18), then a lyrical melody in the upper register, with sparse chordal accompaniment. The station opens with what Alan Walker has called the 'Madonna' chord, which is, in Walker's words:

> an emotional blend of pain and love, tinged with eroticism. It cannot be explained in terms of traditional harmony, and Liszt himself would have been the last to insist on such an explanation. A later age would call it a 'tone-cluster' and perhaps wonder how it came to be introduced into music as early as 1878. But by now Liszt was standing on the brink of the extraordinary music of his old age, and all things were possible for him.[47]

It is possible also to view the chord as a verticalization of two versions of the *Vexilla Regis* motif (F-G-B flat and B flat-C sharp-D sharp). Station IV is repeated, with only slight abbreviation, in Station XIII, along with further thematic recollections from other Stations. Roland Moser describes Station XIII as 'pure music of recollection'.[48] The instrumental quotation of the 'Stabat mater' section of the stations in which Jesus falls directs attention towards Mary's suffering. As with the preceding appearance of this section, in Station IX, the Gregorian melody is chromatically distorted (figure 6.7; the repeat of Station IV begins in b. 25, with the 'Madonna' chord on the first beat of b. 26).

The station ends with a recollection of the *Vexilla Regis* motif that had previously begun Station VI, and preceded Jesus' solo in Station VIII. While the first appearance of this motif had stated the B-A-C-H motif, this is now interrupted midway, and extended with a slow, plainly illustrative, chromatic descent.

46 Compare Saint Léonard, p. 100: 'We have just contemplated Jesus hanging on the tree of the cross, facing death, and now he is resting, cold and without life, in the bosom of his mother'; compare also the meditation on the same station in the *Paroissien romain*: 'Consider, my soul, what affliction the Mother of God experienced when she received the body of her divine Son in her arms, pale, and deprived of his blood and life. Ah! Holy Virgin, obtain for me the grace to no longer make Jesus die by committing new sins, but to make him live in me forever, by the practice of Christian virtues'.   47 Walker, *Franz Liszt*, p. 382.   48 Moser, 'Unitonie – Pluritonie – Omnitonie', p. 141.

6.7 Station XIII: recollections of 'Stabat mater' and Station IV.

THE THEOLOGICAL MESSAGE OF LISZT'S MASTERPIECE

It is better not to approach the Via Crucis through the normal way of musico-
logical commentary. This is not a piece of music. It escapes the concert and has
no place in the liturgy. Its 'otherness' belongs to the realm of faith. ... It escapes
the musician. Only the man of faith can penetrate in this work, because the
Invisible reveals itself in the silence which one finds there. This work is made of
silence, not just the silences which the composer has determined in his score, but
even the notes provoke silence. It is in silent meditation that this work reveals
all its dimensions[49]

Liszt's most important theological message in the *Via Crucis* is his firm belief in the
salvific value of the cross. Liszt's decision to start and end his *Via Crucis* with the
ancient hymn *Vexilla Regis* was clearly motivated by such an aim. In the words of this
hymn in general, and in the strophes selected by Liszt in particular, the emphasis is
not on repentance, but on the victory of the cross: 'Regnavit a ligno Deus'. As
enumerated above, the message is carried through the rest of the work by a three-note
musical motif derived from the opening pitches of the Gregorian *Vexilla Regis*
melody.[50]

Maybe Liszt also wanted believers to find comfort in the example of the suffering
but faithful women disciples. Liszt clearly knew that the tradition of the Way of the
Cross linked together those Stations which evoke the tender presence of the holy
women: Jesus meeting his holy Mother (Station IV), Saint Veronica (Station VI), the
women of Jerusalem (Station VIII), and Jesus taken down from the cross (Station
XIII). This concern is further focused by Liszt's decision to insert the first strophe of
the *Stabat Mater* into the Stations commemorating Jesus' stumbling, and by
entrusting the confirmation of Jesus' final words on the cross, 'consummatum est', to

---

49 Sichler, 'La *Via Crucis* de Franz Liszt', p. 61.   **50** For further consideration of this motif, see Georges Byron,
'Franz Liszt et la dévotion à la croix', *La Maison-Dieu*, 171 (1987), 99–109, and Dorothea Redepenning,
'Meditative musik: Bemerkungen zu einigen späten geistlichen Kompositionen Franz Liszts', *Hamburger Jahrbuch
für Musikwissenschaft*, 8 (1985), 185–201 esp. 187–8.

a trio of female soloists. The spiritual exercises of St Léonard remind the reader that the Way of the Cross was in fact a continuation of Mary's daily practice, performed until her death, of visiting the places where her Son had suffered.[51]

CONCLUSION

The *Via Crucis* is not an easy work. For Dorothea Redepenning, its homophony, unison passages, moments of silence or near-inaudibility, preference for slow tempi and long note-values express 'private religiosity, personal impressions, religious senti-ments … perhaps also … obedience and humility in confrontation with the contents of faith'.[52] Yet the *Via Crucis* irritates her, as she is convinced it did the publisher who refused it, because it refused to take the aesthetic standards of its time into account. The present essay has attempted to argue that, with an understanding of some of its musico-theological elements, it is possible to approach it with more sympathy. As Cecil Hill put it at the end of his reflections on the work, in experiencing Liszt's *Via Crucis*, we are given the opportunity 'to languish in its stark primitive splendour; to be humbled by it; and to be richer in the end'.[53]

STRUCTURE AND TEXT OF *VIA CRUCIS*

Introduction

CHOIR

Vexilla regis prodeunt,	The royal standards advance,
Fulget Crucis mysterium,	The mystery of the Cross shines out,
Qua vita mortem pertulit,	That Cross on which life endured death
Et morte vitam protulit.	And, through death, brought forth life.
Impleta sunt quae concinit	Now fulfilled are those events
David fideli carmine,	Whereof David sang in a truthful poem,
Dicendo nationibus:	Proclaiming to the nations:
Regnavit a ligno Deus. Amen.	God has reigned from upon a tree. Amen.
O crux, ave, spes unica,	O Cross, hail, our sole hope
Hoc passionis tempore	In this Passiontide
Piis adauge gratiam,	Increase Thy grace to the pious,
Reisque dele crimina. Amen.	And efface the sins of the guilty. Amen.

Station I: Jesus is condemned to death

INSTRUMENTAL INTRODUCTION
PILATE (bass soloist)

Innocens ego sum a sanguine justi hujus.   I am innocent of the blood of this just person.

---

51 Saint Léonard, p. 3: 'How encouraging it is to know that paying a daily visit to the places which Jesus Christ consecrated by his suffering was an inspiration for the grieving heart of the Mother of our Lord. She did this, as she has revealed to Saint Brigit, during the entire period in which she outlived her son on Earth'. **52** Redepenning, 'Meditative musik', 192: 'The standard aesthetic criteria clearly play a very minor role here. Religious devotion and meditative recollection take their place. Yet it remains open to question whether this can compensate for the absence of aesthetic qualities'. **53** Cecil Hill, 'Liszt's Via Crucis', *The Music Review*, 25 (1964), 202–8 esp. 208.

Station II: Jesus receives his Cross
INSTRUMENTAL INTRODUCTION
JESUS (baritone soloist)

Ave, ave Crux!   Hail, hail, O Cross!

Station III: Jesus falls
VERY SHORT INSTRUMENTAL INTRODUCTION
CHOIR (tenors & basses in unison)

Jesus cadit.   Jesus falls.

    SOLOISTS (2 sopranos; 1 alto)

Stabat mater dolorosa   The grieving Mother
Juxta Crucem lacrymosa,   Stood weeping beside the Cross
Dum pendebat filius.   where her Son was hanging.

Station IV: Jesus meets his Blessed Mother
PURELY INSTRUMENTAL

Station V: Simon of Cyrene helps Jesus to carry the Cross
PURELY INSTRUMENTAL

Station VI: Saint Veronica
INSTRUMENTAL INTRODUCTION
CHOIR

O Haupt voll Blut und Wunden,   O head covered in blood and wounds,
Voll Schmerz und voller Hohn!   Weighed down by pain and scorn!
O Haupt, zum Spott gebunden   O head mockingly wreathed
Mit einer Dornenkron!   In a crown of thorns!
O Haupt, sonst schön gezieret   O head once beautifully adorned
Mit höchster Ehr und Zier,   With supreme honour and splendour,
Jetzt aber höchst beschimfet,   But now supremely abused,
Gegrüßet seist du mir!   I hail thee!

Station VII: Jesus falls for the second time
VERY SHORT INSTRUMENTAL INTRODUCTION
CHOIR (tenors & basses in unison)

Jesus cadit.   Jesus falls.

    SOLOISTS (2 sopranos; 1 alto)

Stabat mater dolorosa   The grieving Mother
Juxta Crucem lacrymosa,   Stood weeping beside the Cross
Dum pendebat filius.   Where her Son was hanging.

Station VIII: The women of Jerusalem
INSTRUMENTAL INTRODUCTION
JESUS (baritone soloist)

Nolite flere super me,   Weep not for me,
Sed super vos ipsas flete   But weep for yourselves,
Et super filios vestros.   And for your children.

Station IX: Jesus falls for the third time
VERY SHORT INSTRUMENTAL INTRODUCTION
CHOIR (tenors & basses in unison)

Jesus cadit.	Jesus falls.

SOLOISTS (2 sopranos; 1 alto)

Stabat mater dolorosa	The grieving Mother
Juxta Crucem lacrymosa,	Stood weeping beside the Cross
Dum pendebat filius.	Where her Son was hanging.

Station X: Jesus is stripped of his garments
PURELY INSTRUMENTAL

Station XI: Jesus is nailed to the Cross
CHOIR (tenors & basses in unison)

Crucifige, crucifige!	Crucify him, crucify him!

Station XII: Jesus dies on the Cross
JESUS (baritone soloist)

Eli, Eli lama Sabachthani.	My God, my God, why hast thou forsaken me?
In manus tuas commendo spiritum meum.	Into thy hands I commend my spirit.
Consummatum est.	It is finished.

CHOIR

Consummatum est.	It is finished.
O Traurigkeit, o Herzeleid,	O sadness, O heart's distress,
Ist das nicht zu beklagen?	Is this not worth bewailing?
Gott des Vaters einigs Kind	The only child of God the Father
Wird ins Grab getragen.	Is borne to the tomb.
O Traurigkeit, o Herzeleid!	O sadness, O heart's distress!

Station XIII: Jesus is taken down from the Cross
PURELY INSTRUMENTAL

Station XIV: Jesus is laid in the tomb
CHOIR (STB) + MEZZO-SOPRANO SOLOIST

Ave Crux, spes unica,	Hail, Cross, our sole hope,
Mundi salus et Gloria.	Salvation and glory of the world.
Auge piis justitiam,	Increase thy justice to the pious.
Reisque dona veniam! Amen.	Grant thy pardon to the guilty! Amen.

CHOIR (SATB)

Ave Crux, ave Crux!	Hail, O Cross! Hail, O Cross!

7 The return to Byzantine painting tradition: Fotis Kontoglou and the aesthetical problem of twentieth-century orthodox iconography

GEORGIOS KORDIS

The icon is deeply embedded in Orthodox devotional life. Opened to the historically revealed Divine reality, it is a door through which God encounters man, and man prostrates before Holiness. The icon is important, and thus every reflection on what an icon is and how it should appear to man through the ages is of significance, aesthetically, theologically and devotionally. The question of past and present is always crucial; it involves asking what can be changed and what must for ever remain the same, a question of discipline and creativity. It raises the issue of authenticity, of the dynamic elements in an apparently static ecclesial tradition and, ultimately, how the icon as a picture, a physical instrument of devotion, can address the actual life, horizon and experiences of every new Christian generation. Hence, such questions are relevant in the context of devotional instruments, since ultimately they are questions of authenticity and efficiency. In this respect, the present essay briefly discusses a fundamental problem caused by the reintroduction in the 1920s of Byzantine style in Greek religious painting: the loss of the tropological dimension of the icon.

Although the Orthodox Church never officially 'consecrated' any specific style for the rendering of icons of Christ and saints, she has always expressed herself in the artistic language formulated during the Byzantine period. This language, characterized by special and very recognizable ideals and principles, was continuously developed until the mid-nineteenth century, adopting a number of stylistic details and iconographic elements, mainly from Western religious art of the Renaissance. The dialogue between Byzantine art and western naturalism began in Crete during the fifteenth century, during which time the island was occupied by the Venetians, and this resulted in very interesting stylistic trends, which enriched the long Byzantine tradition.

Unfortunately, for reasons not yet the subject of in-depth studies by art historians, this dialogue was interrupted and Byzantine artistic language was now substituted by naturalistic Nazarene style (see plate 10).[1] The dominance of the new Nazarene painting over traditional Byzantine art was due to the preferences of Russian monks in Mount Athos and even more so to the policy of the new Bavarian king, Otto, who came to rule the newborn Greek state after the victorious war of 1821–33 against the Turks.

---

[1] For Nazarene painting in Greece see: A. Xuggopoulos, *Sxediasma istorias tis Thriskeutikis zwgrafikis meta tin alwsi* (Athina, 1957), pp 357–9; E. Georgiadou-Kountoura, *Thriskeutika Themata sti neoelliniki zwgrafiki* (Thessaloniki, 1984); Zias, 'Neoelliniki ekklisiastiki zwgrafiki', *Synaxi*, 24 (1987), p. 46; I. Friligkos, *O agiografos Kwnstantinos Fanelis kai to ergo tou* (Athina, 2005), pp 54–63.

All these factors created a new artistic environment in which traditional Byzantine painting could not survive, and consequently it disappeared from the churches. Now, icons were painted in Nazarene style. The traditional iconography, types/forms, of the persons depicted, was usually maintained in these Nazarene icons, so that the believers could easily recognize the saints and prostrate themselves before the icons accordingly. It is important to realize that during the following decades, people in Greece became convinced that the proper artistic manner of rendering religious icons was naturalistic and not Byzantine – the latter was considered ugly and false, since the ideals of Renaissance art as defined by the great masters could not be found anywhere in this strange artistic language. Nazarene style became synonymous with 'authentic religious painting'.

FOTIS KONTOGLOU

In 1923, Fotis Kontoglou (1895–1965),[2] a young painter and writer from Asia Minor (Aivali), visited Mount Athos and discovered a real treasure covering the walls of Athonite Churches: Byzantine painting.[3] He was fascinated and shocked. He realized that Byzantine painting was an integrated system that functioned especially well when painting murals on church walls. Through this experience, he started studying traditional painting, and a few years later he himself began to work in this style – abandoning the Western style in which he had been working for so many years.

His first attempts were to use Byzantine style in his secular art, and he painted a series of non-religious themes that proved a great inspiration to contemporary Greek artists.[4] Soon after that, he tried to paint icons applying the Byzantine painting system, and worked in several small private chapels. St Lucia's chapel in Rio, a small town close to Patras, was the first.[5] St Irene's chapel in Athens was the second.[6] In 1939, he received a great commission and decorated the City Hall of Athens with a large series of scenes inspired by Greek mythology, and in addition a series of portraits of famous Greek heroes, philosophers and other prominent figures. This monumental work is unique in modern Greek art and is testimony to Kontoglou's intention to continue the Byzantine tradition even in secular painting.

After the Second World War, Kontoglou fought strongly to establish Byzantine artistic language as the legitimate and canonical style for rendering icons. This was not easy, since most Orthodox Christians at the time could not understand the benefits of reviving a Byzantine tradition, which in their eyes was less beautiful than Nazarene painting, which was characterized by the soft, aerial rendering of pictorial forms, and

2 For Kontoglou's biography, see N. Zias, *Fotis Kontoglou zwgrafos* (Athina, 1991), pp 15–24.   **3** Zias, *Fotis Kontoglou zwgrafos*, p. 17.   **4** For Kontoglou's secular painting, see Karakatsani, 'I kosmiki zwgrafiki toy Kontoglou' in *Oi Ellinies zwgrafoi, tom. II, 20th century* (Athina, 1976), p. 220.   **5** The wall paintings were executed in 1934 (Zias, *Fotis Kontoglou zwgrafos*, p. 69).   **6** The wall paintings were executed in 1938 (Zias, *Fotis Kontoglou zwgrafos*, p. 82).

7.1 Fotis Kontoglou, 'Fighters', Egg tempera on canvas, 1932 (private collection).

the emotional faces and sentimental movements of the holy figures. In his writings, and especially in his letters to Mavrikakis, one of his beloved pupils,[7] Kontoglou described in detail the difficulties he faced in attempting to bring Byzantine painting back into the Church.

7 F. Kontoglou, *Pros agiografon Euaggelon Mayrikakin* (Athina, 1997).

To achieve his goal, Kontoglou used theology as his most efficient weapon. Since the contemporary audience in Greece failed to acknowledge the beauty of the old traditional icons, he had to persuade them that these icons, although not beautiful in the Nazarene sense, were canonical – and therefore beautiful in a theological sense. In this regard, he attempted to do what Russian theologians had done a few years earlier.[8] He tried to explain that behind the strange artistic forms of Byzantine icons, theological meanings and truths were hidden – this particular style was their very language. In his writings, Kontoglou endeavoured to define the theological dimension of Byzantine icons, and to present the argument that traditional painting was necessary since it was the only canonical, artistic language for proper or adequate rendering of icons.

The way he argued against western naturalism was simple. The icon is not a portrait of some individual; rather, it is a portrait of a saint, a holy person who is already an inhabitant of the Kingdom of God. Therefore, the art of iconography had to find the proper artistic mode to render this new existence of the saints depicted in icons.[9] The painter had to handle the artistic means of line, colour and composition in a particular way in order to visualize the spiritual condition of the person depicted.[10] Believers looking at the icon must be able to see this spiritual dimension – otherwise the icon was false and non-authentic and they should not venerate it.

Originally, the strange features of the saints in Byzantine icons were an intentional invention of iconographers in order to reveal the 'transfigured humanity' of the saints before the eyes of believers.[11] The big eyes, for example, were painted in this manner because the saints always contemplate Divine glory. Large ears signify that saints always listen to God's will, and the small mouth indicates that the saints always fast and do not speak idle or sinful words.

Although he did not write a special monograph on the theology of the icon, in his writings Kontoglou supported the idea that Byzantine painting was the only artistic language qualified to express the depth of Christian faith and the truth of Holy Scriptures.[12] He accused Western naturalism of a lack of respect for the holiness of the saint depicted. To Kontoglou, the ultimate goal of Western naturalism was the pursuit of fleshly beauty, which was incompatible with spiritual beauty.[13] Most of his arguments were borrowed from Russian theologians, who, nevertheless, also defended the legitimate character of traditional Western European iconography.[14]

---

8 See P. Florenskii, 'On the Icon' in *Eastern Churches Review*, 8:11 (1976); Trubetskoi, *Icons: theology in color* (New York, 1973).   **9** According to Kontoglou 'in the icon of the Church the saints are depicted in a state of eternity'. F. Kontoglou, *Ekfrasis tis Orthodoxou eikonografias* (Athina, 1979), p. 16 (ιστ).   **10** 'The icon is not natural because its purpose is not to describe nature but supernatural things': F. Kontoglou, 'I byzantini zwgrafiki kai I alithini tis aksia' in F. Kontoglou, *Ponemeni Rwmmiosuni* (Athina, 1974), p. 97.   **11** 'The art of icon painting uses natural shapes and colours but these are transformed and are covered from spirit, these are changed from material to spiritual. Shapes and colours in Byzantine art are becoming mystic in order to be able to describe the secret world of Spirit' (Kontoglou, 'I byzantini zwgrafiki kai I alithini tis aksia', p. 98).   **12** According to Kontoglou, 'Byzantine iconography is the only painting which is adaptable to Christian religion and achieved to express the spiritual essence of Gospel' (F. Kontoglou, 'I byzantini zwgrafiki kai I alithini tis aksia', p. 119).   **13** Kontoglou, *Ekfrasis tis Orthodoxou eikonografias*, p. 10 (κ).   **14** See Doolan, *La redecouverte de L' Icone: la vie et*

7.2 Fotis Kontoglou, 'The raising of Lazarus', wall painting in the Church of
the Fountain of Life, Paiania, Attika, 1946 (photograph by the author).

l'oevre de Leonide Ouspensky (Paris, 2001); Baggley, *Doors of perception: icons and their spiritual significance* (New York, 1988); Ozolin, 'The theology of the icon', *St Vladimir's Theological Quarterly*, 31:4 (1987); Ouspensky, *Theology of the icon* (New York, 1978); Ouspensky, Lossky, *The meaning of icons* (New York, 1983).

Finally, Kontoglou succeeded in establishing Byzantine painting as the sole canonical manner of rendering icons in Greece. In 1963, he visited Mount Athos and met Meletios, a monk iconographer who had been persuaded by Kontoglou to abandon the Nazarene style and return to traditional painting. Meletios was the first in Mount Athos to paint icons in Byzantine style after a century of Nazarene painting. Eventually, most of the iconographers in this monastic castle of Orthodoxy returned to Byzantine painting. Today, nobody continues the naturalistic Nazarene style. In this respect, one might regard the mission of Fotis Kontoglou – to restore Byzantine painting in Greece – to have been successfully completed. The consequences of the return to an old traditional style affected almost all aspects of ecclesiastical life in Greece. Therefore, this phenomenon has to be examined carefully – including the proper artistic criteria – in order to fully estimate its effects.

STYLE AND SUBSTANTIAL FORM

The consequences of Kontoglou's endeavour are both positive and negative. The continuation of the long artistic tradition of the Orthodox Church seems to be the most positive result of what Kontoglou achieved. This continuation sustains the tradition and offers a steady base upon which the functional role of iconography can be established. On the other hand, the reality of the art of iconography in Greece today cannot serve as proof of Kontoglou's success in achieving what he desired according to his writings. Although he wanted to continue Byzantine tradition in a creative manner[15] – and his paintings testify to that[16] – the iconographers who followed him sooner or later abandoned his creative relationship with traditional art and started copying old masterpieces of the fourteenth and sixteenth centuries. Quite soon, then, some of them attempted to support this practice by invoking theological arguments to sanction their static repetition of older models. Hence, the art of iconography in Greece today is in an unacceptable situation, as it is characterized by static repetition, displaying neither originality nor creativity.

Thus, the dogmatic establishment of the Byzantine style seemed inevitably to lead to static repetition of old icons. The problem lies in the fact that Kontoglou, in his attempt to ascertain the legitimate character of Byzantine icons against western naturalism, seems to have equated a specific historical style with an ahistorical and general theological meaning. This concept of style – and its practice – was absolutely unknown in the Byzantine age and it had negative effects on the art of iconography, totally changing its identity. It is important to note that during the iconoclastic period in eighth- and ninth-century Byzantium, Church Fathers who defended the legitimate

---

15 J. Chatziphotis, introducing Kontoglou's book, *Thallases, kaikia, karavokyrides* (Athina, 1978), p. 18, states that the artistic ideal of Kontoglou was the continuation of Byzantine tradition, and not the repetition of the old masterpieces.   16 For creativity and originality in Kontoglou's painting, see Kordis, *Paradosi kai dimiourgia sto eikastiko ergo toy Foti Kontoglou* (Athina, 2007).

character of iconography against iconoclastic arguments never attempted to speak about the art of iconography. Therefore, they did not describe the role of art, and of course they never made a connection between stylistic elements and theology. On the contrary, immediately after iconoclasm had been overcome, the Church tried to establish what constitutes the *substantial* element of the icon; that is, the forms of the person depicted. That practice actually reflects the iconology of the Church according to which the substantial element of every icon is the external form of the person depicted, and not the particular style in which a painting might be executed.[17]

In Byzantine patristic theology, formulated during the iconoclastic era, the art of painting did not have an essential role in the creation of authentic icons. According to the Fathers, who defended the existence of such devotional objects against the icono-clastic policy of the Byzantine emperors, the icon must be identical to the external form of the person depicted. According to St Theodore Studite (759–826), one of the most important theologians of the ninth century, the icon of Christ and every icon is legitimate, since Logos, the second Hypostasis of God, was incarnated and assumed a human body. It is not the artist who describes Christ and visualizes Divinity. God became human and created His own image assuming a specific human form. *This form* constitutes His icon. He states that Christ 'had already been depicted derived from the womb of His Mother Theotokos, otherwise he could not be a real and shaped man'.[18] With these data, he asserts that the icon is identical to the external form of the person depicted, which brings all the features of his face: 'the shape of His body, namely the form carrying the features of his face and all the other external character-istics is the unique artistic icon of Christ, and that is why this icon has His name'.[19] This is a given, and consequently the painter does not create the icon *ex nihilo* – from nothing.[20] The icon pre-exists an actual painting, and it is the task of the artist to present it in the proper manner to the faithful.[21] While the Fathers thus made a subtle, but essential, distinction between 'external form' and 'style', it was precisely this distinction that was lost in the twentieth-century effort to explain why Byzantine style should be reintroduced in contemporary icon painting. To do so, style was made identical with this pre-existent external form; it was canonized and became static.

Unfortunately, the original Byzantine aesthetic theory is not very well known today, but it granted art a notable function and avoided the identification of stylistic elements with a specific theological content. Since the icon – the image – already exists, it is not

---

17 For a more thorough discussion of this, see Kordis, *Ierotypws: I eikonologia tou ieroy Fwtiou kai I texni tis meteikonomaxikis periodou* (Athina, 2002), pp 40–5. **18** St Theodore Studite: 'Letter 8', *PG* 99, 1132 D. **19** St Theodore Studite: 'Chapters against Iconoclasts', *PG* 99, 496 B. **20** According to the Seventh Ecumenical Council in 787, the creation of the icons is not an invention of painters, but it is an old tradition of the Church. Painters offer their art-craftsmanship that the icons may be properly presented: 'the making of the icons is not an invention of painters but an old insitution and tradition of the Catholic Church. The task of the painters is restricted to the artistic level' (Mansi, 13, 252 BC). **21** According to St Fotius, patriarch of Constantinople, the task of iconographers is to purify the icons from useless and spiritually unprofitable elements, and to present the new purified form to believers in a proper pictorial manner. See Kordis, *Ierotypws*, pp 25–36.

created by any artistic language; an authentic icon only articulates what is already given. While that which is given must remain unchanged, the language by which it is articulated may change according to circumstances, provided it is faithful to the pre-existing image; that is, the external form. Style is nothing more than a manner capable of properly rendering this form of a holy icon. Consequently, since the style does not have any theologically specific meaning in itself, it is free to be developed and to undergo change. For that reason, Byzantine painting was always dynamic, characterized by continuous progress at the stylistic level. Therefore, it is not surprising that stylistic changes in painting were never discussed in Byzantine society. To Orthodox Byzantines, stylistic development was considered a natural phenomenon of this world, since style was simply a *modus* (τρόπος) of painting and not visualized theology.

THE PROBLEM OF TWENTIETH-CENTURY ARTISTIC CREATIVITY

Endeavouring to reintroduce Byzantine style as the authentic alternative to Nazarene style, Kontoglou overplayed the role of style as such. Attempting to prove that traditional icons were authentic by attaching theological meaning to stylistic elements, he inadvertently destroyed the traditional concept of art. Based on the original Byzantine concept of the function of style, it is not difficult to realize the problem he thereby created for a truly contemporary and creative art of icon painting. Iconography was no more a proper mode for presenting the icons, but it was the very revelation of Divine Truth. Now, art was regarded as the way in which the *hidden* and the *unapproachable* in the icon was defined, revealed and expressed. Style had ceased to be a way to render the truth, no longer merely a tropos of already revealed Truth, but now identical with Revelation itself.

Of course, it was not the intention of Kontoglou to destroy the traditional character of Byzantine art; on the contrary, he tried to prove its superiority to western naturalism. Unwillingly, however, he gave the art of iconography a 'metaphysical-ontological' character, yet in doing so he neglected or denied its creative potential. It could be said that after Kontoglou, the art of iconography 'died', since no room was left for either inventiveness or creativity. If identical to theological content, Byzantine style is no longer art, but dogma, and consequently cannot be further developed.

Within this framework, there is no room for beauty and aesthetics. All elements of the icon are vehicles of the Truth, even identical with it, and the only criterion of style, therefore, is its unchangeable truthfulness. This, however, is a genuinely modern way of thinking about icons as such artistic conceptualism was absolutely unknown in Byzantine tradition, where the functional role of stylistic elements can be easily traced. Many years ago, Otto Demus stated that pictorial space in Byzantine painting lies in front of the surface of the painting.[22] Today, this notion is almost totally accepted by

---

22 'The image is not separated from the beholder by the "imaginary glass pane" of the picture plane behind which an illusionistic picture begins: it opens into the real space in front, where the beholder lives and moves.

the community of scholars. It is also very well known that the structure of colours in Byzantine compositions presupposes a realistic concept, aimed at producing forms alive and discernible to those who look at them.[23] The place of the icons in the iconostasis[24] also indicates that Byzantine painters always attempted to communicate with or refer to the senses of the spectators – they were not exclusively concerned with visualizing theological concepts.

The function of stylistic elements mentioned above always provided the icon with a realistic dimension, referring to the experiences of ordinary people; this was necessary if an icon as a devotional object was to have the capacity of truly uniting Heaven and earth and being a channel through which the Kingdom of God approached believers. The icon painted in Byzantine mode indeed addressed the senses of its beholders, who could thus more efficiently connect their common experiences with the Divine reality depicted before them. After Kontoglou, however, the art of icon painting in Greece lost this kind of realism. Today, many iconographers do not use stylistic elements in the proper way, not least when copying features from wall paintings in portable icons and vice versa. More often than not, icons appear to be reduced to mere signs or symbols of ideas instead of conveying the true presence of the person, represented before the eyes of the faithful.

In conclusion, it can be said that although Kontoglou's attempt to bring the art of icon painting back to its Byzantine tradition did have some positive implications – not least the reintroduction of Byzantine style as the sanctioned ecclesial mode – he nevertheless had an unfortunate influence on the development of iconography by disregarding it as a creative process. The concept of style as intrinsically linked to dogma, instead of being no more than a τρόπος, a mode, soon led to the bulk of iconographers faithfully copying selected, historical models instead of displaying a continuation of the original Byzantine artistic creativity.

His space and the space in which the holy persons exist and act are identical. The Byzantine church itself is the "picture space" of the icons' (Demus, *Byzantine church decoration* (London, 1976), p. 13). According to G. Mathew, 'the "picture space" of Byzantine art was primarily that of the church or palace room in which it was placed ...' (Mathew, *Byzantine aesthetics* (London, 1963), p. 31). See also Hans Belting, *Likeness and presence: a history of the image before the age of art* (London, 1994), pp 173–4. **23** See Liz James, *Light and colour in Byzantine art* (Oxford, 1996), pp 128–38. **24** The icon of Christ is always placed on the right side of the Royal door, as seen by believers. The Pantokrator on the dome of the Church is also always painted in order to be correctly seen by the viewer who enters the church. This demonstrates that the icons are depicted in a mode which facilitates their aesthetic communication with the audience of believers standing in the Church.

8 Fighting the disenchantment of the world: the instrument of medieval revivalism in nineteenth-century art and architecture

HENRIK VON ACHEN

'Religious belief now exists in a field of choices'
Charles Taylor, *A secular age*, 2007

'In welchem Style sollen wir bauen?'
Heinrich Hübsch, 1828

An interesting comparison can be drawn between the history of architecture since the eighteenth century and the process of secularization in the same period. In both developments, pluralism, the acknowledgment of a number of equally valid styles or ideologies, played an important, even constitutive role. In terms of architecture, it made it possible to choose a style according to a specific statement or set of associations, while religion was reduced to one option in 'the steadily widening gamut of new positions', thus creating a profound change in the conditions of belief, which Charles Taylor in 2007 defined as a major constituent of secularization.[1] In this essay, I shall attempt to show that the introduction of alternatives in styles created an equally profound change in architectural theory and practice, making it possible to use medieval styles as instruments of creating a counter-culture to the secularity of contemporary society.

This society, a French Jesuit, de Franciosi, lamented passionately in 1878, was one which:

> [...] renounced miracles and was preoccupied with mean and worldly things. Never before, since the birth of Christianity, had bodily wellbeing been sought with such passion. Always the word 'progress' on its lips, the century had prided itself on being a great emancipator of thought; despising and detesting authority – be it of men or of God.

It was truly an age 'of misery and calamities, of indifference and coldness towards God; a century of great impudence to God, His Christ, His Church. Finally, it had seen the birth of the unheard monstrosity of political Solidarity (Solidarisme)'.[2]

---

1 Charles Taylor, *A secular age* (Cambridge, MA, 2007), p. 423. The introductory quote from Taylor is on p. 437. Our second introductory quote is the title of a short book, published by Hübsch in Karlsruhe 1828. In its precise formulation of the new basic question in architecture, the text became widely known and was translated into French in 1831. From 1837, Hübsch was an honorary member of the Royal Institute of British Architects.   2 X. De Franciosi SJ, *Le Dévotion au sacré-Coeur de Jésus et au saint-coeur de Marie: notions doctrinales et pratiques*

Based on the general tendency of nineteenth-century Catholic political, devotional, edificatory and educational texts, there is no question about the general perception that religion was engaged in mortal battle with contemporary secular forces as never before. The modern world was frightening precisely because it had effective means at its disposal, having undeniably achieved progress in a number of areas, progress which everyone had to acknowledge and enjoy. However, the spiritual danger facing any Christian on the micro level of personal faith, through an immoral and unbelieving age, was mirrored on a macro level by the secular society fighting religion and its influence in all areas but individual faith within the family.

In the fight between Rome and Berlin during the *Kulturkampf* in Germany, Protestant churches became almost invisible, embedded in the (Protestant) state. While the Catholic Church came out stronger and more unified through external pressure, Protestant churches seemed to pay a price for their protected and integrated place in the establishment. Though they did share in the rejection of many features of the modern age, they never quite managed to appear as obvious alternatives to secular society.

Endeavouring to present one basic feature of the age between the Enlightenment and the First World War in a short essay may be foolhardy, indeed. There always seems to be evidence to the contrary of what one suggests as the root or core of any phenomenon. The simplistic model of explanation provides a neat and ordered picture, yet does not do justice to the ideological complexity of nineteenth-century society. The abundance of historical source material and scholarly publications is intimidating; and what is offered here must necessarily be a rather crude sketch, where complex matters are somewhat simplified and much material left aside. However, the point of such a sketch – rendering the period as an ongoing battle between religion and secularism, where religion tried to re-enchant a disenchanted world – is to cultivate just this one feature to make it stand out. In doing so, I realize, of course, that tension between faith and the world is a basic feature in Christianity, and that criticism of the lack of faith of contemporary society is no novelty. Did not another concerned Jesuit, Fr Rapin, lament the old and tired faith towards the end of the seventeenth century, the lack of enthusiasm and the coldness of his own age as opposed to the more spiritually glorious past of the Church?[3] Nostalgia and its implicit

---

(Paris, 1878), pp 139–7: 'Notre siècle nie le miracle. … Notre siècle se destingue tristement par ses préoccupations grossières et terrestes. Jamais avant lui, depuis l'avénement du Christianisme, on n'avait poursuivi le bien-être du corps avec un semblable fureur. Toujour il a sur les lèvres le mot de *progrés* … Notre siècle se vante d'être le grand emancipateur de la pensée … Notre siècle méprise et déteste l'autorité, celle des hommes et celle de Dieu, … la dévotion que Notre-Seigneur a révélée à la bienheureuse Marguerite Marie prêche au contraire le respect et la soumission … Notre siècle est un siècle de misères et de calamités. … Notre siècle est un siècle d'indifférence et de froideur à l'égard de Dieu … Notre siècle est le siècle des grandes audaces contre Dieu, son Christ, son Église. Notre siècle enfin a vu naître la monstruosité inouïe du Solidarisme'. **3** R. Rapin SJ, *La Foy des dernieres siecles* (Amsterdam, 1695). See, for example, pp 314–43 where an entire catalogue of faults and deficiencies of the present age is presented, among which Rapin mentions 'l'amour de la nouveauté' (p. 331).

critique of contemporary secular culture had become a basic element in the view on western culture since romanticist awakenings towards the end of the eighteenth century represented by authors like Schlegel in Germany or Chateaubriand in France, to name a few.[4] Yet, maintaining that fundamental conflict, not merely tension, marked the relationship between religion and society in the nineteenth century, I shall consider, then, one remedy, one instrument, which was applied to fight disenchantment and to visualize the return to, or the aspiration towards, an enchanted world: medieval revivalism as the language of re-enchantment. Nostalgia had obtained a visual language.

While this essay offers no in-depth analysis of the phenomenon or process of secularization, it is sufficient to note that the protagonists of a return to religion or of secular progress themselves perceived the underlying conflict to be between the religious and the secular establishment. To them, the result of the ongoing process was clear: relegated to the domain of personal faith, Christianity had lost its influence on society and its presence in the public space, constantly and aggressively attacked by secular forces like science and politics. In addition, the new means of entertainment provided by secular culture was deemed a great danger to the souls of the faithful. In this contemporary view of the state of affairs, we recognize many of the components later presented in various theories of secularization.

Medieval revivalism and the cultural/religious environment it tried to reinvent was an instrument used by an embattled Christianity in order to regain a visual presence and thus re-enchant the world.[5] Together with the combination of classicist features and a return to early Italian Renaissance in painting, coated with a bourgeois decorum and sweetness, Gothic revival became the visual appearance of Christian revival. Attempting to outline the religious rationale behind the use of medieval designs and forms, the text discusses the choice of 'Christian styles' in a situation where Christianity fought to preserve faith, devotion, piety and their visible, tangible role in modern society. When Pugin (1812–52) in his *Contrasts* of 1836 presented his two worlds, the enchanted world of faith found its adequate expression in the Gothic style – contrasted with the drab shape of contemporary disenchantment.[6] A sense of cultural polarization of the century was succinctly expressed and visualized in this illustrated book, where Gothic style was so much more than just a style or an aesthetic

---

4 F. Schlegel: 'Rede über die Mythologie', *Athenaeum*, vol. 1, fasc. 1 (Berlin, 1800); François-René Chateaubriand, *Génie du christianisme* (Paris, 1802). **5** Magnificent, and today rather rare, examples of neo-Gothic churches with their interiors completely preserved are William Butterfield's Anglican All Saints Church in Margaret Street, London, completed in 1859, and the Jesuit St Francis Xaverius church in the Krijtberg in Amsterdam, by Alfred Tepe, completed in 1883. A neo-Romanesque example of the same is Christoph Hehl's St Cäcilia, built in 1886 in Harsum, Niedersachsen, its interior painted in the 1890s. **6** A.W.N. Pugin, *Contrasts or a parallel between the noble edifices of the Middle Ages, and corresponding buildings of the present day; shewing the present decay of taste* (Reading, 1836). The book may be said to be the first fruit of his conversion to Catholicism in 1834. An echo of this is found in the Catholic weekly magazine for Scandinavians, *Skandinavisk Kirketidende for katholske Christne*. København. No. 4/1856, 247–9, comparing the dignified state of the poor in medieval England with contemporary misery in that same country.

choice. His illustrations contrasted the glorious past of the Middle Ages, the age of faith, with the drab, grey, inhumane ugliness of contemporary secular society.

DISENCHANTMENT

In his famous lecture at the University of Munich in 1918, Max Weber described the existential situation of man in modern society, summing up developments since the French Revolution. In this new society, religion was no longer needed to explain the human condition and existence, its traditional explanations now regarded as pious superstition testifying to an intellectual deficiency. In principle, everything was accessible to and explicable by modern science:

> The increasing intellectualization and rationalization do not, therefore, indicate an increased and general knowledge of the conditions under which one lives. It means something else, namely, the knowledge or belief that if one but wished one could learn it at any time. Hence, it means that principally there are no mysterious incalculable forces that come into play, but rather that one can, in principle, master all things by calculation. This means that the world is disenchanted. One need no longer have recourse to magical means in order to master or implore the spirits, as did the savage, for whom such mysterious powers existed. Technical means and calculations perform the service. This, above all, is what intellectualization means.[7]

This process of disenchantment (*Entzauberung*) had marked the entire previous century as the very sign of progress and civilization. It might, of course, be regarded as an exaggerated description, overrating the effect of secularization, yet his perception of a basic conflict between religion and modern science was shared by most religious authors of the nineteenth century.[8] Likewise, it does not matter if Catholic nostalgia perceived a schism that may not have been a truly significant feature of nineteenth-century life and society in terms of historical reality, as long as those who wrote and talked about religion acknowledged that 'the tension between the value-spheres of "science" and of "the holy" was "unbridgeable"', as Weber put it.[9] At least mentally and

---

7 M. Weber, *Wissenschaft als Beruf*, originally a speech at Munich University in 1918 (München, 1919). 'Die zunehmende Intellektualisierung und Rationalisierung bedeutet also *nicht* eine zunehmende allgemeine Kenntnis der Lebensbedingungen, unter denen man steht. Sondern sie bedeutet etwas anderes: das Wissen davon oder den Glauben daran: dass man, wenn man *nur wollte*, es jederzeit erfahren *könnte*, dass es also prinzipiell keine geheimnisvollen unberechenbaren Mächte gebe, die da hineinspielen, dass man vielmehr alle Dinge – im Prinzip – durch *Berechnen beherrschen* könne. Das aber bedeutet: die Entzauberung der Welt. Nicht mehr, wie der Wilde, für den es solche Mächte gab, muss man zu magischen Mitteln greifen, um die Geister zu beherrschen oder zu erbitten. Sondern technische Mittel und Berechnung leisten das. Dies vor allem bedeutet die Intellektualisierung als solche'. See *Gesammelte Aufsätze zur Wissenschaftslehre* (Tübingen, 1922), pp 524–55. **8** In retrospect, one may realize to what degree Weber, and so many like him, underestimated the resilience of religion, but in this context I am concerned with how he summed up the development in the nineteenth century. **9** Weber 1919,

rhetorically, the conflict between the sacred and the secular was a fact. Religion found itself in an ongoing battle against a relentlessly growing and self-assured secularism. An important strategy was to employ devotional tools to fight this 'disenchantment': the introduction of new or rejuvenated devotions, the enlisting of lay people in numerous pious confraternities and sodalities, the 'explosion' of Marian visions and large-scale building and decoration of churches as true '*demonstrationes catholicae*'. In many rural Protestant areas, the same situation was responded to by religious revivals, concentrating on individual conversion and a reclusive life outside secular society.[10] To both denominations, medievalist design, which visualized faith and tradition, served the same purpose: to be the voice of (re)enchantment – props to remind people that the enchanted world of faith had not ceased to exist; it still made sense to kneel before God.

DESIGN AS AN INSTRUMENT

To Christianity, then, style became the visualization of a nostalgic urge to return to a world where religion in the form of a visible institution, a given ecclesial structure, still dominated society – its hopes and fears, values, ideas, performances in the arts and sciences, and its entire system of thought. The world thus longed for was the medieval world, and its visible form, was, therefore, the neo-Gothic style. In fact, if one reflects on medieval revivalism and the Church of England, the 'medievalization' came in the middle of the nineteenth century, and it obviously was a matter of more than just forms. Thus, the spiritual revivalism of traditional Christian beliefs and virtues, as well as its institutions, was accompanied and most adequately expressed by a medieval revivalism in terms of art, architecture and design.

Medieval forms were instrumental in articulating the presence of religion in an increasingly secular society, and in fighting the disenchantment of the world by being itself an 'enchanted' language of form. Such use of historical forms was possible because particular associative potencies were embedded in specific historical form systems. So, when the architect Heinrich Hübsch in 1828 programmatically asked 'In what style should we build?', the answer depended on another question: what are you building and for what purpose? What associations do you wish those who look at your design to make?[11] If the answer encompassed something of the Christian religion, then most likely a medieval style was suggested. However, that such a question could be posed, and answered like this, was itself the heritage of both Enlightenment and Romanticism of the previous century.

op. cit.: 'die Spannung zwischen der Wertsphäre der "Wissenschaft" und der des religiösen Heils [ist] unüberbrückbar'. **10** Cf. H. Sanders, *Bondevekkelse og sekularisering. En protestantisk folkelig kultur i Danmark og Sverige 1820–1850* (Stockholm, 1995), pp 17 and 254ff. **11** See introductory quote. The question was repeated throughout the century; see Rosenthal 1844, Gottgetreu 1855 and Hoffmann 1890. Hübsch himself preferred 'Rundbogenstil', mainly neo-Romanesque variants, a style which occupied a strong position in Munich in the 1830–50s; see St Bonifaz 1835–50 (Ziebland), and the University Church, St Ludwig, 1829–43 (v. Gärtner).

THE EMANCIPATION OF STYLE

Before the stylistic pluralism of the later eighteenth century, the chosen form – or style
if you will – was by and large a given. Yet, when the slow, locally based, organic development of form was substituted by a variety of possibilities provided by books and
magazines, 'style' was no longer born out of a certain tradition; it became a matter of
choice.

Style, then, was emancipated and emerged as a set of forms, derived from architecture, but possible to apply to any object, be it a church or a medal, according to the
whims or preferences of either patron or architect. To some architects, the virtue of
Gothic style lay in the fact that it seemed to consist of forms derived from a pure structural system, form and structure blending into one. To others, Gothic style carried all
the right connotations concerning the national or the religious. Even if many architects never ceased to be moralistically concerned with the truthfulness of a given style,
the stylistic pluralism led to an emancipation of style from construction. It became a
set of referential forms recreating a historical atmosphere with all its associations,
forms in which any building might be clothed. Art was no longer a given derived from
'the static system', but the result of a choice – decoration of certain basic building
elements. This line of thought was brought to a logical formula in 1860/3, when
another German architect, Gottfried Semper, defined architecture as a clothing of
certain basic structures, style being a carpet or clothing covering the wall (playing on
the German similarity between 'Wand' and 'Gewand', wall and cloth).[12] It was hardly
surprising, then, that Semper was less occupied with the functional aspects of architecture than with the symbolic meaning of forms.[13] So, if a certain style was not linked
to a specific way of building by necessity, it was truly a matter of choice. A row of
columns may thus have a very simple functional task: to keep a roof from falling
down, but it makes no functional (or static) difference whether they are designed as
Doric or Gothic columns. The definition of architecture, then, even medieval architecture, thus developed into the opposite of the old love for its structural qualities:
architecture, the art of building, as it were, consisted precisely in everything that was
not necessary. The emancipation of style from specific building structures entailed
emancipation from certain periods; hence style became something in which you could
clothe anything, and therefore all styles were at the disposal of anyone who needed to
design something. Each choice, however, was rooted in history: the historical
monuments and spiritual heritage of a given style remained important factors,
providing the values, associations and models needed for re-employment.

12 G. Semper, *Der Stil in den technischen und tektonischen Künsten oder Praktische Ästhetik*, I–II (München, 1860,
1863). See also M. Hvattum, *Gottfried Semper and the problem of historicism* (Cambridge, 2004). **13** See M.
Onsell, *Ausdruck und Wirklichkeit. Versuch über den Historismus in der Baukunst* (Braunschweig/Wiesbaden, 1981),
p. 11.

GOTHIC STYLE AS CRITICISM OF CONTEMPORARY CULTURE

Of course, both the religious and the secular world of the nineteenth century were 'modern' in the sense that they belonged to their own age. Though clothed in medievalism, the retrospective (sometimes even regressive) world of traditional Christianity was a contemporary phenomenon, articulating ideas and positions that might have found their inspiration in Christian history, but which were basically modern and aimed at dealing with current problems.

Knowledge about historical form-systems, styles, their accessibility and legitimacy of use was not only valuable in expanding the means of designing, but it was eagerly sought after, since contemporary art was unable to hold its own.[14] Thus, historicism had the insufficiency of contemporary culture – sometimes even the decadence of western urban culture in general – as its point of departure, and the use of historical styles was, therefore, in itself an expression of culture criticism. Just as those in favour of medieval styles accused their own age of secularism, those favouring the Antique accused contemporary culture of being decadent. This pre-Romantic and Romantic lamenting of the loss of coherence and morality, of one great noble idea that could bind everything together, anticipated the religious revivalist endeavour of the nineteenth century. Programmatically, moonlit Gothic ruins testified to this loss, which was offered by Friedrich Schlegel (1772–1829) at the very beginning of the century as a general explanation for the poor state of the arts.[15] To the Gothic revivalists, the Middle Ages were precisely the age where everything was connected by a vast, lofty system of thought: the theology of the Church, encompassing all spheres of human existence, reached its finest and most adequate expression in the great Gothic cathedrals.[16] Hence, neo-Gothic style became the expression of this great idea that current times so desperately lacked. Simultaneously, the use of Gothic style implicitly criticized a secularized and fragmented contemporary culture, and suggested an alternative. To the protagonists of the early nineteenth century, a Catholic revival was the very condition for a new Christian art.[17] However, might it, then, work the other way round too – could a new art evoke a new religiosity?

By and large, this new Christian art was Gothic. While more or less direct copying

14 On the situation of religious painting in the latter part of the eighteenth century, see M. Schieder, *Jenseits der Aufklärung* (Berlin, 1997). 15 Friedrich Schlegel, 'Rede über die Mythologie', *Athenaeum*, vol. 3, fasc. 1 (Berlin, 1800), pp 94–105. In this we find an anticipation of Hans Sedlmayer's opposition to modern art in *Verlust der Mitte* from 1948; see H. Sedlmayer, *Verlust der Mitte* (Salzburg, 1998). In the same way, de Boylesve 1851 attacked Voltaire while exalting Chateaubriand and his *Génie du Christianisme* from 1802 (p. 75). 16 In this we detect a certain analogy with the way in which Erwin Panofsky explained Gothic style as an expression of scholastic theology; see *Gothic Architecture and Scholasticism* from 1951. It may be seen to correspond with Blumenberg's definition of secularization as the establishment of various institutional 'ideologies': H. Blumenberg, *Die Legitimität der Neuzeit* (Frankf.a.Main, 1966), p. 19. 17 Explicitly formulated by Chateaubriand in *Genié du Christianisme*, 1802, and Friedrich Schlegel in his articles in *Europa*, 1803, nos 1–2; see Kritische Ausgabe, *Ansichten und Ideen von der christlichen Kunst* (1823), ed. Hans Eichner (Paderborn, 1959), pp 48ff. A few publications on behalf of models from classical antiquity for churches did appear; see, for example, L. v. Klenze, *Anweisung zur Architektur des christlichen Cultus* (München, 1822/4).

of historic monuments was common, greatly aided by a wealth of new publications, the employment of medieval styles was not seen as regression, or sheer copying, but as the creative development of a tradition that had been halted with the Renaissance or Reformation. This view, expressed from time to time by the architects themselves, makes it particularly clear how medieval revivalism was always conceived as a basically modern phenomenon. Hence, the work of the Middle Ages could be completed, as in Cologne in 1842–82 or Ulm in 1844/90, or a new 'medieval' architecture could be introduced; both were obvious tasks for pious Catholics or Lutherans at the time.

In the visual arts, the Nazarene tradition – also a historicist practice combining the ideals of Classicism and early Italian Renaissance – strongly influenced the pictorial style of devotional painting. Even though in trivialized versions, the bulk of holy cards, pious reproductions for devout homes – or indeed the vast amount of 'Nazarene late Gothic' sculptures, testify to the great influence of the Nazarenes and their followers.[18]

Even in neo-Gothic altarpieces, or on holy cards with Gothic framing, the pictures themselves most often do not appear in Gothic style, but in this tradition of the Nazarene movement in which sweeter versions of classicist features, perhaps in medieval costumes, lived on throughout the nineteenth century.[19] In the 1860s, the Benedictine art school of Beuron represented a creative development of this tradition, anticipating the development around 1900.[20]

THE POSSIBILITY OF CHOICE

To combat modern secular culture, medieval styles were chosen. The new age had several alternatives at its disposal, and the style adopted was no longer a given – a continuation within the existing, obvious form tradition – but had inevitably become a matter of choice. As noted above, a curious analogy can be drawn between stylistic pluralism and a definition of secularity based on the existence of viable alternatives, making Christianity truly optional. The possibility of choosing a Gothic design, due to the message conveyed by its historical form, may be regarded as one fruit of the Enlightenment.

That history and historical forms influenced contemporary design (architecture) was not something new. It suffices to point to the obvious example of the Renaissance

18 See, for example, Y. Herzig, *Süddeutsche sakrale Skulptur im Historismus* (Petersberg, 2001). **19** On this tradition, see H. Schindler, *Nazarener – Romantischer Geist und christliche Kunst im 19. Jahrhundert.* (Regensburg, 1982); C. & M. Hollein, *Religion Macht Kunst. Die Nazarener. Katalog zur Ausstellung in der Schirn Kunsthalle Frankfurt* (Köln, 2005). On the afterlife of this tradition in mass-produced devotional pictures, see S. Metken, 'Nazarener und nazarenisch – Popularisierung und Trivialisierung eines Kunstideals' in *Die Nazarener*, Catalogue, ed. Klaus Gallwitz for an exhibition in Städel'sches Kunstinstitut und Städtische Galerie, Frankfurt am Main. On the 19th century mixture of neo-Gothic and Nazarene elements, see the interesting study by Yvonne Herzig, *Süddeutsche sakrale Skulptur im Historismus. Die Erberlesche Kunstwerkstätte Gebr. Mezger* (Petersberg, 2001). **20** On the art of Beuron, see H. Krins, *Die Kunst der Beuroner Schule* (Beuroner Kunstverlag, 1998). A late example of monumental use of this style, 1907–13, was in the German, neo-Romanesque abbey of Eibingen, Rheinland-Pfalz, by Fr Paul Krebs OSB.

8.1 Jesus and His Sacred Heart. Frontispiece of the devotional book by Jesuit Fr Francois-Xavier Gautrelet, *Manuel de la dévotion au sacré coeur de Jésus*, published in Brussels in 1851. The picture in the Nazarene style was 'Eigenthum des Vereins zur Verbreitung relig. Bilder in Düsseldorf', engraved by Friedrich Seifert after a very popular painting by the German painter Peter Molitor (1821–98).

to find a historicist architectural practice insinuating a re-established continuity, a similarity, between contemporary culture and a certain age in history. Yet, this should not negate the fact that the situation in the middle of the eighteenth century was qualitatively new.[21] What we call 'historicism' in architecture does not mean that some features or forms from the history of design are used again; rather, the term describes an entirely new situation where possibilities were not provided by tradition. The constant increase of the knowledge of other ages and their culture and monuments through the Enlightenment seems to have led to a break in the slow, organic development of form. Suddenly, those who designed – or commissioned designs – found themselves as if on a mountain top from where they had an overview of all periods and styles, from the beginning of culture until the present day.

Even if the Baroque had mediated a classical heritage that was still strong, there was a growing acceptance of the contribution of all periods, even of all cultures, to the

---

21 Not all agree on this. W. Goetz saw this historicist practice as a constant in West European art history: see W. Goetz, 'Historismus: ein Versuch zur Definition des Begriffes', *Zeitschrift des Deutschen Vereins für Kunstwissenschaft*, 24 (1970), 196–212 at 201.

progress of humanity and its art forms. In 1750s, the Picturesque movement allowed one to build in one's garden a Chinese house, a grotto, a classical ionic temple or a Gothic ruin. Combined with a growing archaeological and architectural knowledge of the actual historical models through surveys published ever more frequently, monuments from antiquity and from the Middle Ages became known and their forms accessible, but also legitimate to use. The pluralistic attitude provided architects and patrons with a very real possibility of choosing a style, which, in its turn, charged any style with the power of articulating something special, pertaining to its particular form language. So, there was not only 'architecture in the age of reason',[22] but also an inter-national 'architecture of reason', namely the classicist tradition. Likewise, there was 'architecture of faith and fatherland' articulated through medieval forms. A style became the vehicle of associations, political or religious statements – the choice became important.

When Batty Langley published his *Gothic architecture restored and improved* in 1742, it presented Gothic in the manner of the 'Picturesque', while John Milner's survey of historical monuments in Winchester, published 1798–9, signalled an archaeological turn towards medieval architecture. A few decades later, architects like Britton, Pugin and Willson surveyed and published major medieval monuments, providing their colleagues with tools for a historically correct neo-Gothic, finally capable of matching neo-Classicism. At the same time, the romantic religious sentiment with its melancholic acknowledgment of loss, was turned into a specific criticism of secular society. The 'loss' became a contemporary spiritual and moral problem to be solved by a religious revival expressed through medieval forms. Hence, putting follies of the Picturesque aside, Pugin could advocate Gothic style as simply 'the only current expression of the faith, wants and climate of our country'.[23]

In the later part of the nineteenth century, though, medievalism lost much of its specific religious context. In England, for instance, artists like Tennyson, Morris and Rosetti still sought enchantment, but not of a Christian hue. With his model village for workers in Yorkshire in 1859, his impressively neo-Gothic St Pancras railway station in London, opened in 1868, or a secular shrine, the Albert memorial, opened four years later, George Gilbert Scott may have wanted the same thing. In France, Viollet-le-Duc – the architect of the restoration of Notre Dame in Paris in the 1840s – had few problems combining fervent medievalism with equally fervent anticlericalism. In a society erecting a large number of buildings with new functions and free access to history, the use of Gothic style was not always a religious statement, but simply a standard repertoire of architectural forms.

---

22 The very title of the architectural history of the Baroque and post-Baroque in England, Italy and France, by Emil Kaufmann, published by Harvard University Press in 1955. On the ideas behind neo-Gothic architecture, see G. Germann, *Neugotik: Geschichte ihrer Architekturtheorie* (Stuttgart, 1974).   **23** A.W.N. Pugin, *An apology for the revival of Christian architecture in England* (London, 1843), quoted from A. Bøe, *From Gothic Revival to functional form* (Oslo, 1957), p. 21.

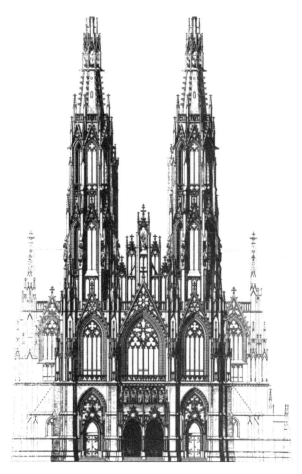

8.2 The west façade of the Votivkirche in Vienna, designed in 1854–5 by the
Austrian architect Heinrich von Ferstel (1828–83), and erected in 1856–79.

By and large, however, particularly Gothic style became the style par excellence of
religious institutions, a 'Christian' style. Only when a choice among others, and not a
given provided by tradition, could a style be defined as 'Christian'. Of course,
sometimes it was just a matter of taste, but more often the choice of style dictated the
associations that were created and values articulated, incorporating an item or a
building into a specific tradition. In Germany, August Reichensperger (1808–95), a
great fan of Pugin, combined the religious and the national into what he then called
a 'Christian-Germanic' architecture, regarding it as an expression of precisely what was
about to become lost in modern times: a people brought up in Christianity.[24] From

24 August Reichensperger, *Die christlich-germanische Baukunst und ihr Verhältnis zur Gegenwart* (Trier, 1845), p.
11: the architecture of the 'im Christenthum aufgezogenen Volksthums'.

this perspective, it was hardly surprising that medieval revivalism was canonized as the appropriate form of true Christian contemporary culture. So it had been during the 'reign' of Catholic Pugin in England, and so it was stated to be in the Protestant Eisenach regulation of 1861, which recommended that no Lutheran church be built except in Gothic style.[25]

CONDEMNING REVIVALISM

However, the dawning twentieth century reacted against what was regarded as the tyranny of history and lack of contemporary authenticity and creativity in art and architecture. Although we have seen examples of a creative approach to old forms in order to find a new style, there was a long tradition of remaining safely inside the magnificent examples of the past. In 1852, the German periodical, *Organ für christliche Kunst*, had recommended that ancient designs be chosen for exact imitation,[26] and sixty years later, in 1912, the hierarchy of the archdiocese of Cologne still decreed that only medieval forms were appropriate in ecclesial art and architecture. As late as the new Code of Canon Law of 1917, canon 1164, §1 stated that when churches were built, forms received from Christian tradition should be used.[27]

Since religion had turned to history and tradition, secular society embraced progress and the world of machines and science while often explicitly rejecting the authority of religion, history and tradition. It was as if the anti-modernism of Pius X was met by an equally resolute opposition, articulated in early twentieth-century art theory: Marinetti's Futurist manifesto of 1910 rejected the cult of the past, copying, old subjects, morality and history, and praised the victorious science.[28] History had no longer any decisive role to play, and religion could not be kept alive by 'medieval' properties. Medieval revival, then, was not authentic and could not be regarded as a genuine expression of faith.

This criticism seemed to indicate that lack of modernity and originality reflected a deeper lack of truth, questioning the religious authenticity of the entire medieval revival of the previous century. According to Weber, it simply testified to

> [...] the need of some modern intellectuals to furnish their souls with, so to speak, guaranteed genuine antiques. In doing so, they happen to remember that religion has belonged among such antiques, and of all things religion is what they do not possess. By way of substitute, however, they play at decorating a sort of domestic chapel with small sacred images from all over the world.[29]

25 The *Eisenachacher Regulativ* 1861 dealt with Protestant church building in sixteen paragraphs, in which §3 stated that historically developed Christian styles should be used, preferably 'den sogenannten germansichen (gotischen) Stil'.   **26** *Organ für christliche Kunst* (Köln) 1852, no. 2, pp 201 ff, in a review of a new church in Düffelward/Kleve, Germany.   **27** *Codex Iuri Canonici* 1917, ca. 1164, §1: 'Curent ordinarii ... ut in ecclesiarum edificatione ... serventur formae a traditione christiana receptae'. On Cologne 1912, see *New Catholic encyclopedia* (NCE), vol. 3 (1967), p. 827.   **28** C. Baumgarth, *Geschichte des Futurismus* (Reinbek, 1966), pp 49–52.   **29** Weber, *Wissenschaft als Beruf*, op. cit. The larger context of the quote: 'Noch nie ist aber eine neue Prophetie

Weber maintained, then, that these acted as substitutes for authentic religion or faith.

Within the Catholic Church, this almost moralistic attitude had its counterpart in the Liturgical Movement, which rejected the contemporary 'decadence of sacred art', as Cingria wrote in 1917.[30] The triumph of the movement came with Vatican II. Its text on the Sacred Liturgy stated that the Church had 'never adopted any particular style of art as her very own, admitting styles from every period', and went on to welcome modern art.[31] Denouncing the phenomenon of visualized nostalgia, the text does seem to have conveniently forgotten much of what the Church had actually said and done for more than a hundred years. To the post-Vatican II era, the alleged lack of authenticity in nineteenth-century medievalism made it a sign of secularization, 'an illegitimate acquirement of certain foreign cultural elements, by which Christianity masked a basic conversion to the world', a parallel to Weber's 'Hauskapelle'.[32]

SECULARIZATION

In 1878, a particular devotion could be perceived as a weapon, arming the faithful for the battle between the sacred and the secular. Indeed, its very existence renounced the main result of the secularization process: the existence of a new autonomous secular society outside religion and its influence. Fr Franciosi complained of protagonists of the secular break with tradition, that they 'proclaim that the separation between the religious and the civil society is something desirable, an indispensable necessity. The devotion to the Sacred Heart (…) reproaches indirectly, yet energetically this monstrous system, which was never known among the nations until now'.[33] A Gothic building might serve the same purpose.

However later research may have defined the phenomenon of secularization, there can be no doubt that nineteenth-century Christianity regarded contemporary society as secularized, finding its institutions propagating an ever more uninhibited secularism, aggressively turning on religious authority in every conceivable way,

dadurch entstanden […] dass manche moderne Intellektuelle das Bedürfnis haben, sich in ihrer Seele sozusagen mit garantiert echten, alten Sachen auszumöblieren, und sich dabei dann noch daran erinnern, dass dazu auch die Religion gehört hat, die sie nun einmal nicht haben, für die sie aber eine Art von spielerisch mit Heiligenbildchen aus aller Herren Länder möblierter Hauskapelle als Ersatz sich aufputzen oder ein Surrogat schaffen in allerhand Arten des Erlebens, denen sie die Würde mystischen Heiligkeitsbesitzes zuschreiben und mit dem sie – auf dem Büchermarkt hausieren gehen. Das ist einfach: Schwindel oder Selbstbetrug'.   **30** A. Cingria, 'La décadence de l'art sacré', *Cahiers Vaudois* (Lausanne, 1917).   **31** *Sacrosanctum Concilium* (Constitution on the Sacred Liturgy) 1963, art. 123: 'Ecclesia nullum artis stilum veluti habuit, sed … modos cuiusvis aetatis admisit'. And: 'Nostrorum etiam temporum … ars liberum in Ecclesia exercitium habeat…'   **32** M.M. Olivetti, 'Le problème de la sécularisation inépuisable' in E. Castelli (ed.), *L'Herméneutique de la sécularisation* (Paris, 1976), pp 73–86 at 81, commenting on the position of Blumenberg, *Die Legitimität der Neuzeit*: 'une appropriation illégitime des certains elements culturels étrangers, par quoi le christianisme a masqué sa substantielle conversion au monde'.   **33** de Franciosi, *Le Dévotion au sacré-Coeur de Jésus et au saint-coeur de Marie*, op. cit., p. 141: 'Ils proclament que la separation entre la société religieuse et la société civile est une chose désirable, une nécessité indispensable. Le Dévotion au Sacré-Coeur de Jésus … réprouve indirectement, mais énergiquement ce monstreux système inconnu jusqu'ici à tous les peuples'. See also pp 14 and 142–56.

militarily, politically, intellectually, scholarly and morally. Today, the once underestimated resilience of religion is recognized, and the idea that religion and modernity are ultimately incompatible no longer seems to hold. Hence, new definitions of secularity and secularization appear, endeavouring to find explanations that acknowledge the fact that the process and result of secularization would rather comprise a responsive transformation of religiosity than its disappearance. Undoubtedly, Christianity did experience a loss of status, relegated to take its place among a variety of cultural phenomena.[34] Yet, our current experience of how religious beliefs and practices have been transformed, or adapted to the needs of individual believers, but also to what extent religion remains a major political force, makes it reasonable to reconsider what seemed to be the inescapable truth about secularization only a few decades ago. Hence, we may need a new 'master narrative' on the subject,[35] a more varied view of the phenomena involved. Nevertheless, a considerable 'secularization' of European society did take place in the nineteenth century, as religion had to fight for its survival in the public sphere and as an authority on human existence.[36]

All definitions of secularization aside, the faithful perceived themselves under pressure – gasping for air in an increasingly hostile environment that delusively appeared as a bright, liberal, self-assured society based on progress and science. This perception coloured sermons and edifying books, and led to an introduction, or reintroduction as it often was, of a number of both individual and communal devotional practices, which served to shelter the exposed souls by building a sanctified habitat, literally a 'sanctuary', in which they could survive the seductive forces of the bright new world. The phenomenon of 'Secularization' might, to a considerable extent, have been a rhetorical construct, but it did have massive political consequences, and it did define the world in which Christians fought the good fight. Thus, in 1785, an introduction to reading edifying books complained that in those days everybody was his own casuist and theologian, having an opinion, deciding, using nice excuses to side with those who had new ideas – against the formal authority of the Church.[37] No wonder that the ecclesiastic establishment longed for a past where its

---

34 See two somewhat older contributions: the important questioning of the concept of secularization as a main feature in the development of society after the Middle Ages in Blumenberg, *Legitimität der Neuzeit*, and the interesting panel of contributions in Castelli (ed.), *L'Herméneutique de la secularisation*.   **35** J. Cox, 'Master narratives of long-term religious change' in Hugh McLeod (ed.), *The decline of Christendom in Western Europe* (Cambridge, 2003), pp 201–17. One such new narrative is presented by Taylor in *A secular age*. In McLeod, *The decline of Christendom*, p. 3, significantly, it seems to me, he defines secularity as a state when belief in God is no longer axiomatic, since viable alternatives exist.   **36** See, for example, O. Chadwick, *The secularization of the European mind in the nineteenth century* (Cambridge, 1975).   **37** Fr C. de Pontalier, *Le trésor du Chrétien* (2nd ed., Paris, 1785), pp 40–1: 'Mais le malheur de notre siècle, c'est qu'aujourd'hui la plupart des fidèles peuvent à peine être regardés comme des catechumènes. … ces Chrétiens qui n'en portent le nom que pour le profaner. D'un autre coté, parmi ceux qui passent pour être plus instruits, nous voyons, hélas! Jusqu'où s'étend la licence des pensées et des discourse. Chacun est son casuiste, chacun est son docteur; chacun tranche, decide, prend parti pour les novateurs soux des beaux pretexts, contre l'autorité formelle de l'Eglise'. Interestingly, this lament is not found in the 1st edition dated 1778.

authority was unchallenged in all matters of life – similar complaints echoed throughout the nineteenth century. Our age, Pope Pius X stated in 1907, in his syllabus, *Lamentabili sane*, condemning Modernism, pursues novelties and rejects tradition, 'thus it falls into very serious errors, which are even more serious when they concern sacred authority'.[38]

Both Christianity and secular society came to conceive the situation dichoto-mously: progress versus religion, science versus faith, liberalism versus morality. The tension – if not confrontation – between the two spheres, acknowledged by both Church and society, remained a basic feature in modern society. The emancipation of the secular and the establishment of a new rationalism would eventually gain hegemony and banish the rationality of faith to an obscure corner of human imagi-nation. Even within Catholicism, popular piety in rural areas seemed to secular progress and Catholic bourgeoisie alike to be a somewhat naïve, and intellectually undeveloped faith filled with traditional practices close to superstition. This too, might be viewed as a result of the Enlightenment, and this divide within the community of faithful itself became quite clear in 1797, when the head of the Virgin Mary miraculously appeared on the window pane in a farmhouse in Absam, Austria. While the diocesan commission in a very Max-Weberian way concluded that it was no miracle at all – even if inexplicable – the rural population continued to venerate it regardless, and after some decades it was eventually recognized by ecclesiastical author-ities. Later, however, miraculous events were not rejected, but published, the Church cultivating particularly the role of uneducated, simple people as vehicles of divine manifestation – a corrective comment on the scientism of the day, as outlined in Eli Seland's contribution to this volume. Nevertheless, throughout the nineteenth century, a certain alienation of Catholic bourgeoisie from traditional forms of religious celebration did take place.[39] The actual *modus operandi* of secularization remains a subject for research, demanding a more varied notion of religion and 'secular' society.

In the perspective of secularization as it was perceived, then, medieval revivalism may be viewed as a struggle to de-secularize a world where religion was increasingly relegated to the private sphere of personal belief. For such was the logic of the modern secular movement: if religion could not provide valid (that is, scientific) explanations of the world and of human existence, it had lost its operational value, and hence, its political importance. Religion became a private matter. In its domesticated form, as part of the establishment, it might still be promoted by those in power to ensure that people remained docile and adhered to certain morals.[40] Eventually, however, the basic

---

38 *Lamentabili sane exitu,* 3 July 1907.   39 Cf. J. Sperber, *Popular Catholicism in nineteenth-century Germany* (Princeton, NJ, 1984), pp 10f. See also Schieder, *Jenseits der Aufklärung*, who registers the discrepancy between popular piety and the emerging Eucharistic cult of the Catholic 'Enlightenment', pp 253–71 at p. 259. A similar attitude disregarded the expressions of much popular piety in the decades following Vatican II.   40 The continued political importance of the Church of England in the nineteenth century was already registered by Christopher Dawson in his essay 'The secularization of western culture' (1943); see G.J. Russello (ed.), *Christianity and European culture: selections from the work of Christopher Dawson* (Washington, 1998), pp 170–81

truth of Christianity, its general relevance and even its legitimacy, would be questioned.

TWO WORLDS

The acknowledgment of a conflict between the two worlds was found everywhere in contemporary descriptions of the current situation. Everything seemed encompassed by the conflict, and anything might be instrumental in fighting the good fight, as practical, visual and instrumental dimensions of devotion were incorporated into this holy warfare.

Such a confrontation could not be expected to leave the physical and cultural framework of existence untouched. Art, architecture and design, also encompassing instruments of devotion, was a most visible field, where battles were fought and ideas reflected. Already in the beginning of the Enlightenment, one of the lesser art critics of his age, Daniel Webb, voiced the secular concern in an important essay: compared to the artists of Antiquity, he asked, 'how unequal is the lot of the modern artist? – employed by priests, or princes who thought like priests'. According to Webb, what may indeed be edifying is not, therefore, picturesque, or a worthy subject. Instead, pious pictures leave their audience cold: 'the genius of painting wasting its powers on crucifixions, holy families, last suppers, and the like, wants nerves, if at any time the subject calls for the pathetic or sublime'.[41] In the 1760s, lamenting the poor quality of Christian art compared to the art of Classic Antiquity – and hence promoting Classicism – was still primarily a question of aesthetics; of art and taste, not a rejection of Christian subjects as such. Thus Webb simply stated that a (Christian) 'subject great in conception, may become little in the execution',[42] thereby rejecting most of the popular religious art with its discrepancy between lofty iconography conveying holy messages, yet, by crude or inadequate forms.

Rejecting the support of priests and patrons thinking like priests, art would emerge liberated and free – which meant free to serve the secular world. In 1806, the German art critic Carl Ludwig Fernow expressed the new state of affairs when he wrote that in the future, the liberated art, which had now lost both the support and the constraints of religion, would have to rely on itself.[43] What was a matter of taste and choice in the eighteenth century had become much more serious around 1800. The search for the picturesque had become a hunt for meaning, and rejection of Christian iconography

at pp 178–80. See also the furious attacks on the established church in Denmark by Søren Kierkegaard in the 1850s, not least in the ten issues of his magazine *Øieblikket*, May to Aug. 1855; vol. 19 of his *Samlede værker* (København, 1991), 91–330.   **41** D. Webb, *An inquiry into the beauties of painting; and into the merits of the most celebrated painters, ancient and modern* (London, 1769), 145/147; see reprint in 1998 of the expanded and revised 3rd edition as *Aesthetics: sources in the eighteenth century*, vol. 7 (Bristol). The first edition was published in 1760, with two German editions following in Zürich 1765 and 1771.   **42** Ibid., p. 170.   **43** C.L. Fernow, *Leben des Künstlers Asmus Jakob Carstens*, quoted from the 2nd ed. (Hanover, 1867), p. 163: 'Die freigewordene Kunst, der Stütze aber zugleich des Zwanges der Religion enthoben, muss hinfort auf sich selbst ruhen'.

the very instrument of artistic emancipation to serve a new world. Not only certain topics, but style itself, had become an exponent of a world view, a reflection of Christian or secular (Classical) virtues and values.[44] Henceforth, art had to relate to these two worlds, which both claimed supremacy.

The dissolution of the German monasteries in 1803 testified to the incompatibility of these two worlds, as governmental need for control and power – and cash – could not tolerate the independence of large abbeys. As in the Reformation era, the emerging national states seemed to believe that they could only prevail if the Church and its institutions were either annihilated or severely domesticated. Indeed, in the nineteenth century, the tension between the two worlds developed into open conflict. The fight was not only spiritual or ideological: what was anticipated by the French Revolution and the rigorous secularization of German monasteries was later continued through military campaign in Italy, and hostile legislation in both Germany and France.

To the devout and those rejoicing in secular progress alike, there could be no spiritually peaceful coexistence between religion and modern society, between traditional and contemporary values, between faith and science. Human existence, or the soul, was the field on which the battle was fought, and all possible means applied: pious congregations, societies and confraternities, devotions of all kinds using instruments like medals equipped with indulgences, edifying books, rosaries, statues, pilgrimages and masses etc. It was a century marked by important Marian visions, the last one in Fatima, Portugal, taking place shortly before Weber's Munich lecture. What better way than such visions for religion to insist that the world was still enchanted? Visions, Gothic churches and altars, guardian angels, saints, sacraments and public processions were all signs serving the preservation or reinstatement of God as a reality and the Catholic Church as the true herald of that reality. The signs were there to see and to interpret. The Disenchantment of the world, Ricoeur commented on Weber, is precisely the erosion of a common religious symbolic.[45] Catholic nostalgia, politics and devotions, the pious structuring of lay life in congregations and confraternities, the weekly or daily mass, pilgrimages to holy sites, prayers and devotions within the family etc., provided life with a general symbolic frame of reference. In addition, they were practical religious measures to ensure that faith survived and did not crumble under the pressure from a bright new world answering to no one but itself.

The public display of piety in pilgrimages and processions was only the tip of the iceberg; below the surface, the nineteenth century was filled with an immense variety of devotions and practices, in groups, in families or in the private life of individuals. No wonder that a handbook was needed to provide the faithful with a practical guide

---

44 Even if the first decades of the nineteenth century saw some major classicist churches, like the cathedrals in Lutheran Copenhagen, begun in 1811, and Catholic Dublin, begun in 1815. The Catholic St Ludwig in Celle, Niedersachsen, Germany, was completely classical, built 1835–8.   45 P. Ricoeur, 'L'Herméneutique de la secularisation' in Castelli (1976), p. 49.

to all these instruments of devotion, preferably with an indulgence attached, and Abbé Giraud met the demand with his *Manuel des principales devotions et confréries auxquelles sont attachées des indulgences*, published in Lille in 1844. Responding to the pressure of secular society, simultaneously new and traditional devotional forms were found and cultivated – as in architecture.

Interestingly – and logically – it seems that some of the more important devotions expressed a revitalized Counter-Reformation spirit, with devotions to the Guardian Angel, St Joseph or the Sacred Heart, while what we may call the 'design-profile' of current religiosity by and large fetched its forms from the Middle Ages – even if the Oratorians in England preferred the Baroque. Religious culture might not encompass all sectors of society any more, but perhaps it continued as the interior life of pious families or dedicated groups, where elements of a new religious culture emerged as a response to the secular threat.[46] To counterbalance this reclusion, public displays became important as *demonstrationes catholicae* – pilgrimages for instance, or the reintroduction of religious processions as in Lille, France, where processions with the Blessed Sacrament began again on 15 June 1852 – the event commemorated by a special bronze medal (see plate 11).

Facing the dire circumstances of faith in a disenchanted world, the Church fought to re-enchant it by promoting the revival of a devout spiritual life with all its elements, orchestrated by the religious hierarchy. A phenomenon like Lourdes articulated the religious alternative to the great development of contemporary medicine and science; the message of this miraculous event told the world that sickness, pain and suffering made sense, viewed in the context of faith, yet cure was always a possibility, due to divine intervention. In this way, a corrective to the heroes of modern science was presented: an uneducated girl was granted knowledge of a deeper nature. Events occurred that could be explained by neither medicine nor science; a holy place emerged drawing a multitude based on faith and hope. Lourdes and other such places or events served the re-enchantment of the world, at the same time confronting the finest achievements of its secular forces. The devotions expressed the 'depressive, defensive and anti-modern mentality' of a beleaguered people.[47] *Appel à la jeunesse catholique contre l'esprit du siècle*, published by a Jesuit father in 1851, met the require-ments for defending faith and morals against the values of a secularized society, whose main instruments were identified as a hostile press and immoral literature. No, the light of modern independence and science was no light at all, but darkness masked as light: 'Beware of the spirit of this century, because it is a wrong and perverse spirit; its breath blows out the light and reinstates the night again everywhere'.[48] Indeed, the

46 See C. Taylor, *A secular age*, p. 436.   47 As Norbert Busch has shown in his interesting study of the Sacred Heart devotion in Germany in the late nineteenth and early twentieth centuries; see N. Busch, *Katholische Frömmigkeit und Moderne: die Sozial-und Mentalitätsgeschichte des Herz-Jesu-Kultes in Deutschland zwischen Kulturkampf und Erstem Weltkrieg* (Gütersloh, 1997).   48 M. De Boylesve SJ, *Appel a la jeunesse catholique contre l'esprit du siècle* (Paris, 1851), pp 11–12: 'Prenez garde à l'esprit du siècle; car c'est un esprit faux et pervers; son

Church found herself in a battle against the spirit of the age of industry and material science, and she could save only those who rallied to her colours.[49] With the attacks on the Papal States in Italy, eventually stripping the pope of any temporal power, this confrontation gained archetypical character. From all over the world, the spontaneous collections of money for a beleaguered Pius IX in Rome introduced a new and optional form of the old 'Peter's pence'. It contributed to compensate the papacy for the loss of the Papal States, but more importantly, it served as an overwhelming sign of allegiance to the papacy. To gather around the pope gave the religious faith of Catholics, so often relegated to the domestic sphere, the opportunity of public display on the level of national and international politics.

LIVING IN OVERLAPPING FRONTIERS

Even if it remains the point of this essay to regard the spiritual/ideological conflict between the religious and the secular as a major component in the post-Enlightenment era, particularly to those in the trenches on each side, it must not be forgotten that believers lived in both worlds. Two independent worlds was the result of secularization, and the situation may from a theological and moral viewpoint have been depicted as two opposite and incompatible spheres fighting each other. Yet, any devout Christian still had to live in both worlds, hence the devotional efforts to minimize the damage from that fact; and it was obviously not a question of Christianity versus paganism – even if concerned clerics sometimes explicitly suggested just that.

So, the idea of this strict divide in the nineteenth century should be somewhat modified. The basic conflict was obvious and had a history going back to the gospels, but both Catholics and Protestants belonged to both worlds, living their everyday lives where these worlds overlapped.[50] As has been suggested above, we may have to make a distinction between the tamed, conformist religion as an integral part of the estab-lished (secular) society, the state church, so furiously attacked by the Danish philosopher Søren Kierkegaard in the 1850s, and religion as a basically independent competitive system of authority, insisting on alternatives to that society. Any aggressive secularism would be directed against this latter 'undomesticated' version of Christianity.

Another area where Christianity was as modern as any secular institution was the employment of modern technologies. One might be concerned about the unfortunate effects of industrialization, and architects rejected mass-produced elements, but

---

souffle éteint lumière, et partout répand la nuit'; ibid., pp 9–10.   **49** Ibid., p. 66: 'L'Eglise ne sauvera pas que ceux qui se rangeront sous son drapeau, et qui la seconderont dans la lutte contre l'esprit du siècle', and p. 96: 'siècle de l'industri et de la science matérielle', which cannot solve the problem of Job (contrary to spiritual science, that is, theology).   **50** See, for example, Sperber, *Popular Catholicism*, p. 13; also H. Blumenberg, *Die Legitimität der Neuzeit*, p. 15.

Christian institutions made ample use of the means of mass production, and so did architects despite their rhetoric. Indeed, the overwhelming product culture of nineteenth-century Christianity – most of the cultural history of devotion of that age – depended heavily on the new capability of producing all kinds of items in huge numbers, and hence affordable for everybody. Did not pilgrim sites and railroads enter into a mutually fruitful union? On the relationship between modernity and religion, through the impact of technology on Catholicism, one must agree with Michel Lagre's conclusion, that technology itself was not the main agent of the world's disenchantment, far from it.[51]

If one component of nineteenth-century secularization was the relocation of religion to areas of less institutional and general social control, this would evidently reduce the impact of religion and its institutions on society. However, religion still exerted influence or even dominated certain important sectors: family life and individual religious activity organized in religious societies. Thus, while participating in a society growing still more secular, the individual remained attached to sectors where he or she could practise and articulate his or her faith. The abundance of nineteenth-century practices and devotions testifies to the still massive influence of religion in these sectors of society. The practical everyday task of any Christian would be to establish a life outwardly compatible with the demands of the secular world, yet interiorly shaped by faith and its various practices. The question of safeguarding one's spiritual life from destructive influences of secularism remained a constant challenge – hence the new popularity of a phenomenon like guardian angels. In a few instances, the two worlds officially merged; one such instance is the decision in 1842 to complete the great Gothic cathedral in Cologne, a project which for a short while united the concept of Germania and Ecclesia (see plate 12).

Using the term 'Christianity' does suggest that the Christian world was homogeneous; a united whole confronting rising secularism. It was not – at least not in Northern Europe. Even if religion as such was under pressure, Christianity existed as a variety of denominations. Hence, in some areas the confrontation between denominations was an ongoing phenomenon, sometimes fierce, and may have contributed as much to the self-consciousness of any denomination as did the conflict with secular society. In this perspective, the practice of one's religion, its devotional profile, was developed precisely to strengthen a specific denominational identity. In such cases, the battle between denominations and churches was crucial in maintaining the 'purity' of the sector to which religion had been relocated. Hence, it should not surprise that Catholics lamented the present situation where 'infidelity raged in the intestines of the nations'. Contemporary Europe was in a sad state, they thought, having turned its back on religion and virtue, torn apart by politics and denominational differences.

---

51 M. Lagrée, 'The impact of technology on Catholicism in France (1850–1950)' in McLeod (ed.), *The decline of Christendom*, pp 163–83 at p. 179.

Longing for the day when all European leaders, peoples and nations would sing their Halleluia in the 'mighty Gothic cathedral of the Catholic Church', it could not be denied that many had left the faith that once made that very Europe; left it to follow heresy or secularism.[52] Therefore, while both fronts were important, the denominational battle was often perceived as the more immediate and important, the 'enemy within', as it were, while fighting secularism after all remained secondary. In denominationally mixed areas, the very building of a church and the choice of style became a public political act. The entire shaping of both individual and communal religious life, then, was not only an aid to survive secularism, but (at least in religiously divided Northern Europe) to forge a denominational identity. Thus, when Protestants in the kingdom of Hanover had used Gothic style extensively, it could no longer serve Catholics, who, then, had recourse to neo-Romanesque style.[53]

CONCLUSION

Fighting the 'disenchantment of the world', neo-Gothic style provided a visual manifestation of a re-enchanted world: the forms of a resurrected *Civitas Dei*. In Gothic revival, the ghost of a devout past turned into firm matter, a piety-evoking framework signifying a restoration of traditional beliefs and values – together with Marian visions, Sacred Heart or Holy Family devotions, saints and indulgences, processions with the Blessed Sacrament, devout confraternities and papal authority. Medieval revivalism appeared as the materialization of religious nostalgia, in itself an implicit criticism of contemporary secular culture. The very possibility of style making such a statement was the result of development in architectural theory and practice since the middle of the eighteenth century.

Faith received its form-language, through which it could visualize an alternative to a modern society emerging as self-assuredly secular. To Protestants, the obvious 'Catholic' connotations triggered by a pre-Reformation style did little to diminish the attraction of Gothic forms. Hence, neo-Gothic style and design became simply the 'Christian style', the truly appropriate form of everything pertaining to faith. Indeed, medieval style became so closely linked to the world of faith that it became a sign and symbol of it, visualizing and reviving a world that was about to be lost. In that respect, sometimes designing in medieval style in itself came close to a devotional practice, as it was to a Pugin or a Reichensperger – or at least provided the basic symbolic and traditional form of all material instruments of Christian devotion in the hundred years between neo-Classicism and the First World War. The form-language of medieval

---

52 The article 'Opstandelse!', by an anonymous author, perhaps an Austrian, published in the weekly *Skandinavisk Kirketidende for katholske Christne* (København, 1855), no. 14, pp 211, 213–14. **53** U. Knapp, 'Restauratio Ecclesiae. Die Erneuerung einer Kirchenlandschaft' in Ulrich Knapp (ed.), *Restauratio Ecclesiae: das Bistum Hildesheim im 19. Jahrhundert* (Hildesheim, 2000), pp 27–70 esp. pp 27–9.

styles spoke of the enchanted world of faith; therefore, it could be used to re-enchant a secularized, and hence, disenchanted world.

Neo-Gothic architecture and design, then, was enlisted in the fight against a modern, secular society. Viewed from the nostalgic perspective of loss, Gothic design was a useful instrument in the hands of those who were given the task of visualizing the ever resilient presence of Christianity, its spirit and its institutions. Christians returned to the old world of faith by reinventing it. Hence, it seemed only natural that some pious Belgian in 1885 should use a devotional book styled like a late medieval Book of Hours, when he immersed himself in the Passion of Christ and was offered some 'pratiques de piété' in honour of the sufferings of Jesus (plate 13).

Throughout the nineteenth century, this battle was fought in the hearts of men, but also on the world stage. The character of this ideologically divided century may be appreciated if one considers the contraposition of the public displays or expressions of the two halves. These two adversaries struggled for power and allegiance, putting their essential features on display for public veneration: Christianity, particularly the Catholic Church, celebrated its major events like jubilees, proclamation of dogma, or Marian visions, its progress in sanctity by glorifying great saints, and promoted loyalty by glorifying the papacy. The modern world, on the other hand, celebrated its achievements with great exhibitions, its progress by glorifying great scientists and artists, and promoted loyalty by glorifying the national state, its law and rulers. However, to those trying to uphold a religious tradition under attack, the self-assured celebration of secular progress was tantamount to a new heathendom, much worse than the old one conquered so long ago. 'There cannot be a higher degree of evil, wickedness and sin', a Scandinavian Catholic weekly pointed out in 1861, 'than what presently appears in its devilish blindness and diabolic pride'.[54]

---

[54] The editorial 'Gammel og ny hedendom', accusing the spirit of the present age, *Skandinavisk Kirketidende for katholske Christne* (København), no. 1 (1861), p. 6.

PART III

Devotional instruments

9 'When wicked men blaspheme Thee': constructing the religious Other in English hymnody

PETER McGRAIL

INTRODUCTION

Among my childhood memories from the 1960s, one of the most vivid remains that of the two major processions that were held each year by the Roman Catholic (hereafter, Catholic) community of the Lancashire mining village in which I lived. On two Sunday afternoons, the first in May and again in June, hundreds of people would first gather in the church and then process around the adjacent cemetery before re-entering the building for solemn Benediction. In May, the procession would accompany an image of the Virgin Mary, carried on a flower-bedecked bier by four senior boys from the parish school. In June, the focus would be the monstrance containing the consecrated Host, carried by the priest under a golden canopy along cemetery pathways strewn with rose petals by a carefully drilled team of veiled school-girls. These were more than acts of devotion; they emotively imprinted on the participants and spectators a collective memory and identity, focusing upon the two great markers of pre-Vatican II popular Catholicism – devotion to Mary and to the Eucharist. The perambulation of the graveyard reinforced a common sense of identity and shared memory between current worshippers and previous generations. And as we processed we sang hymns that had been used for generations in the community and which expressed a highly developed myth of Catholic recusancy, of persecution, of survival and of religious aspirations for the future. Singing and walking together, we affirmed who we were, and we also sang who we were not – at least hinting, darkly, at the Other. 'When wicked men blaspheme thee', we sang to Mary, 'I'll love and bless thy Name'.[1]

English Catholics, of course, were far from alone in harnessing hymnody for socio-logical purposes; historically, a parallel – and, arguably, richer – seam of sectarian hymnody was produced within various English Protestant communities. When compared, these two sets of hymns demonstrate a striking commonality: each seeks to map out an account of English history and national identity. Within the Protestant corpus, England (and later, Britain) was portrayed as the subject of divine election, miraculously preserved from the ever-present threat of papist overthrow; religious and political liberty were dominant themes. The Catholic corpus, on the other hand, understood England's authentic identity to be not so much a Protestant homeland as

---

1 'I'll sing a hymn to Mary', by John Wyse (1825–98).

'the dowry of Mary', a beacon of fidelity to Rome and to Catholic orthodoxy. Concrete historical events were woven into the texture of the hymns; for both it was the often tragic events of the English Reformation itself. Outside the Catholic community, there was a focus on the defeat of the Spanish Armada, the Gunpowder Plot against James I (1605), the 'Glorious Revolution' and accession of William III (1688–9), and the securing of Protestant succession in the Hanoverian dynasty (1714). Later events such as the process of Catholic Emancipation (1778–1829) and the restoration of the Catholic hierarchy in England and Wales (1850) fed into the hymnody and songs of both sides. What emerges from these hymns is the construct of an opposing Other: be it Rome as Whore of Babylon or the reformers as spoilers of England's true religious identity. Such an Other could never be a mere political agent; diabolic forces were recognized, hinted at, and sometimes named.

This essay explores the hymn production of both parties in this religio-political contest across the 'long nineteenth century'. With regard to the Catholic community in England and Wales, this period calls for further clarification. The key battleground mapped out by nineteenth-century sectarian polemic was the impact of the progressive relaxation of penal laws against Catholics and the growing confidence of the Catholic community in the wake of the restoration of the Catholic hierarchy in 1850. It thus seems most appropriate to take the date of the first Catholic Relief Act of 1778 as marking the beginning of the period under discussion.[2] As the Protestant tradition of anti-Catholic hymnody was much longer, and as older hymns enjoyed continued currency at least during the early part of this period, I shall discuss that corpus first, moving then to consider the Catholic hymns.

PROTESTANT HYMNODY

The original English Reformers had tended towards a Calvinist rather than a Lutheran approach to church music. The dominant form of congregational singing across the sixteenth and seventeenth centuries was thus the metrical psalm rather than the hymn, and it was not until the eighteenth century that hymn-singing became securely established in English Protestant worship. That having been said, there exist a few examples of English vernacular hymnody from the mid-sixteenth and seventeenth centuries that offer glimpses of the expression of anti-Catholic sentiments within the hymn form.

For example, the *Old Version* of the Psalter – effectively the official song book of the Anglican Church from 1662 until the early eighteenth century – contained a hymn to the Holy Spirit that prayed:

---

2 18 George III, c. 60. The process of Catholic emancipation was completed by two of the subsequent Relief Acts of 1791 (31 George III, c. 32) and 1829 (10 George IV, c. 7).

O blessed spirit of truthe, keep us,/ In peace and unitie:
Keep us from sects and errours all,/ And from all papistrie.[3]

Opposition to Catholicism and its doctrines can also be detected in later seventeenth-century hymns that sat on the edge of the mainstream. Thus the Anglican George Wither (1588–1667) published two versions of a hymn for the time of administration of the sacrament that is a systematic rebuttal of Tridentine Eucharistic doctrines:

We do no gross realities/ Of flesh in this conceive;
Or, that their proper qualities/ The bread or wine do leave.[4]

Similarly, the Baptist Benjamin Keach (1640–1704), an early advocate of congregational hymn-singing, expressly identified the Catholic Church with the Babylon of the Book of Revelation.[5] It comes as no surprise, therefore, to find that in inviting his worshippers to be grateful to God for having been born in England, he exhorts them to be particularly grateful that they did not hail from other lands where:

Dumb pictures might we all ador'd,/ Like papists in devotion;
And with Rome's errours so been stor'd,/ To drink her deadly Potion.[6]

In the preceding illustrations, we see the foundations of the genre that in Protestant circles was extremely prevalent during the earlier half of the long nineteenth century. Particularly important is the manner in which Keach's work counterbalances the construct Babylon-Rome with that of Britain/New Israel. This theme of the divine election of Britain re-emerged later, especially in the metrical psalms of Isaac Watts (1674–1748).[7] Watts' psalm settings came to replace the *Old Version* in popular use;

---

3 John Day, *The whole booke of psalms, collected into English metre by T. Starnhold I. Hopkins & others: conferred with the Ebrue, and apt notes to synge the withal, faithfully perused and allowed according to thordre appointed in the Quenes maiesties iniunctions. Very mete to be used of all sortes of people primately for their solace & comfort: laying apart all ungodly songes and ballades, which tende only to the nourishing of vyce and corrupting of youth* (London, 1562).   **4** *The hymnes and songs of the church. Divided into two parts. The first part comprehends the canonicall hymnes, and such parcels of Holy Scriptures, as may properly be sung: with some other ancient songs and creeds. The second part consists of spirituall songs, appropriated to the several times and occasions observable in the Church of England* (London, 1623). No. 83; *Halelujah or, Britans second remembrancer, bringing to remembrance (in praisefull and poenitentiall hymns, spirituall songs, and morall-odes) meditations, advancing the glory of God, in the practice of pietie and virtue; and applied to easie tunes to be sung in families, &c.* (London, 1641). Printed for the Spencer Society 1879. Part I, no. 53.   **5** See *Antichrist stormed: or mystery Babylon, the great whore and great city, proved to be the present Church of Rome. Wherein are all objections answered* (London, 1689).   **6** *Spiritual melody, containing near three hundred sacred hymns* (London, 1691), hymn 97, stanza 3. Similar sentiments are expressed in the hymn 'Divine breathings', contained in Keach's *War with the Devil: or the young mans conflict with the powers of darkness: in a dialogue. Discovering the corruption and vanity of youth, the horrible nature of sin, and the deplorable condition of fallen-man. Also a definition, power, and rule of conscience, and the nature of true conversion*, 3rd impression (London, 1675), p. 126.   **7** *The psalms of David imitated in the language of the New Testament, by I. Watts* (London, 1719). Based on information from English short title catalogue, eighteenth century collections online. Gale Group.

they were reprinted and incorporated into various collections across most of the long nineteenth century; several of them continue in use even today – for example, 'O God our help in ages past' (Psalm 90).

In several of these psalms, Watts quite deliberately replaces the original references to Israel with direct reference to Britain.[8] A particularly long-lived hymn was his setting of Psalm 67, subtitled, 'The nation's prosperity, and the Churches increase.' The opening words set the tone:

> Shine, mighty God, on Britain shine,/ with beams of heavenly grace;
> Reveal thy power thro' all our coasts,/ and show thy smiling face.

In the remaining stanzas the nationalist note is increased – Britain is a 'favourite land',[9] a 'chosen isle', protected by God like a 'wall of guardian fire'.[10] This hymn was reprinted in numerous hymn books across the eighteenth and up to the end of the nineteenth century.[11] The religious and political implications of this divine election are played out most fully in hymns written for the annual celebrations of 5 November. These hymns not only map concrete historical events on to the myth of Protestant Britain as uniquely favoured, but also identify the (Papist) Other against whom Watts' construct of the Guardian God was protecting it.

After the restoration of Charles II, from 1662 until 1859, 5 November was celebrated as one of three State Holy Days in the Anglican Book of Common Prayer.[12] In 1790, William III instructed that the commemoration of his landing in England – also on 5 November, in 1688 – should be added to the celebration.[13] This thus became a national celebration of the trials, but especially of the success of the Protestant cause in England. The Prayer Book prayers written for the commemoration are strongly anti-Catholic: the intended victims of the Gunpowder Plot were, 'by Popish treachery appointed as sheep to the slaughter, in a most barbarous and savage manner'; the arrival of William of Orange was 'for the deliverance of our Church and nation from Popish tyranny and arbitrary power'. These prayers were used in public worship until the abolition in 1859 of the State Holy Days,[14] though their popularity had waned by then.[15] At their height, these State Holy Days occasioned the production of a body of hymnody that vigorously reflected the sentiments expressed in the formal prayers.

---

8 Nos 19, 47, 50, 67, 75, 96, 100, 114, 115, 135, 145 and 147.   **9** Stanza 6.   **10** Stanza 2.   **11** It is no. 81 in a hymn book produced by the Congregational Congregation of Leeds, *Psalms, hymns and passages of scripture for Christian worship* (London, 1894).   **12** 'State Holy Days' in George Harford et al. (eds), *The prayer book dictionary* (London, 1925), p. 769; see also Charles Hefling, 'The State Services' in Charles Hefling and Cynthia Shattuck (eds), *The Oxford guide to the Book of Common Prayer: a worldwide survey* (Oxford, 2006), pp 73–5. **13** Lois G. Schwoerer, 'Celebrating the Glorious Revolution, 1689–1989', *Albion: a quarterly concerned with British Studies*, 22:1 (spring 1990), 1–20 esp. 3. See also David Cressy, *Bonfires and bells: national memory and the Protestant calendar in Elizabethan and Stuart England* (London, 1989), pp 141–89.   **14** 22 Vict., c. 2.   **15** See Philip Williamson, 'State prayers, fasts and thanskgivings: public worship in Britain 1830–1897', *Past and Present*, 200 (Aug. 2008), 121–70 esp. 163.

Benjamin Keach, living at the time of the Glorious Revolution under William III, celebrated the raising of the siege of Derry/Londonderry with a 'Hymn of thanksgiving for our late deliverance'.[16] Several decades later, Isaac Watts' 1719 collection of metrical psalms applies two of the psalms to the Glorious Revolution. Psalm 115, against idol worship, is sub-titled, 'Popish idolatry reproved', and concludes with a direct call to the nation that combines the themes of Britain's special blessedness and divine intervention in its history:

> O Britain, trust the Lord: thy foes in vain/ Attempt thy ruin, and oppose his reign;
> Had they prevail'd, darkness had clos'd our days,/ And death and silence had forbid his praise:
> But we are sav'd, and live: let songs arise,/ And Britain bless the God that built the skies.[17]

A hymn book published in 1842 by W.J. Hall, rector of St Benet and St Peter, London,[18] provides evidence for the continuing commemoration of 5 November as an occasion for the expression of anti-Catholic sentiments well into the mid-nineteenth century proper. The book indexes two hymns under the heading, 'Papist conspiracy (Nov. 5)'. One makes no direct mention of Catholicism as such, but plays upon a theme that Catholics themselves were to invert in their own hymnody – reformation martyrdom. The other includes a stanza demonstrating the continuing currency in some quarters of the combination of the themes of divine intervention in British history and anti-Catholicism:

> What hath God wrought! Let Britain see,/ Freed from papal tyranny:
> Its tenfold night, its iron chains,/ Its galling yoke, its cruel pains.[19]

Publication of hymns for 5 November continued to the end of the century. A small collection of hymns published as late as 1894 includes several that perpetuate the myth of Britain as the favoured, Protestant island.[20] The hymn for 5 November contained in this collection strikes an almost retrospective note, with verses celebrating the defeat of the Armada, the Gunpowder plot and the Glorious Revolution; here, 'the Sons of Rome' are still identified as the enemy and the Glorious Revolution is portrayed as a divine response to a Catholic plot:

> Princes and priests again combine,/ new chains to forge, new snares to twine;
> Again our gracious God appears,/ And breaks their chains and cuts their snares.[21]

---

16 *Spiritual melody*, hymn 179.   17 Stanza 6.   18 *Psalms and hymns adapted to the services of the Church of England* (London, 1842).   19 No. 122, stanza 3.   20 *The Protestant hymn book: for use at Protestant meetings, conferences and lectures* (London, 1894). See hymns 10, 12–16 and 26.   21 No. 27.

However, a truer picture of the waning appetite for the use of 5 November as a vehicle for anti-Catholic sentiments is reflected in a late hymn for the Anglican liturgical celebration of the same date. Published twelve years after Hall's 1842 collection, this hymn is an anodyne prayer for the monarch, shorn of any historic or sectarian references.[22] By the end of the century, the national mood had well and truly changed, and in 1889 the second centenary of the Glorious Revolution passed almost unmarked – in sharp contrast to the exuberant celebrations of 1789.[23]

It would be wrong to imagine that the events of Catholic emancipation and the restoration of its hierarchy went unnoticed in Protestant hymnody and song, or that voices of concern were not raised. This can be seen at the very opening of our slightly extended long nineteenth century, in the aftermath of the first Relief Act of 1778. William Augustus Clarke, minister of Red Cross Street Particular Baptist Church, London,[24] was personally involved in at least the anti-government demonstrations that followed (if not the riots). Four years after the Relief Act, Clarke published a collection of his own hymns that appear to be responding to the new situation.[25] In hymns of repentance, intended for use on a public fast day, Clarke condemns the new dispensation as inherently sinful; it has allowed 'Rome's infectious horrid tide into the British isle'.[26] This is, for him, a national calamity, drawing down divine wrathful judgment upon the nation.[27] 'O Lord', Clarke has his congregation sing, 'forgive this dreadful sin/ In letting cursed Pop'ry in';[28] yet, in the final instance he remains confident that,

> ... tho' injurious Rome and hell,/ Together should combine,/
> Striving to crush protesting saints,/ yet Christ will keep his vine![29]

Anxieties provoked by the growing confidence – and, indeed, visibility – of the Catholic community after the passing of the final Relief Act may have played into the hymn 'We won't give up the Bible', by the Anglican priest William Whittemore (1820–94). This piece went through a number of significant revisions (one might, more appropriately say, mutations) across the century. In 1845, Whittemore published a musical setting of it, under the title 'The young Protestant's hymn', which is used here as the base text.[30] The anxiety that undergirds this hymn is that young Anglicans might well be tempted to 'give up the Bible' – not least in the face of the twin threats of a

22 Hugh Stowell, *A selection of psalms and hymns suited to the services of the Church of England* (London, 1854), no. 141.   **23** See Schwoerer, 'Celebrating the Glorious Revolution', pp 8–12.   **24** For a near-contemporary account of Clarke's colourful career, see Walter Wilson, *The history and antiquities of dissenting churches and meeting houses in London, Westminster and Southwark; including the lives of their ministers from the rise of nonconformity to the present time* (London, 1810), pp 322–3.   **25** *Sacred hymns, for the use of the elect family of Jesus, in this militant state; by W. Augustus Clarke* (London, 1782), from *Eighteenth-century collections online*. Gale Group, http://galenet.galegroup.com/servlet/ECCO.   **26** Hymn 61, stanza 3.   **27** Hymn 62, stanza 1.   **28** Ibid., stanza 3.   **29** Hymn 70, stanza 4.   **30** The Young Protestant's Hymn, 'We won't give up the Bible', the words written and adapted by a clergyman of the Church of England; the music arranged for three voices, with symphonies and a separate accompaniment for the piano forte, by W.H. Kearns, organist of the Verulam Episcopal Chapel, Lambeth (London, ?).

resurgent Catholicism, coupled with ritualism within the Anglican Church, and the rise of the scientific method. These threats are brought together in the third stanza of the hymn:

> We won't give up the Bible,/ No need what scoffers say;
> Nor romish craft of those who would/ This treasure take away;
> For they would fain enshroud our minds/ In gloom of moral night;
> But to this blessed book we'll cleave;/ And God defend the right!

An echo of Whittemore's approach is found later in the century. In 1865, Revd D.T. Barry invited the schoolchildren and families of his Anglican parish to sing their prayer for the mission of the Church in familiar terms:

> Arm of the Lord, Thy power extend; / Let Mahomet's imposture end;
> Break superstition's papal chain,/ And the proud scoffer's rage restrain.[31]

However, the general mood had shifted, and the anti-Catholic vehemence that once was common became associated with the political and religious extremes. Not surprisingly, Ulster Protestantism and mainland Orange Lodges maintained the sectarian tone. Thus, from these quarters comes a near-panicked response to the 1850 restoration of the Catholic hierarchy in England:

> Up Protestant Britain! And arm for the strife,
> Your Bible is perill'd, far dearer than life;
> O'er Westminster's court, o'er the home of our queen,
> Floats the old scarlet banner in popery's sheen.[32]

Similarly, as the Irish Home Rule issue intensified across the first two decades of the twentieth century, we find a British parliamentarian quoting in debate a gross variant of Whittemore's hymn sung by the 'Ulster mobs'. In the crucible of events, the text employs extreme imagery that intensifies even Keach to portray an Other who is both feared and reviled:

> We won't give up the Bible,/ the beacon of our hope.
> For all the powers of darkness,/ the devil or the pope.
> What though the drunken woman/ should gnash her blood-stained jaws,
> Their strength is more than human/ who fight in God's own cause.[33]

---

31 *Psalms and hymns for the church, school and home* (London, 1865), no. 14.   32 *The national orange and Protestant minstrel: being a collection of constitutional and protestant songs, hymns, toasts, sentiments and recitations, original and select* (Kirkgate, 1853), pp 9–10.   33 *New York Times,* 22 June 1913.

However, mainstream popular Protestant hymnody had long departed from this sectarian route, and focused increasingly upon the devotional rather than the sectarian, particularly under the influence of American mass-evangelism.[34] Whittemore's hymn was far more likely to be softened than intensified in its sectarian thrust. For example, in a Sunday School hymnbook published *c.*1905,[35] the original third stanza had been stripped of its direct sectarian references:

> We won't give up the Bible!/ For pleasure or for pain:
> We'll buy the truth, and sell it not/ For all that we might gain.
> Though men may try to take our prize/ By guile or cruel might,
> We'll suffer all that men could do,/ And 'God defend the right'.

Yet, here is the paradox. As by the turn of the twentieth century, mainstream English Anglican and other Protestant congregations had moved away from direct sectarianism in their hymnody, so the Catholic community had moved in the opposite direction, publishing and singing hymns in which the Other is clearly drawn. It is to this Catholic corpus that we now turn.

CATHOLIC HYMNS

The development of a vernacular English Catholic hymnody was limited by two factors. The first was the circumscribed nature of English Catholic life. From the mid-eighteenth century until well into the nineteenth, the primary resource for Catholic devotion in England was *The garden of the soul* by Bishop Richard Challoner (1691–1781).[36] This much reprinted volume mapped out a sober, restrained devotional style, and contained only five vernacular hymns, three being translations of Latin Office hymns. There was nothing sectarian here, and the restrained style reflected the political and social restraints against overt displays of Catholic worship. The second limiting factor was the very nature of Catholic liturgy itself. The celebration of the Mass – which through the penal period had been the very touchstone of Catholic identity – was conducted in Latin and was subject to stringent rubrical control; its celebration offered no sanctioned opportunities for vernacular song. However, progressive Catholic emancipation not only led to a growth in confidence among Catholics – and the possibility of increasingly elaborate liturgical display – it also afforded space for the development of extra-liturgical devotions, such as Lenten Stations of the Cross or Benediction of the Blessed Sacrament. The spread within England from the 1830s onwards of these continental devotions was to no little extent

---

34 For example, witness the popularity of *Sacred songs and solos: nos I and II combined: (441 pieces) compiled and sung by Ira D. Sankey* (London, 1885).   **35** *Songs of gladness: a hymn book for the young* (London, *c.*1905), no. III. **36** *The garden of the soul: or a manual of spiritual exercises and instructions for Christians who (living in the world) aspirre to devotion* (1st ed., London, 1740); frequent republications.

due to the increasingly confident activity of continental religious orders of men and women, who led missions, ran schools and staffed parishes.[37] Devotional expression was also linked to the development – again frequently under the guidance of the afore-mentioned religious orders – of sodalities and pious associations of lay people.

This devotional explosion coalesced in what became across the pre-Vatican II English Church the primary venue for vernacular expression of Catholic piety – namely, the Sunday afternoon or early evening service. This service, whose form and content varied according to the liturgical season, drew upon a number of elements, such as Marian devotions, Benediction, the recitation of litanies, and processions (originally indoor, but – as my own experience witnessed – eventually outdoor). This service became the locus *par excellence* for the emotive and vernacular expression of later nineteenth- and early twentieth-century popular Catholicism, and was progressively furnished with a body of vernacular hymnody that expressed the aspirations and concerns of the community. Paradoxically, therefore, the period that witnessed the decline in the expression of sectarian sentiments in the hymnody of the mainstream English Protestant population nonetheless saw the rise of popular vernacular hymns through which the Catholic community laid claim to a different version of English history and hinted at or named the non-Catholic Other.

These hymns, therefore, counterpoise the shrinking body of anti-Catholic hymns written in the same period. The texts are composed in response to similar stimuli – for example, the events of Catholic emancipation, the restoration of the Catholic hierarchy, or the need to construct a meaningful account of English history. However, very different conclusions are reached from those of their Protestant counterparts; an alternative account of the events of the Reformation is articulated, and the growth of religious tolerance is understood as heralding a Catholic revival. The confluence of these two themes, and the broader, triumphalist expectations at play in the Catholic community can be most clearly seen in the hymn *England! Oh, what means this sighing?*, written by Nicholas Cardinal Wiseman (1802–65), and first published in 1860.[38]

Created the first archbishop of Westminster by the 1850 restoration of the Catholic hierarchy, Wiseman embodied the confident tone of the English Catholic community in this period, drawing on a long familiar theme – whereas the Protestant hymns discussed earlier had spoken of post-Reformation England as the divinely favoured new Israel, the Catholic hymns that emerged in the mid-nineteenth century offered a more desolate perspective. The rupture that the Reformation introduced into the fabric of English religious history is represented for Wiseman by the ruins of the medieval monasteries. This was not a new concept – he is probably developing Shakespeare's image of the 'bare ruined choirs where late the sweet birds sang':[39]

37 For the ritual implications of the activities of these religious congregations, see Peter McGrail, *First Communion: ritual, church and popular religious identity* (Aldershot, 2007), pp 15–17. **38** John Julian, *A dictionary of hymnology, setting forth the origin and history of Christian hymns of all ages and nations* (London, 1892, 1908), p. 1729. **39** Sonnet 79, line 4.

England! Oh what means this sighing from those heaps of mossy stone;
As of spirits music trying on some harp left crushed and lone?
Through carv'd shaft of aisles deserted, breezes murmur still the song,
Which in cadence sweet concerted! rais'd once there the cloister'd throng.[40]

After establishing this vision of past desolation, Wiseman offers an interpretation of his present: a Catholic community resurgent in the wake of religious and political developments in which he himself had been a primary player:

Whence this clang of pick and hammer, blent with cheers in field and town?
Ha! Whence that unearthly clamour, 'neath earth's lowest deeps far down?
There is faith once more restoring Church and Convent, cross and spire:
Here perdition's host is roaring: cries of vengeance, howls of ire.

The cries of 'vengeance' and 'ire', of course, had been expressed in the response to the restoration of the Catholic hierarchy; Wiseman here offers a construct of those such as Whittemore who opposed Rome as 'Other' in the most negative terms – the almost demonic 'perditions' host'.

The corpus of nineteenth-century Catholic hymnody weaves two other themes through Wiseman's twin motifs of a Catholic English past and contemporary restoration. Both themes flow out of the sense that contemporary developments represented a re-suturing of a disrupted English Catholic history; they are the notion of England as the dowry of Mary, and the cult of the Catholic martyrs of the Reformation era. The potency of the Dowry theme to encapsulate the theme of an authentic, non-Reformation English historical religious identity was expressed in an extraordinary ceremony conducted by Cardinal Herbert Vaughan (1832–1903) in June 1893. Over the course of a day, Vaughan, accompanied by almost the entire English Catholic hierarchy, solemnly consecrated England to Mary and to St Peter.[41] The lengthy sermon devoted to the Marian aspect of the event played heavily on the conviction that the title 'Dowry of Mary' had a venerable pre-Reformation history. By offering England back to Mary, as it were, Vaughan was inviting his fellow countrymen to discover their natural and authentic religious identity. There were, naturally, howls of protest.[42]

The sense of a lost history, and of the recovery of the Dowry, is found in an unattributed hymn in the 1864 *Crown of Jesus music*, written to celebrate the Assumption of Mary into heaven. Once she has assumed her celestial throne, the Virgin is asked to

---

40 *Crown of Jesus music* (London, 1864), no. 92, stanza 1.   41 For a full account of the Consecration, see *The Tablet*, 82:2,773 (London, 1 July 1803), 5–21. See also Robert O'Neill, *Cardinal Herbert Vaughan; Archbishop of Westminster, Bishop of Salford, founder of the Mill Hill Missionaries* (London, 1995), pp 359–60.   42 For example, the stridently anti-Catholic pamphlet, *The Roman Catholic 'dedication of England' to the Virgin Mary as 'Our Lady's Dowry'. A manifesto to the people of Great Britain. By an Englishman* (London, c.1893).

> Look on this isle from the azure sky,/ That bask'd so happy in days gone by,
> Beneath thy dove-like reign.
> Fallen away from its faith of old,/ O bring it back to the Catholic fold,
> And claim thy dowry again.

The theme is even more insistently driven home in the hymn, 'Peal, ye bells', which was printed by *The Tablet* immediately after its account of the 1893 Consecration. The hymn also appears in the 1905 *Notre Dame hymn tune book.* Every stanza concludes with a reference to the Dowry image. The second stanza, for example, reiterates the theme of the English Reformation as historic rupture, and constructs the reformers, and particularly the physical destroyers of England's Marian sanctuaries, as the Other:

> Men have robbed our Queen of her Dower,
> Robbed Thy Dower of Thee, sweet Queen;
> Dark and dreary without Thy smiles
> Our meads and cities for years have been.
> Queen of our hearts! Queen of the world!
> Rend Thine own from the spoiler's power;
> Come back again,
> Over us reign,
> Take us once more for Thy Royal Dower.[43]

This was the hymn book used in the early twentieth century in my childhood parish: my grandparents and their contemporaries grew up singing of their aspirations for English Catholicism in terms that approached a Marian Second Coming.

The sixth stanza of the same hymn links the theme of Reformation-era martyrdom to the Dowry image.[44] In the Catholic reversal of the Protestant account of that period, the figures of the martyrs came to play a pivotal role – a new body of heroes, and advocates before God for the restoration of the pre-Reformation state. Published slightly later, 'Tyburn's days are long forgiven' by Fr Joseph W. Reeks (d. 1900) has those who were executed for their Catholic allegiance at Tyburn, London's traditional place of execution, crying out before God for vengeance:

> Tyburn's days are long forgiven, unforgotten is the pain;
> Time can never dim the traces of the cruel blood-red stain.
> And the martyrs' cry for vengeance rises up before thy throne:
> 'Save the land we love so well, Lord! Claim its children for thine own'.[45]

---

43 *The Notre Dame hymn tune book.* Compiled and arranged by Frank. N. Birtchenall and Moir Brown (Liverpool, 1905), no. 89.   44 As also does the hymn, 'O Lord! Behold the suppliant band' by Thomas Edward Bridgett (1829–99), ibid., no. 128; see also, 'The conversion of England' by T.J. Potter (1828–73), *Arundel hymns and other spiritual praises. Chosen and edited by Henry Duke of Norfolk and Charles T. Gatty, FSA* (London, 1902), no. 265.   45 *Westminster hymnbook* (1st ed.), no. 197, stanza 1.

Reeks then applies the metaphor of the martyrs' spiritual warfare to the Catholics of his own time, effectively inviting his singers to identify a continuity and sense of comradeship between themselves and their ancestors:

> Look upon this land, deep watered with the blood of martyrs slain,
> Surely these who were our kinsmen have not bled for us in vain;
> We, like them, are stoutly fighting for the souls of men today,
> And we claim them for our brothers who have fallen in the fray.[46]

This nobly embattled vision of the modern English Catholic is, rather more prosaically, but no less defiantly, expressed in a hymn by Lady Georgiana Fullerton (1812–85), a society convert to Catholicism. For her the opposing Other appears rather close: 'Though friends may entice me, and fortune may frown, my faith and my Church until death I will own'.[47] In the face of all this, however, she invites those Catholics gathered in their churches on Sunday evenings to sing:

> They call me a Papist and they laugh at my creed,
> 'Tis the faith that will save in the dread hour of need;
> Let them talk, let them laugh, but when death is at hand,
> The priest is the only true friend in the land.[48]

The hymn does express a common concern in nineteenth-century English Catholicism that it was surrounded by a hostile, mocking majority. This concern fed particularly into an anxiety that young Catholics were particularly vulnerable to Protestant proselytizing. The institutional Catholic response was the establishment of a network of Catholic schools during the mid- to late nineteenth century. These schools served a significant social function in maintaining the distinctiveness of the Catholic community as well as ensuring the completeness of its children's ideological formation. It is not surprising, therefore, that hymns written for Catholic children and young people should strike a particularly defiant and, indeed, sectarian, note – rather as had done Whittemore's hymn for young Protestants. A strongly worded example was the hymn, 'I am a faithful Catholic'.[49] This appears to be an extended version of the hymn 'I am a little Catholic' written by a female religious who, like many other such authors, simply gives her initials – Sr M.B. The second stanza of the hymn reads:

> I shun the haunts of those who seek/ To ensnare poor Catholic youth;
> No Church I own, no schools I know, /But those that teach the Truth.[50]

The hymn marries this contemporary social concern to an appeal to the myth of England's Catholic past: 'I love to pray where saints have prayed, and kneel where they

---

46 Ibid., stanza 4.   **47** *Notre Dame hymn tune book*, no. 133, stanza 1.   **48** Stanza 4.   **49** *Notre Dame hymn tune book*, no. 134.   **50** *Notre Dame hymn tune book*, no. 134, stanza 2.

have knelt'.[51] It also fixes in the imagination of the child the importance of key Catholic religious symbols as tokens that define them against the Other:

> I love my Cross, I love my Beads,/ Each emblem of my faith;
> Let foolish men rail as they will, I'll love them until death.[52]

Such love unto death in the face of Protestant abuse, however, was presented as still potentially leading to martyrdom. John Wyse's hymn 'I'll sing a hymn to Mary', with which this chapter opens, presented Catholics with a vision of the fragility of what they were constructing by transforming the image of Mary as all-powerful heavenly queen to one of the Virgin as vulnerable, virtually defenceless against the blasphemy of the 'wicked men' of its refrain:

> And now, O Virgin Mary, my Mother and my Queen,
> I've sung thy praise so bless me, and keep my heart from sin.
> When others jeer and mock thee I'll often think how I,
> To shield my Mother Mary, would lay me down and die.

CONCLUSION

The Notre Dame hymn tune book seems to have been published at the high-water mark of Catholic sectarian hymnody. 1912 saw the publication of the first edition of the *Westminster Hymnal*, commissioned by the bishops of England and Wales for use in churches in England and Wales.[53] With this book we find a marked decrease in the number of hymns in which English Catholics were invited to sing against a threatening Protestant Other. The second edition of 1940 reduced the presence of such hymns still further. For example, 'Tyburn's days are long forgiven' does not feature,[54] and while both editions contained 'I'll sing a hymn to Mary', the hymn was shorn of its original final verse (quoted above) by the editors of the 1940 revision.[55] Therefore, by the time I took part in the parish processions of the 1960s, a more irenic regime was in place; or, perhaps not entirely. The congregation at those processions reserved its most enthusiastic vocal participation for the hymn with which the event always ended – irrespective of whether the occasion was the May or June procession. The hymn was Faber's classic, 'Faith of our Fathers'. Sung beneath the stained-glass windows depicting the Reformation-era martyrs that ringed the church, the hymn's stirring words set to a soaring melody invited that parish community, once again, to understand itself as the local heir to an alternative and costly account of English history:

51 Stanza 6. **52** Stanza 7. **53** London: R. & T. Washbourne. For a discussion of the relationship between this and earlier hymnals, see Brian Plumb, 'Hymnbooks revisited' in *North West Catholic History*, vol. 27 (2000), pp 68–91. **54** London: Burns, Oates and Washbourne. **55** 1912 ed., no. 122; 1940 ed., no. 182.

Our Fathers chained in prisons dark
Were still in heart and conscience free;
How sweet would be their children's fate,
If they, like them, could die for thee.
Faith of our Fathers, Holy Faith, we will be true to thee till death.[56]

To me, a small child during the 1960s, the third line was always troubling – perhaps the broader context of the narrative was already weakening. At any rate, the events came to an end in the early 1970s. What I was experiencing, therefore, in the years just after the Second Vatican Council constituted, perhaps, the last corporate expression of the long nineteenth century of the Catholic Church in that Lancashire village.

---

56 *Hymns by Frederick William Faber, D.D. New Edition* (London, 1861), no. 93.

10 The Spanish Civil War *detentebalas*: some notes on the materiality of the Sacred Heart*

EWA KLEKOT

Objects and symbols perceived as originating in the field of religion and endowed by their users with deep religious meaning have often been used in politics because of their power to mobilize people's emotions and actions. However, it is only since the time when modern religion started becoming invisible, having been removed to the private sphere of life, that many people in the Western World started to feel uneasy about religious symbols being used in political contexts, or even more generally in the public sphere. One of the most powerful Catholic religious symbols that mobilized human actions and emotions in Europe far beyond the realm of privatized modern religion was the Sacred Heart of Jesus.[1]

In spite of the fact that the iconography approved for the public cult by the Holy See in 1891 was of Jesus himself showing his burning heart to the world, in popular imagery the Sacred Heart was mostly represented separately, without any connection to Jesus' body, and this makes it less an image and more a symbol. It is in this symbolic form that the Sacred Heart of Jesus appears on small badges called *detentebalas* (stop-bullets) used by some groupings of counter-republican troops during the Spanish Civil War of 1936–9. This essay follows the origins of *detentebalas*; small, portable objects made of embroidered fabric or printed paper, sometimes called 'scapulars of the Sacred Heart'. Their iconography consists of the image of a burning heart crowned with thorns and a motto that states: '*Détente! El corazón de Jesús está conmigo!*' ('Stop! The Heart of Jesus is with me!'). The contexts in which these *detentebalas* appear may provide us with important insights into modern material religiosity.

ICONOGRAPHY AND DEVOTION TO THE SACRED HEART

Until the end of the sixteenth century, devotion to the Heart of Jesus was generally limited to the monastic environment and related to private visions and devotions of mystics, especially female ones such as St Gertrude or St Catherine of Siena, and later St Mary Magdalene de Pazzi or Jeanne de Valois.[2] On a more popular level, the concept of Jesus' Heart and its sufferings had been developed within the cult of Five

---

* The author wishes to thank the editors for their assistance in preparing this essay for publication. 1 The political power of the image of the Black Madonna, and other religious symbols in resistance movements against the regime of state socialism in Poland in 1980s, extensively discussed by Jan Kubik, is notable here; however, the way an image works, and even more a miraculous one, is different from the way a symbolic graphic form such as the Sacred Heart (or the cross) does. 2 See Jean Vincent Bainvel, *Kult Serca Bożego: Teoria i rozwój* (Kraków, 1934), transl. from French.

APPARITION DE N.S. A LA B^{se} Mre MARIE

Tout en Dieu et rien en moi.
Tout à Dieu et rien à moi — Tout pour Dieu et rien pour moi.

10.1 Vision of St Margaret Mary Alacôque, devotional print,
France, early twentieth century (private collection).

Wounds, introduced in the thirteenth century and spread in particular by the
Franciscan order.[3] Therefore, the early iconography following the devotion's development represents Jesus' heart as a wounded, symbolically represented human heart,
mostly depicted among four other wounds.

However, the situation changed in the seventeenth century, which has been called
'the age of the religion of heart' by religious historians such as Jaroslav Pelikan[4] or Ted
Campbell.[5] Generally speaking, both the human heart and Jesus' heart became

3 Sixten Ringbom, *Icon to narrative: the rise of the dramatic close-up in fifteenth-century devotional painting* (Åbo,
1965). 4 Jaroslav Pelikan, *The Christian tradition: a history of the development of doctrine*, v (Chicago, 1989).
5 Ted A. Campbell, *The religion of the heart: a study of European religious life in the seventeenth and eighteenth
centuries* (Columbia, SC, 1991).

important subjects of theological discussion and devotional practice in relation to important developments in philosophy and theology, both Catholic and Protestant, which focused on God's love, free will, grace and predestination. Pelikan and Campbell both see the development of 'affective theology' or 'theology of the heart'[6] as a reaction to the rationalist bias in theology and philosophy and emphasize the fact that the 'religion of heart' is by no means limited to Catholic Christianity. The strong religious focus on the heart – both the human heart and the heart of Jesus – seems also to result from the end of medieval (pre-Thomistic and Thomistic) anthropology described by C.S. Lewis in the metaphor of the 'discarded image'[7] and the beginning of the modern dichotomy of heart and reason, grounded in the Cartesian *res extensa* and *res cogitans* that later proved seminal to the modern dualistic concept of man as 'the animal with culture'.

The fully developed devotion to the Sacred Heart is directly related to the visions of the French nun Margaret Mary Alacôque of the Visitation Order. However, the visions she received in 1673–90 in the convent of Paray-le-Monial had been preceded by half a century of dissemination of the cult of the Sacred Heart, especially by the Jesuits and the Eudists (the latter tended to combine devotion to the Heart of Jesus with its counterpart, the Immaculate Heart of Mary). In the devotion, male orders with a strong missionary charism saw a chance, on the one hand, to revive popular piety, and on the other, to use it in theological discussions on free will and grace, which resulted in the common understanding of devotion to the Heart of Jesus as an example of 'warm religion of heart' as opposed to the 'cold religion of reason' standing for Jansenism. The first Brotherhood of the Hearts of Jesus and Mary was established in 1666 by the Eudists in Morlaix, some years before the visions of Margaret Mary who may, therefore, have been familiar with the devotion already before entering the Visitation convent. However, had she not known of it before, she must have soon become acquainted with it as it had been practised by the Visitandines almost since the establishment of the order, according to the personal advice given by Francis de Sales to the founder, Jeanne de Chantal.[8] Besides, Margaret Mary had a Jesuit confessor, Fr Claude de la Colombière, who was well acquainted with the rules of 'the religion of the heart'.[9]

In spite of its powerful promoters within the most influential order of the early modern Catholic Church, namely the Jesuits, the devotion had not been officially ratified and was allowed only in a private capacity in several convents of the Visitandines and the Eudists. In 1704, a book describing the visions of Sister Margaret Mary, written by a Jesuit, Fr Jean Croiset, was put on the Index.[10] However, the popular appeal of the devotion was so strong that in spite of the official lack of enthu-

6 *Theologie affective* by Louis Bail was published in Paris in 1659; *La theologie du Coeur, ou recueil de quelques traits qui contiennent les lumieres les plus divines des ames simples et pures* by Pierre Poiret in Cologne in 1690.   7 Clive Staples Lewis, *The discarded image: an introduction to Medieval and Renaissance literature* (Cambridge, 1964). 8 Bainvel, *Kult Serca Bożego*, pp 357–70. 9 Ibid.   10 Ibid., p. 501.

10.2 Vision of Bernardo de Hoyos, devotional print, Spain,
before 1936 (private collection).

siasm (in 1729 the Congregation for Rites dismissed the request for approval of the liturgy and the feast of the Sacred Heart signed by the monarchs of Poland and Spain) it continued to spread and the 'scapular of the Sacred Heart' soon made its first appearance.

ARRETE! LE COEUR DE JESUS EST LÀ!

Having received her visions, Margaret Mary made an image of the Heart of Jesus that was exposed for veneration in the convent chapel in 1685. It was a simple drawing representing a heart with a cross on the top and a horizontal wound with drops of blood on its edge, surrounded by three smaller wounds pierced by nails. The heart was encircled by flames and the crown of thorns. According to the visions of 1685, many graces had been promised to believers who would copy the image and carry it around on their person, as well as to the houses where it would be exposed.[11] The Visitandines, in spreading the devotion, were also popularizing the image.

11 Ibid., pp 81–2.

10.3 Antonio Molle Lazo, a requeté from Jerez de la Frontera, died in 1936 in the Civil War; a devotional print with a prayer for his beatification; Spain (private collection).

In 1720, the city of Marseille was struck by the plague. In the atmosphere of general despair, one of the local Visitandines, Anne-Magdalene Remuzat, started distributing small paper images made according to Margaret Mary's prototype with a motto saying: *Arrete! Le couer de Jesus est là* (Stop! The Heart of Jesus is here!),[12] which proved to be quite effective protective talismans against the plague. The images received the French name of *sauveguardes*, and their fame in protecting people against all kinds of dangers and evils spread beyond the city.

During the French Revolution, these images were adopted as royalist symbols. The main reason was on account of one of Margaret Mary's visions in which she was commanded to tell the French monarch to offer the whole nation to the Sacred Heart of Jesus. However, the visionary never succeeded in seeing the king. In 1792, according to the widespread royalist tradition,[13] King Louis XVI, imprisoned in the ancient Parisian fortress known as the Temple, and apparently informed about the vision, made a vow to offer all France to the Sacred Heart, but was then guillotined. The

---

12 Ibid., p. 522. **13** Michael Paul Driskel, *Representing belief: religion, art and society in nineteenth-century France* (Philadelphia, 1992), p. 47.

image of the Heart of Jesus became a symbol of loyalty to the king and spreading them, or even possessing them, during the 'Reign of Terror' was punishable by death.[14] These royalist associations led to 'sacred heart scapularies' or embroidered badges of a heart crowned with a cross being sported on the left side by the Vandée uprising fighters.[15]

NINETEENTH-CENTURY ASSOCIATIONS OF THE SACRED HEART: FRANCE

In 1765, the Congregation for Rites repealed the decision of 1729 and the feast of the Sacred Heart was approved, although not without serious reservations. Its opponents were aware of the dangers of subjectivism resulting from the 'doctrine of the heart' claiming that non-intellectual religious experience could lead to people confusing God's inspiration with the inspiration originating in the human soul.[16] Charges against the anti-intellectualism of the devotion were expressed in pamphlets such as *Lettre aux Alacoquistes dits Cordicoles* published in 1781–2 by one Fr Reynaud, a priest from Vaux, which derided 'une theologie musculaire'.[17]

The anti-revolutionary meaning of the Heart of Jesus in France was reinforced after 1814: the year of the restoration of the Bourbons and the Jesuits. The strong political associations of the Sacred Heart badge can be seen in the painting executed by Ary Scheffer in 1827, representing the death of Pope Clement XIV, in which the murderer who has just poisoned the pope is wearing the Burning and Wounded Heart emblem attached to his garb; with an accusatory (or maybe also cursing) gesture of his left hand, he points to the dying pope, while with his right hand he reveals the badge worn under his cloak as a sign of his identity and as a supposed explanation of the authorship of the pontiff's death.[18] The painting was reproduced in the form of prints, adding to the general association of the Heart of Jesus emblem with Catholic conservatism and the Jesuit order, and later also with Ultramontanism.

The last quarter of the nineteenth century and the beginning of the twentieth century seem to be marked by a vigorous Sacred Heart devotion, visible both in the Vatican regulations concerning the cult, as well as in the employment of representations of the Sacred Heart in political debate both within the Catholic Church and outside it. The popularity of the badge among pious Catholics had grown after 1872 when a papal indulgence was granted to the devotees of the Sacred Heart. An important factor shaping the Sacred Heart's associations was the pronouncement of the Congregation for Rites in 1891 concerning the Sacred Heart iconography that was then approved for use in the official public cult. The figure of Jesus showing his burning, thorn-crowned heart to the world was to be the only valid representation to be displayed at roadside shrines, hermitages, chapels and churches. However, as in the

14 Victor Alet, *La France et le Sacré-Coeur* (Paris, 1889), p. 284; Bainvel, *Kult Serca Bożego*, p. 531. **15** Bainvel, *Kult Serca Bożego*, pp 530–1; see also iconography of Vandee uprising fighters. **16** Pelikan, *The Christian tradition*, p. 163. **17** Bronisław Mokrzycki (ed.), *Zawierzyliśmy Miłości: Kult Najświetszego Serca Jezusowego* (Kraków, 1972), p. 53. **18** Driskel, *Representing belief*, pp 27–8.

case of the Sacred Heart badge (still allowed for the private use), this iconography would also be harnessed for political purposes.

In July 1872, a year after the Commune, the French Assembly passed a law approving the construction in Paris on the hill of Montmartre of a great national expiatory basilica dedicated to the Sacred Heart.[19] From the outset, the project was taken by the republicans and liberals as a 'monument to obscurantism', as 'the cult of the Sacred Heart had occupied a special place in the authoritarian imagination since the beginning of the century'[20] because of its Bourbonic associations. In this way, the Sacred Heart took its place in one of the most important conflicts of modernity – the conflict between republic and monarchy. However, the Montmartre image of Jesus standing with wide open arms and showing his heart to the world could be associated with another political – and theological – debate, this time within the Church itself, and especially the French Catholic Church: the debate on Jansenism. According to Michael Paul Driskel, there was a particular representation of the Crucifixion associated in France with Jansenists and referred to as 'Christ aux bras étroits', which was supposed to symbolize the Jansenist doctrine on the 'narrow way' to salvation:[21] 'the vertical arms, which can embrace few individuals, were thought to be a signifier for the heretical [Jansenist] doctrine'.[22] Therefore, the wide open arms were supposed to convey the opposite, anti-Jansenist doctrine of 'probabilism' and God's grace associated with the Jesuits. Wide open arms of the Sacred Heart of Jesus had then the character of an ideological – and not only theological – statement; especially given the fact that most of the Sacred Heart representations previous to the 1891 pronouncement, adhering to approved iconography, showed Christ with his heart on hand or pointing to the heart represented on his chest.

THE TWENTIETH-CENTURY CONTEXT: SPAIN

These anti-republican, monarchist (namely Bourbon) associations of the Sacred Heart images adopted in late eighteenth- and nineteenth-century France crossed the Pyrenees. In 1919, in a solemn ceremony at Cerro de los Ángeles near Madrid, Spain was 'offered to the Sacred Heart of Jesus' by King Alphonse XIII (of the Bourbon dynasty), and a huge monument representing Jesus with open arms and his heart on the left side of his robe was inaugurated. The consecration of Spain to the Sacred Heart – similar to the act required by Jesus from the French king according to the visions of Margaret Mary Alacôque – had won local 'divine favour' in the form of the private visions received by a Jesuit novice, Bernardo de Hoyos in 1733 (and known in Spanish Catholic tradition as the Great Promise). In this instance, the Sacred Heart which appeared to Hoyos as an organ separated from Jesus' body (as it had been represented in several early eighteenth-century images) made a promise that it would 'reign in Spain and be more venerated there than in any other place'.[23]

19 Ibid., p. 47.   **20** Ibid.   **21** Ibid., pp 88–97.   **22** Ibid., p. 88.   **23** *El Santuario Nacional de la Gran*

10.4 *Detentebalas*, Spain, twentieth century (private collection).

The monarchy in Spain was abolished in 1931 with the Second Republic, and King Alphonse XIII went to exile. However, in July 1936, the armed rebellion against the Republican government provoked the three-year civil war, which would be won by the anti-republican party. The 1936–9 Spanish Civil War meant a political and military mobilization of huge sectors of Spanish society by both sides of the conflict. Among the old symbols associated with the rebel anti-republican side was the Sacred Heart of Jesus. Already in August 1936, the monument to the Sacred Heart at Cerro de los Ángeles was blown up, having been previously 'shot' by a 'firing squad' of republican militia-men,[24] and this act, deeply symbolic for both parties, was presented by the Catholic press as the symbolic martyrdom of Jesus followed by the martyrdom of several innocent pilgrims (children among them) present at the spot.

On the other hand, during the civil war, the Sacred Heart badges – *detentebalas* – became strongly associated with the *requetés*, the paramilitary formations of the Carlist movement. This movement, which was of nineteenth-century origin, had, by the early twentieth century, a very strong traditionalist and localist dimension, matched by its particularly powerful presence in Navarre (conquered by the rebels already in July 1936). However, nineteenth-century Carlism had also contained a strong absolutist component related to the dynastic claims of the Don Carlos line,[25] while its fundamentalism was expressed in its demands to re-establish the *ancien régime* based on the union of Throne and Altar,[26] with some factions demanding also the re-establishment of the Inquisition.[27] This image of nineteenth-century Carlism was still vivid at the outbreak of the civil war, and was mobilized by both sides. The twentieth-century Carlists proudly pointed to the continuity of their cause since the nineteenth-century wars and used the Catholic symbols politicized already during the nineteenth-century struggles as 'allegorical symbolism […] to oppose the Republic'.[28] On the other hand,

Promesa (Valladolid, 1963), pp 211–45.   **24** Rafael Cruz, 'Old symbols, new meanings: mobilizing the rebellion in the summer of 1936' in Ealham & Richards (eds), *The splintering of Spain* (Cambridge, 2005), pp 168, 171. See pl. 14, this volume.   **25** The dynastic claims of Carlists were based on the fact that the Pragmatic Sanction of 1830 established the succession to the throne against the Salic Law practiced by the Bourbon family, making the heiress to the king Ferdinand VII his elder daughter Isabel instead of his younger brother Charles (Carlos).   **26** *Los Carlistas, 1800–1876* (Vitoria, 1991), p. 62.   **27** Josep Carles Clemente, *Raros, heterodoxos, disidentes y viñetas del Carlismo* (Madrid, 2005), p. 127.   **28** Francisco Javier Caspistegui '"Spain's Vendée": Carlist identity in Navarre as a mobilizing model' in Ealham & Richards (eds), *The splintering of Spain* (Cambridge, 2005), p. 182.

SAGRADO CORAZON DE JESÚS.

10.5 Sacred Heart in form approved for official cult,
devotional print, France, early twentieth century
(private collection).

in 1937 Arthur Koestler, at the time war correspondent of the *News Chronicle*, dubbed Navarre 'Spain's Vendée', trying to explain its role in the civil war and its regional identity very much in terms of the Carlist variant of traditionalism.[29] However, it should be not forgotten that the Carlist *requeté* troops were not only of Navarre origin but also of Catalan and Valencian provenance.

Devotion to the Sacred Heart as well as to the use of the emblem became associated with the Carlists both by themselves and by their opponents, which is not surprising in the context of the royalist-absolutist, anti-republican and Bourbon associations of the cult and the badge as already established in France. The Carlist *requeté* flags exposed in the Museum of Tabar in Navarre, dating from the civil war onwards, include the image of the Sacred Heart emblem in the royal Spanish coat of arms with the Bourbon lily in the centre; the emblem is placed under the royal crown and surrounded by the motto saying *venga a nos el tu reino* (thy kingdom come upon us). However, the nineteenth-century Carlist flags do not bear the Sacred Heart emblem.[30] The Sacred Heart was also mobilized within the rhetoric and imagery presenting the war against the Republic as a Crusade:[31] '… centuries have passed. The wheel of the

29 Ibid., p. 177.   **30** See *Los Carlistas*.   **31** Cruz, 'Old symbols, new meanings', pp 171–5.

Crusades keeps turning. There is now a heroic Crusade against unbridled communism. When the moment of truth came, Spain could not fail ...' wrote Antonio Pérez de Olaguer in his book, *Lagrimas y sonrisas*, published in 1938, calling an eleventh-century crusader from Navarre a *requeté*.[32] The fact that for the public acts of consecration of the *requetés* to the Sacred Heart the feast of St James had been chosen[33] might be interpreted as the same type of 'Crusade' contextualization of the symbol: St James Matamoros [the Moor-slayer] was the patron of the Christian cause against the infidels. This association of a religious symbol of the Sacred Heart with the war presented as the Crusade was confirmed also by Alfonso Carlos, the Carlist pretender to the throne, who wrote in August 1936 to the Carlist council of war in Navarre: 'We are singularly pleased to hear that our *requetés* have the banner of the Sacred Heart and are fighting this war to save religion'.[34]

The Civil War *detentebalas* bearing the Sacred Heart emblem had, therefore, a very complex religious and political meaning, which contributed to their widespread use among the *requetés*. However, the connection between the emblems allegedly used by the Carlist fighters from the war of 1872–6 and the badges used during the Civil War seems to be the result, rather, of family legends and twentieth-century Carlist propaganda than of the material continuity of objects, a consequence of the wartime mobilization of a 'particular kind of self-image, of a certain emotional state and of memories that were channelled to this end'.[35] Therefore, even if the nineteenth-century Carlist fighters had used any protective Sacred Heart badges and passed them on to their grandsons' generation, they had apparently not worn them attached to their uniforms in any visible way, as had been the case both in Vandée and during the civil war; at least any Carlist-related nineteenth-century iconography fails to show the fighters wearing the Sacred Heart badges. Certainly, they could have been worn under their garments, in the same way scapulars were, but if that were the case, then they could never have possessed political meaning. Therefore, the idea of the generational flow of the *détentes* being a symbol of Carlist allegiance, conveyed also by *Three generations*, the famous illustration by Carlos Saenz de Tejada, seems to be the result of a strong desire for the confirmation of continuity by the twentieth-century Carlists.

However, as always with objects endowed with supernatural or sacred characteristics, the interesting point is more their supposed origin than their material identity. The *detentebalas* with the Sacred Heart were actually made a kind of Carlist sign of allegiance, one of the most frequently used – the others were the Cross of Burgundy and the monarchist red-and-yellow flag, used at the beginning of the civil war almost exclusively by the Carlists, which, in a few weeks, became the flag of all the rebels, opposed to the republican tricolour.[36] The allegiance meant a particular political identity that was inseparable from religious identity and practice. Wearing the emblem

---

32 Caspistegui, '"Spain's Vandée"', pp 180–1.   **33** Ibid., p. 181.   **34** Quoted in Caspistegui, '"Spain's Vandée"', p. 183.   **35** Ibid., p. 179.   **36** Cruz, 'Old symbols, new meanings', esp. pp 165–70.

with the Sacred Heart meant also that the *requeté* was a devotee of the cult, and following the advice given in the *Prayer Book for the requeté* published in 1936, repeated several times a day the prayer 'Sacred Heart of Jesus, I trust thee', even in battle.[37] The protective and religious meaning of the badge seems to be as important as its meaning as an allegiance identifier. The presence of *detentebalas* in the visual material originating in the time of the civil war and especially directly afterwards suggests their importance. The wartime photographs show that the embroidered or paper (printed) badges were worn on the left side of the *requeté* clothes; however, as noted above, the Sacred Heart emblem was also included in the Spanish coat of arms embroidered on the flags of *requeté* troops. The same Spanish coat of arms with the Sacred Heart was placed on the title page of *Ordenanza del requeté* (The Rules of the Requeté). In at least one instance, the image of a *détente* with the Sacred Heart emblem and motto was printed on the corner of a photograph representing a marching *requeté* squad and then reproduced as a postcard.[38]

It seems however, that the credit for the most successful image of a Navarre Basque *requeté* proudly wearing the Sacred Heart badge has to be given to an artist: Carlos Sáenz de Tejada. He was one of the illustrators of two gargantuan propaganda enterprises meant to glorify the troops that won the 'glorious crusade', namely two publications in several volumes, entitled *Laureados de España*, published in Madrid in 1939 and 1940, and *La Historia de la Cruzada Española*, published in Madrid in 1940–4 (of the latter he was also one of the editors). The illustrations produced by Sáenz de Tejada for these books were afterwards reproduced in the form of postcards. The success of the pictures had been so significant that they were sometimes later 'falsified' or manipulated in order to make their ideological content more clear and obvious.[39]

Sáenz de Tejada, as a very talented draughtsman, developed a very particular and recognizable style characterized by 'linearism, baroque flair and monumentality'.[40] At the outbreak of the war, Tejada had been collaborating as an illustrator with the Johnson Agency in London, apparently staying in his summer house in Laguardia in the Basque province of Álava. However, from 1937 he began collaborating with the Delegation for Press and Propaganda in Salamanca and with *Vértice*, the magazine of the Spanish Falanga.[41] His contribution to the *Laureados* and *Historia de la Cruzada* includes popular representations of the strong Basque Carlist fighters wearing *détentebalas*. Among them is also the aforementioned picture entitled *Three generations*, showing three Carlist figures of different ages sporting the badges with the Sacred Heart on the red-and-yellow background of the monarchist flag. In *The standardbearers of Tercio de Lácar*, the fighters bearing a cross (as in the photograph of the marching squad) and several flags are also sporting the Sacred Heart badges but not wearing uniforms: they are dressed in chequered flannel shirts and loose trousers,

37 Caspistegui, '"Spain's Vendée"', p. 185. 38 Ibid., p. 183. 39 Prieto Dario, 'Los investigadores reivindican la figura de Carlos Sáenz de Tejada', *El Mundo*, 28 Jan. 2007, no. 6251. 40 Angel Llorente, *Arte e ideología en el franquismo (1936–1951)* (Madrid, 1995), p. 196. 41 Prieto, 'Los investigadores reivindican'.

which allowed the artist to indulge in executing the baroque folds of loose fabric. There are several more illustrations of the Carlist fighters by Sáenz de Tejada, and in them all, strong, sinewy, tall Basques dressed in loose draperies of uniforms, or equally loose workman's trousers and shirts with rolled up sleeves, heads covered with Basque berets, are wearing the Sacred Heart badges on the left side of their wide, masculine chests. The artist's fascination with a figure of a stereotypical sinewy, weather-lashed, strong Navarre Basque and its successful rendering could be related to the time spent by the artist in his summer family house in Laguardia.

Apart from the victorious troops, Sáenz de Tejada represented also martyrs of the crusade, such as Captain Eugenio Perea Urquijo, wearing a Basque beret and sporting the Sacred Heart on the red-and-yellow background. The theme of the fallen martyr of the Crusade had been widely exploited by many different artists, also in relation to the Carlist fighters, and the aforementioned booklet on *The rules for the requeté* contained an illustration of a young fighter wearing a Basque beret, with a motto saying: 'Before God you will never be an anonymous hero'.[42] However, it is almost impossible to see the badge that the fighter is wearing on his left breast as it is covered with his cloak. From what can be seen, one might imagine there the Cross of Burgundy, and not the Sacred Heart. The picture was not the work of Carlos Sáenz de Tejada, although his seems to be the picture used as inspiration by the producer of the cover image in one of the 1939 issues of *Pelayos*, a Carlist magazine for children. It represents a dying Crusade martyr accompanied by an angel holding the red-and-yellow flag, while the battle is being fought in the background. The martyr is wearing a red beret and a familiar loose, chequered shirt; on his left breast, the Sacred Heart *détente* is clearly visible.

CONCLUSIONS

Material objects in the form of badges with the Sacred Heart emblem and the accompanying motto (*Détente …*) were endowed with very complex meanings related to the long history of the devotion and iconography of the Sacred Heart of Jesus. In spite of its late medieval origin, the cult developed and gained importance when the Heart of Jesus could embody not only God's love towards humankind but also some basic dichotomies of modernity: heart/reason, religion/science, autocracy/democracy etc.

With modernity, the idea of human cognitive powers had changed in such a way that reason became reduced to its non-bodily discursive dimension, while the remaining cognitive powers, including the heart (which, within the 'discarded image', had played a very important role in attaining wisdom) were placed within the body and therefore submitted to whimsy or chance. Modern ontology changed the whole concept of the human being, including the notion of the heart. The heart of God, in

---

42 Cf. Caspistegui, '"Spain's Vendée", esp. pp 184–5.

spite of its theological meaning as a symbol of love understood as the Cardinal Virtue, also became – following the concept of human heart – the seat of love understood as emotion. This understanding was fostered both by seventeenth-century piety, as well as later by the Romantic concept of love, which, according to Colin Campbell,[43] had itself seventeenth-century pietistic roots.

This image has made regular appearances in a variety of contexts: with the Vendée and Spanish Carlist badges; with the expiatory basilica on the hill of Montmartre and its Christ with broadly open arms; with the solemn acts of offering whole nations to the Sacred Heart. It has also been involved in the main political struggles of modernity, between the modern 'imagined community' of the nation state and the Rome-oriented, hierarchical community of Catholic Church, as well as between the authoritarian *ancien régimes* and democratic republics. Pope Leo XIII wished the Sacred Heart image to become the 'New Labarum' of modern Catholicism, leading it to victory in its struggles. Therefore, the Sacred Heart image seems to sum up the most important and constitutive conflicts of modernity, and the Spanish *detentebalas* and their meaning are both a material realization and a consequence of this fact.

43 Colin Campbell, *The romantic ethic and the spirit of modern consumerism* (Oxford, 1987).

11 Religious emblems and cultural identity in Northern Ireland

E. FRANCES KING

The island of Ireland, at the furthermost reach of Europe, is divided into two territorial areas, Northern Ireland and the Republic of Ireland; a state of partition that has its roots in history and the relationship of the island with its nearest neighbours, England and Scotland. When the partition of Ireland was formalized in 1921, two different Christian mindsets, Protestant and Catholic, were already well developed in Ireland. In this essay, it is argued that over the centuries, but particularly from the 1850s onwards, these different mindsets were supported and sustained by the domestic use of different kinds of material religious artefacts. Around the same time as mass production was facilitating the widespread use of devotional statues, pictures, bibles and framed scriptural mottoes in Catholic and Protestant homes, the symbols of religion were becoming more prominent, and influential, in the public processions and celebrations of these two different cultural traditions.

The view that there are 'two traditions', Protestant and Catholic, in Northern Ireland has become a useful means of encapsulating the debate, supporting the case that cultural differences, while by no means the whole picture, have played a significant part in the constructing of different ways of being in the world.[1] The notion of two traditions also serves to draw attention to the historical contextualization – sometimes seen as the burden of Northern Ireland – where old grievances are aired to justify contemporary differences. The 'differences' in Ireland, both north and south, have been endlessly analyzed and debated – frequently with reference to the historical context that led to the civil conflict that broke out in 1969, and the difficulties that have since been encountered in finding a solution to this same division. In this essay, it is suggested that greater attention needs to be paid to the different kinds of material religion that existed – and still flourish, although to a lesser extent – in homes and churches throughout Ireland; and that we should examine how these differences developed into a form of visual apartheid that, in certain circumstances and with particular symbols, could be described as 'the-differences-that-make-a-difference'.[2]

To explore the role played by religious images and artefacts in sustaining social integration and confirming identity, the author interviewed a number of individuals and family groups in their homes in Northern Ireland between 2005 and 2006.[3] The respondents spoke about the pictures, biblical texts and other religious objects they

---

1 A.D. Buckley and M. Kenney, *Negotiating identity: rhetoric, metaphor and social drama in Northern Ireland* (Washington, 1995), p. 5. 2 R. Jenkins, *Re-thinking ethnicity: arguments and explorations* (London, 1997), p. 115. 3 See E.F. King, *Material religion and popular culture* (New York, 2010), for more details of this research.

still had, or remembered once having, in their homes and gave permission for photographs to be taken. The oldest interviewee, a great-grandmother, was born in 1913 – before the partition of Ireland – and the youngest, a boy of seventeen, was growing up within the new political settlement established by the Good Friday Agreement in 1998, an agreement that reinforced the right of Northern Ireland to remain in union with Britain, until voted otherwise in a referendum.

Initially, the interviewees were all Catholics but, as the research progressed, interviews with Protestants were included because of the tendency of Northern Irish Catholics, particularly those in the older generations, to link their own use of religious images to a perception of Protestant dislike of the same; in the interviews with Protestants a similar tendency soon became evident. For example, a Catholic woman told me there had been no images in her childhood, but this was because her grandmother had been a Protestant. A Protestant woman from a Presbyterian background recalled how the family Bible was carefully displayed on a table in the hall, but added '… we have Jesus in our hearts … we don't need pictures and things like that' – an implicit distinction between her practices and those of others. As they have grown up with the symbols and images commonly displayed in Northern Ireland, each religious persuasion has developed an awareness of the symbols of 'the Other', tending to use these as a reference point for a stereotype of the other. On the one hand, statues, pictures, medals and rosaries are seen as the symbols of Catholics and, on the other, religious signage, mottoes and abstract symbols with Biblical referents are seen as the emblems of Protestants.

Typical of the images that are employed in the Catholic home are those in plate 18, which now are much denigrated, placed '… near the bottom end of any ranking by status, of the artistic and cultural motifs of the home'.[4] However, the significance of such goods does not arise solely from aesthetic or cultural concerns. They are worthy of interest because they engage with deep levels of human experience, in that people associate with them within what Pierre Bourdieu calls the 'habitus', whereby they learn a lasting, general and adaptable way of looking at the world.[5] The pictures displayed in plate 19 are in a Protestant home, and have been brought from another room to be photographed. As the certificates on the back of each picture indicate, these religious texts with secular imagery are awards that have been received for good biblical learning. There can be grounds, as plate 18 and plate 19 demonstrate, for making some distinctions based on the display of material religion in different homes. Yet, these are private images, and our interest lies in how such typical images migrate to become stereotypically representative of an ethnic group; that is, become the simplified mental images that inform attitudes (plates 18 and 19).

Most studies of the visual and material culture of Catholics and Protestants in

---

4 D. Halle, *Inside culture: art and class in the American home* (Chicago, 1993), p. 171. 5 Bourdieu used the concept habitus to describe a culturally specific way of doing, seeing, thinking and categorizing.

Northern Ireland tend towards an examination of public display and performance.[6] Yet it is in the home that different traditions are nourished, where people encounter the material artefacts and bric-a-brac of everyday religious life. Here people make use of artefacts and objects and learn the visual cues and embodied habits that encode different religious identifications. When a society is divided, where attitudes can reflect identity, things change slowly because, even when there is change in social and cultural life, categorization by stereotype can continue to reflect difference.[7]

The particular circumstances that prevailed in the northern counties of Ireland throughout the 'long nineteenth century' provides us with an opportunity to examine how awareness of the culture and the imagery of the 'Other' developed over a specific period of time, and what part it might have played in sustaining a sense of cultural difference between two communities, who otherwise share both language and land. When, in the late 1960s, Northern Ireland became locked in a bitter ethnic dispute, religious overtones were apparent in the worldwide publicity that was generated by the conflict. The accelerating violence was often, it seemed, accompanied by an abundance of colourful visual imagery, ranging from banners to wall murals. Eventually, such imagery became almost iconically associated with the province. For the people who lived in Northern Ireland, however, this was not a sudden proliferation of imagery – nor did it come as a surprise to them.[8] They were accustomed to public displays and parades: they were familiar with much of the imagery called upon to support the political views of one group or the other and, in many homes, they had learnt family and community 'versions' of the stories behind the images.

So, while visitors to Northern Ireland might gain an impression of '... a split and divided society; the two sides each manifesting its existence, its identity and its political positions in simplistic, if colourful, images',[9] these were images that most of the inhabitants of Northern Ireland took for granted. Speaking about her work in Belfast during the worst part of the 'troubles' – as this period of unrest is often called – a senior social worker recalls how, during her home visits in different parts of the city, she would glance quickly around the pictures and artefacts on display so as to know what 'not to say'. Brought up as a Protestant in Belfast, she had, almost unwittingly, become adept at ascribing identifications to both Protestants and Catholics on the basis of their favoured images, artefacts and religious memorabilia. Even now, a few decades later, and with a settlement that has been given the support of the majority of the inhabitants, the religious sensibilities of many in Northern Ireland are still deeply embedded, with feelings that are liable to be as easily hurt by the use of images, as by the words that accompany them.

---

6 An exception can be made for the work of art historian Belinda Loftus, who incorporates both domestic artefacts and public displays in her work on the emblems of Northern Ireland.   7 J. Brewer with G. Higgins, *Anti-Catholicism in Northern Ireland, 1600–1998* (London, 1998), p. 187.   8 Wall murals, however, once the cultural property of Unionists, only began to flourish in republican areas in the 1980s: see B. Rolston, *Politics and painting: murals and conflict in Northern Ireland* (New Jersey, 1991), p. 74.   9 J. Santino, *Signs of war and peace* (New York, 2001), p. 2.

In churches, temples, meeting houses and chapels, people pursue the theology that informs their use of material religion. It is important to note, however, that here we are examining the popular use of different forms of material religion in the home; those images and artefacts people learn to live with, and the religious instruments that help to facilitate their domestic devotional life. Our interest lies with how they ascribe identifications based on material goods and very basic stereotypical ideas – ideas which are often prompted by the emblems, symbols and signage[10] that have helped to shape and define their lived experience in the family and community.

THE DEVELOPMENT OF TWO MATERIAL RELIGIOUS TRADITIONS IN NORTHERN IRELAND

The northern counties of Ireland, generally referred to as Ulster,[11] were 'planted' with Scottish, mainly Presbyterian, settlers from the sixteenth century onwards and, over time, as the newcomers sowed and reaped the land, built their houses and attended their churches, it became their 'homeland', although always with an element of unease, and a sense of being surrounded by those who did not share their faith or their aspirations. When the calls for home rule from Catholic nationalists in the nineteenth century grew louder, such calls were perceived as threatening to a Protestant, and Unionist, way of life. At the same time as demands for political changes were increasing in Ireland, both the Catholic and Protestant populations were also feeling the influence of the evangelical fervour emerging from the United States. As a northern newspaper commented at the time, the opportunity arose for confrontation between 'ultra-Protestantism, which [runs] riot on the one side, and ultramontane Catholicism, which [goes] fanatically crazy on the other'.[12]

In the aftermath of the famine years (1845–8), the Catholic people of Ireland, under the influence of Archbishop, later Cardinal, Cullen, became more 'tridentine' in their religious practices. They adapted to a Roman-style form of liturgy and in their devotional life made increased use of artefacts such as beads, scapulars, medals, missals, catechisms and holy pictures.[13] Protestants, however, especially those in the northern counties – and the census of 1881 showed that three-quarters of all Irish

---

10 The word 'signage' is used here with reference to the hand-made religious texts and mottoes that are frequently displayed on trees and posts throughout Northern Ireland. **11** There are nine counties in the province of Ulster, one of the four ancient provinces of Ireland. Northern Ireland, the official designation of the part of the island in union with Britain, comprises six of these counties but unionists often describe it as Ulster, while for many northern nationalists the preferred terms are 'the north' or 'the six counties'. **12** Quoted in Brewer with Higgins, *Anti-Catholicism in Northern Ireland, 1600–1998: the mote and the beam*, p. 60. **13** 'Tridentine' reform derives from influence of the Council of Trent (1545–63) which comprised a response to the Reformation but also a programme of internal reform. It placed pastoral focus on the parish church as the focus for sacramental celebration. However, Irish Catholics were so poverty-stricken and bereft of church buildings that it was not until the devotional changes of the nineteenth century that the tridentine reforms took hold; M. Drumm, 'Neither pagan nor Protestant: Irish Catholicism since the Reformation' in Denis Carroll (ed.), *Religion in Ireland: past, present and future* (Dublin, 1999), p. 19.

Protestants lived in Ulster – under the influence of the Great Revival of the 1850s, became increasingly scripturally orientated. Andrea Ebel Brożyna, who has searched the pages of Ulster religious literature, both Catholic and Protestant, between the years 1850–1914, notes that religious presses produced poems, stories, sermons and 'improving articles' in unprecedented quantities and that different authors clashed on many points, ranging from theology to politics.[14]

THE INTRODUCTION OF MASS-PRODUCED RELIGIOUS ARTEFACTS INTO NINETEENTH-CENTURY IRELAND

There has always been a material culture of religion, and there have always been simple techniques for the reproduction of the same image or object. However, the nineteenth century saw improved technologies, cheaper reproductive techniques, faster transportation and a market stirred by evangelical fervour; hence the supply of religious goods proliferated dramatically. The development of a religious consumerist culture was not confined to any one religious tradition – religions of all kinds adapted to improved means of communication in the latter part of the nineteenth century, just as speedily as they have learnt to make use of the Internet for spreading their message in the twenty-first.

Much of the popular Catholic religious memorabilia of the early nineteenth century emanated from the workshops on the Rue St Sulpice in Paris, which produced religious artefacts, statues, pictures and other goods. In their day, these *objets de religion* were modern and considered technologically sophisticated, eventually giving rise to a standard form of Catholic iconography – a style that was to reign from 1840 to 1940 – and was so widely copied and disseminated throughout the Catholic world that it could be described as 'an international style of Catholic art'.[15] Along with an increased production of religious images and objects, there was a surge of worldwide Catholic missionary activity that encouraged greater lay participation in devotional rituals; rituals that were supported by an ever-increasing number of paraliturgical devotions to saints and sacred personages. Not only did Catholics go to mass, but they said rosaries, made novenas, joined religious sodalities and confraternities and, with improved educational facilities, more and more could attend Catholic schools.

The influence of Cardinal Cullen's ultramontanism on Irish Catholicism from the 1850s onwards has been well documented,[16] as has the Protestant Revival of 1859 and the renewal of evangelistic and conservative Protestantism.[17] Less attention has been given to the growth in the supply of material goods – by which we mean tracts and

14 A.E. Brożyna, *Labour, love and prayer* (Belfast, 1999), p. 210. **15** C. McDannell, *Material Christianity: religion and popular culture in America* (New Haven, CT, 1995), pp 167–70. **16** See E. Larkin, 'The parish mission movement' in Bradshaw and Keogh (eds), *Christianity in Ireland* (Dublin, 2002), and P. Nic Ghiolla, 'The power of the Catholic Church in the Republic of Ireland' in P. Clancy et al., *Irish society: sociological perspectives* (Dublin, 1995). **17** D. Hempton and M. Hill, *Evangelical Protestantism in Ulster society, 1740–1890* (London, 1992).

biblical mottoes as well as statues and pictures – and how this impinged on a sense of religious identification. Yet the social and communal 'life' of the artefacts of domestic religion was involved in the construction of both religious and ethnic identity in Ireland over a long period. This ranges from the Famine, and subsequent decline in Catholic population, the proselytizing endeavours of both Protestant and Catholic missionaries to the partition of Ireland in 1921, and the first half-century of existence of the Northern Ireland state.

Between 1859 and 1890, missions in Ireland by different Catholic religious orders numbered over two thousand. Although it was Cardinal Cullen's desire to transfer religious celebrations from the home to the chapel, the instruments, that is the beads, leaflets, pictures and statues of saints, scapulars and a huge variety of other goods, could be bought from the religious stalls and markets that flourished outside churches on the occasions of missions and other religious celebrations, as outlined by Brendan McConvery in this volume. From these temporary stalls, all kinds of religious goods – from 'holy pictures', prayer leaflets and rosary beads, to statues and framed pictures – were available for the laity to buy. After being blessed by the missionaries, these mementoes of the occasion were then taken home, where they remained as tangible and visual reminders of the mission, and the devotional habits and rituals it had encouraged, displacing other, more home-based activities, such as the practice of the Station Mass.[18]

With the use of devotional materials spreading among the Catholic laity, there was also a proliferation in the religious tracts, mottoes and memorabilia of Protestantism. At the start of the nineteenth century, there was an evangelical push to distribute cheap copies of the Bible to the poor and the working class. It became a sacred object in the home, with individual texts and mottoes being embellished, embroidered, embossed or printed and then displayed in the home for the edification of the family. Thus, as the century progressed, so too did the use of popular religious artefacts among both Catholics and Protestants, while Victorian notions of sentimentalism and romanticism encouraged Christians of all denominations to understand faith as an element of feeling rather than rationality, and family life as sacred.[19]

Between 1850 and 1921, the visual differences between Catholic and Protestant were more evident in public demonstrations and processions. Surviving artefacts and printed materials show how the cultural spheres of Protestants and Catholics in Ireland became increasingly separate as the century progressed. Previously, the same few heroes, most notably St Patrick and King William, offered simple messages to do with faith, loyalty and identity. But, as the decades passed, the banners used by

---

18 One of the most notable of the devotional changes was the side-lining of the Station Mass, a strong element in popular Irish Catholicism in the eighteenth century. The Station Mass involved the priest visiting a number of homes before Christmas and Easter to hear confession and to celebrate Mass. It almost died out in consequence of the devotional reforms of the nineteenth century but, in the aftermath of the Second Vatican Council, there has been a revival of this practice in many areas: Drumm, 'Neither pagan nor Protestant: Irish Catholicism since the Reformation', p. 27. **19** McDannell, *Material Christianity*, p. 68.

Protestant brotherhoods and Catholic confraternities in public parades and processions, elaborated in greater detail on Ulster unionism and Irish nationalism,
emphasizing both national ideals and local distinctiveness.[20]

After partition occurred in 1921, Catholics in the Republic of Ireland, who were
very much the majority population, lived comfortably and publicly with the familiar
artefacts and objects of Catholicism. In the newly formed state of Northern Ireland,
however, the Catholic population were in the minority, although a substantial one,
and their environment was dominated by the visual expression of Unionist culture,
which had an explicitly Protestant content.[21]

LINKS BETWEEN DOMESTIC RELIGION AND ETHNICITY

Ethnicity is the term for the differences that exist within a social group that otherwise
shares many common attributes. The social markers of ethnicity, such as distinctive
rituals, garments, symbols and emblems, are the visible signs of difference and can
often be minor, arbitrary – and perhaps even, at times, imaginary. But, there are some
emblems and ways of behaviour that are particularly important, that actually speak
loudly of difference between people who otherwise might have much in common; and
when this difference matters, it really can matter – even, in the most extreme cases,
leading to killing or being killed.

When Claire Mitchell argues that the religious content of ethnic identities has been
seriously underestimated and that religion often constitutes the fabric of identity, she
is, in effect, indicating the salience of everyday ways of being religious.[22] In the case of
Northern Ireland, the fact that different forms of *material* religious culture are
associated with two different religious traditions has come to matter a great deal
because these different material forms are the *markers* of difference – they are, as we
have noted earlier, differences that make a difference. When communities within a
society have divergent religious traditions, together with different ethnic identifications, then religious emblems can become supportive of both culture and religion.
This entanglement comes about through a process of learning that, for many people,
first takes place in the home, but eventually it can happen that the private deployment
of religious objects becomes linked to public expressions of affiliation and identity,
charged with emotional undertones and psychological resonance. In Northern Ireland,
religious images, artefacts and texts provide a bank of symbols that have been called
upon to support both religious and ethnic identity.

Too often we think of language alone as constitutive of identity – it constructs as
well as reports on the categorizations of 'us' and 'them'.[23] But, as Paul Connerton

20 N. Jarman, *Material conflicts* (Oxford, 1999), p. 32.   **21** Rolston, *Politics and painting*, p. 72.   **22** C.
Mitchell, 'The religious content of ethnic identities', *Sociology*, 40:6 (2006), 1135–52.   **23** See Brewer and
Higgins, *Anti-Catholicism in Northern Ireland, 1600–1998*, for a discourse on language in common-sense reasoning
and identity construction with particular reference to Northern Ireland, pp 181–6.

reminds us, it is the unpretentious nature of habitual practices – the fact that they are so often unconsciously carried out – that has led to the privileging of the hermeneutics of language over the hermeneutics of incorporated, that is embodied, practices.[24] We are (it cannot be otherwise) embodied in a material world: our family and social history is inscribed in the objects we cherish, our identities are enshrined in our homes; our sense of community is nurtured in the places we move through whether industriously, prayerfully or playfully. Through deeply embedded bodily practices we learn to participate in the ritualistic habits and ways of behaviour that are constitutive of our own identity, our own sense of belonging – but which also are indicators to others of who we are and, perhaps more significantly in certain circumstances, where our allegiances lie.

It needs to be emphasized that the embedding and embodiment of a religious culture in the home need not be associated with division, divergence or conflict with other cultures or traditions. However, as Danièle Hervieu-Léger points out, identity formation becomes extremely salient when it assumes *both* an ethnic and a religious dimension; when there is an attraction between an assumed genealogy, which is one that is affiliated to a faith belief, and a naturalized genealogy, that is one that is related to blood and soil.[25] In such cases, and both history and contemporary life offer innumerable examples, the emblems of religion can become 'markers' that can be seized upon as signs of affiliation.

The development of 'two traditions' in Ireland, especially in the northern part of the island, goes some way towards demonstrating how religious material culture can impinge on identity, bolstering, on the one hand, a sense of self and belonging and, on the other, marking out a very clear sense of difference. As we have seen, most people in Ireland became acutely aware of difference within their habitat – in one tradition the pope was infallible and, in the other, the Bible was the literal word of God.[26] Some grew familiar with statues, beads and pictures, while others emphasized the sacredness of scriptural text and abhorrence of the image. The social world we are referring to is as much about culture as it is about family, it is as much about ethnicity as it is about religion and it is as much about difference as it is about belonging. Statues, religious pictures, family Bibles and prayer manuals and all the other paraphernalia of popular devotion become entangled with ethnicity because they are involved in both the private and the public lives of the family and the community.

Hervieu-Léger famously describes religion as 'a chain of memory' – a concept that enables us to explore how the domestic emblems of religion become vital material links in the chain of religious memory within the period we are considering. Religious goods can be aids in the handing on of religious traditions, practices and knowledge between generations; they are repositories of local and communal memories and stories and reminders of places, events and people, and they can act as emotional

24 P. Connerton, *How societies remember* (Cambridge, 1989), p. 102. **25** D. Hervieu-Léger, *Religion as a chain of memory* (Cambridge, 2000), p. 157. **26** J. Bardon, *A history of Ulster* (Belfast, 1992), p. 348.

triggers, outlets for such sentiments as empathy, sympathy, antipathy or even anger.[27] But these attributes of religious goods are not easy to disentangle, especially not in the home where they are so closely involved with everyday life.

THE EMBODIMENT OF RELIGION IN THE HOME

Religious memorabilia of the popular kind referred to in this essay might seem to be somewhat insignificant, but the 'humility' of such objects – the term used by Daniel Miller in reference to domestic goods – actually belies their power to shape identity, and act as mediators in domestic and family life.[28] Consider the image in plate 20, which shows the well-handled familiar leaflets used by one Catholic interviewee in her everyday devotional life. The worn leaflets can be described as 'humble', but to their owner they are meaningful and intimate, her way of linking the everyday concerns of domestic life with her religious beliefs. Through frequent embodied practices linked to religious goods, she brings the spiritual and material aspects of her religious life together (plate 20).

People develop a sensuous engagement with the things in their environment and complex emotions exist between people and even the most commonplace and banal things that they live with. Alfred Gell has argued that images and objects can be agents affecting human response and, more recently, Stephen Pattison has explored the importance of the haptic (touching) nature of seeing and the importance of the integration of the senses, urging us to recognize that '... the world of persons is full of objects and objecthood that shape humans'. And, he adds, even the most humble and self-effacing of objects help to shape the human and non-human worlds, 'physically, psychologically, culturally and socially' (plate 21).[29]

In plate 21, the objects are closely and intimately related to the owner. Her inter-action with these goods – the intimacy of their dwelling as it were – is an indication of the embodied nature of their use, just as much as the worn texture of the leaflets and the smooth patina of the beads. It is not just the physical nature of the interaction, the tactile qualities of touch, sensation and smell that are significant – although these are extremely relevant. These objects make connections to relationships – they may be linked to times of family trauma, when prayers and appeals for intercession have been

27 The three reasons cited here derive from the reasons supporting the institution of images in the Church summed up by, among others, St Thomas Aquinas. In the translation provided by David Freedberg, *Power of images: studies in the history and theory of response* (Chicago, 1989), Aquinas writes that images are useful '... for the instruction of the unlettered, who might learn from them as if from books; second, so the mystery of the example of the saints might remain more firmly in our memory by being daily represented to our eyes; and third to excite the emotions which are more effectively aroused by things seen than things heard' (p. 162). Previously I have argued that material objects, such as sacred books and displayed religious texts and mottoes, also serve roughly similar purposes (see E.F. King, *Material religion and popular culture*). **28** Daniel Miller, *Material culture and mass consumption* (Oxford, 1987), introduces the term 'the humility of things' to characterise the unobtrusiveness of material goods and objects in everyday life (see pp 85–108). **29** A. Gell, *Art and agency* (Oxford, 1998); S. Pattison, *Seeing things* (London, 2007), p. 176.

a resource for help and a source of comfort; they may symbolize the shared practice and ritual of a community and a common understanding of values and beliefs that is accompanied, perhaps inevitably, by a shared sense of belonging. Since religion is emotional as well as cognitive, people use sight, touch, smell and voice to stimulate pious feelings, and, as McDannell points out, the body is the primary mediator of religious experience.[30]

Immediate evidence of how religion can be materialized in a domestic setting is found in the hallway of a rural home with the display of an embroidered Biblical text hanging. And, half-hidden in a corner, are two inscribed brass plaques, which, the householder explains, once belonged to his grandmother. On one plaque the etched image of a tree is accompanied by the text 'Thou will keep him in perfect peace whose mind is stayed on Thee' and, on the other, the image of a butterfly hovers over a flower with the inscription 'As for God His way is perfect'. Not only are these objects signifiers of a particular religious identity, but they are also in a network of family relationships acting as 'links of continuity, existing in the present yet mementoes of the past and signposts to future goals'.[31]

In recalling her family home at the turn of the century, a ninety-two-year-old woman says 'God bless my mother, she had pictures the size of the wall ... she had statues of the Sacred Heart, Our Blessed Lady, holy Saint Patrick ... and there was St Philomena ...', adding, with reference to the liturgical changes of the Second Vatican Council that happened fifty years later, 'and then they said she wasn't a saint'. Older Catholics, men and women, remember devotions to the Sacred Heart and Our Lady, St Theresa and other saints; they describe practices from their childhood, such as lighting votive lights and setting up May altars, although often adding that 'times have changed'. These familiar devotions, if still practised, are now more likely to be said in private, with the statues and pictures, once so prominent, now confined to less public areas of the house.

The Ulster Folk Museum was established in 1958 and here, in 'Ballycultra Village', original dwellings from both rural and urban areas of Northern Ireland have been brought together and reconstructed, insofar as possible in their original condition.[32] Many of the smaller houses date from the turn of the nineteenth century and were once occupied by large families; they contain the cooking implements, furniture, clothes, worn bedding and sparse decorative items of the day. Plates and other kinds of crockery are displayed on the dresser with, here and there, faded photographs of family members. Even in these reconstructed homes it is possible to 'read' the religious identity of the inhabitants from the material artefacts one sees. In Protestant homes, printed religious texts are often placed over the bed, and inexpensive faded pictures of the Virgin Mary and Holy family hang in the bedrooms and living areas of Catholic

---

30 McDannell, *Material Christianity*, p. 14.   **31** M. Csikszentmihalyi, 'Why we need things' in S. Lumbar and D.W. Kingery (eds), *History from things* (Washington, 1981), p. 23.   **32** Later the name was changed to the Ulster Folk and Transport Museum and eventually subsumed into Museums and Galleries of Northern Ireland.

homes. To the contemporary visitor, the houses are exceedingly small and emphasize the high level of intimacy that must have existed between those who inhabited the house, and even with the objects that they chose, or could afford, to display.

In Ireland since the late fifteenth century, different guilds and other brotherhoods have displayed their public existence and affiliations through parades and processions and such activities were not considered uncommon.[33] However, the emergence of unified Protestantism in the latter half of the nineteenth century was accompanied by the image of the Protestant Prince William of Orange on a white charger, raising a sword over his head as he leads his troops over the River Boyne to defeat the Catholic King James in 1690. This depiction emerged as the iconic symbol of Protestant triumph and, by the turn of the century, was accompanied by the symbols of the Orange Order with banners, flags and arches.[34] Initially, the range of images used (other than that of William of Orange) did little except affirm a loyalty to faith and crown, but at the turn of the century, nineteenth-century biblical and religious history began to merge with the political ideology of Unionism. Eventually, this emphasis on loyalty to the crown became so ubiquitous in the visual displays of the Orange Order that it cannot be divorced from how Catholics in Northern Ireland learnt to perceive Protestants, and Protestants continued to perceive themselves.

In the decades that followed partition, a complex interplay of political, social and economic issues continued to sustain division and the public visual reminders of loyalty and religion could be mirrored in the home (plate 22).

In some homes in Belfast, Bible and crown remain closely entangled. The owner of the memorabilia pictured in plate 22, a woman in her late seventies, recalls that an open Bible had pride of place and was the first object that visitors would see as they came through the front door of her childhood home. The imagery she treasures, and now displays in her home, is a collection of figurines and plates, memorabilia of the British royal family that have been collected over the years, and she says of royalty that 'we were brought up to respect them, that kind of thing'.

In her research into the public and domestic artefacts of Northern Ireland, Belinda Loftus explores how the different ways of seeing not just involve two different sets of emblems but result in two different styles of vision.[35] When we read into the background of how these two ways of seeing emerged, we can see how they have been socially constructed over a long period; because they are so obvious and so easily accessed by both traditions within the community, it may well be that they also obscure what there is that the communities have in common.

In this essay, the most humble and frequently denigrated artefacts of religion have been considered as links in a religious chain of memory. To consider religion as a chain of memory means taking account of the body of practices, and the material goods –

33 A.D. Buckley and K. Anderson, *Brotherhoods in Ireland* (Cultra, 1988).   **34** Rolston, *Material Christianity*, p. 17.   **35** B. Loftus, *Mirrors: orange and green* (Dundrum, 1994).

as well as the institutions and the beliefs – that comprise particular traditions. It has been noted how familiarity with religious artefacts can be part of everyday cultural competence – an everyday way of recognizing difference. Such emblems have been considered in the context of the northern counties of Ireland, where the attraction between what is ethnic – to do with where one belongs – and what is religious – to do with what faith one affirms – has been highlighted, and this has also drawn attention to the complexities of the relationships between religious goods and culture; such relationships are built up over time, influenced and altered by different groups and individuals, at times deemed significant and at other times irrelevant.

In the early years of the Northern Ireland state, the antagonisms of two different religious persuasions were evident in the artefacts and images that both sides associated with religious affiliation – each set of emblems acting as a negative reference point for the other. Today, in dramatically altered circumstances, similar images and artefacts are just as capable of reigniting passions, because, as they are also frequently emblems of identity, they help to establish a sense of 'we' and 'our' in an increasingly complex world. Because these objects might appear to be very ordinary, and are often ignored and sometimes despised, does not mean that they are of little account – they symbolize relationships, family, community and religious beliefs. Remarkably, even the smallest and apparently most insignificant artefact – a Catholic religious medal, a Protestant tract – is an embodied expression of affiliation and, as such, can contain layers and layers of unstated meanings and assumptions.

Bibliography

Aarflot, Andreas, *Hans Nielsen Hauge. Liv og budskap* (Oslo, 1971).

Aarflot, Andreas, *Norsk kirkehistorie* II (Oslo, 1967).

Aarflot, Andreas, *Tro og lydighet. Hans Nielsen Hauges kristendomsforståelse* (Oslo, 1969).

Ajmar, Martha and Catherine Sheffield, 'The Miraculous Medal: an Immaculate Conception or not', *The Medal*, 24 (1994), 37–51.

Aladel, M., *La Médaille Miraculeuse: origine, histoire, diffusion, résultats*. Édition revue et augmenté (Paris, 1881).

Alet, Victor, *La France et le Sacré-Coeur* (Paris, 1889).

Allison, J., *Edward Elgar: sacred music* (Bridgend, 1994).

Amundsen, Arne Bugge (ed.), *Presten – lærer, kollega, lovbryter. Studier i Østfolds prestehistorie på 1700– og 1800–tallet* (Sarpsborg, 1992).

Amundsen, Arne Bugge and Henning Laugerud (eds), *Norsk fritenkerhistorie, 1500–1850* (Oslo, 2001).

Amundsen, Arne Bugge (ed.), *Norges religionshistorie* (Oslo, 2005).

Amundsen, Arne Bugge, '"En lidet forsøgt og mindre skriftlærd dreng": Hans Nielsen på Hauge' in Svein Aage Christoffersen and Trygve Wyller (eds), *Arv og utfordring. Menneske og samfunn i den kristne moraltradisjon* (Oslo, 1995), pp 68–9.

Amundsen, Arne Bugge, '"Mig Engelen tiltalte saa …": Folkelige visjoner som kulturell kommunikasjon' in Arne Bugge Amundsen and Anne Eriksen (eds), *Sæt ikke vantro i min overtros stæd. Studier i folketro og folkelig religiøsitet. Festskirft til Ørnulf Hodne på 60–årsdagen 28 september 1995* (Oslo, 1995), pp 21–59.

Amundsen, Arne Bugge, '"The Haugean heritage": a symbol of national history' in Jens Braarvig and Thomas Krogh (eds), *In search of symbols: an explorative study* (Oslo, 1997), pp 214–33.

Amundsen, Arne Bugge, '"The living must follow the dead": in search of "The religious person" in the nineteenth century', *Arv. Nordic Yearbook of Folklore*, 53 (Oslo, 1997), 107–30.

Amundsen, Arne Bugge, 'Apokalyptikk på norsk – fra Draumkvedet til Hauge', *Humanist. Tidsskrift for livssynsdebatt*, 2–3/99 (Oslo, 1999).

Amundsen, Arne Bugge, 'Books, letters and communication: Hans Nielsen Hauge and the Haugean Movement in Norway, 1796–1840' in Arne Bugge Amundsen (ed.), *Revival and communication: studies in the history of Scandinavian revivals, 1700–2000* (Lund, 2007), pp 45–64.

Amundsen, Arne Bugge, 'Hans Nielsen Hauge i dobbelt grep', *Humanist. Tidsskrift for livssyns-debatt* 1/01 (Oslo, 2001).

Amundsen, Arne Bugge, 'Haugeanism between liberalism and traditionalism in Norway, 1796–1845' in Jonathan Strom (ed.), *Pietism and community in Europe and North America, 1650–1850* (Leiden and Boston, 2010).

Andersen, Øivind, *I retorikkens hage* (Oslo, 1995).

Anon., 'Opstandelse!', *Skandinavisk Kirketidende for katholske Christne*, 14 (København, 1855).

Ár bPaidreacha Dúchais: Cnuasach de Phaidreacha agus de Beannachtaí Ár Sinsear ('Our native prayers: a collection of our ancestors prayers and blessings') (Dublin, 1975).

Archer, Antony, *The two Catholic churches: a study in oppression* (London, 1986).

Arundel hymns and other spiritual praises. Chosen and edited by Henry Duke of Norfolk and Charles T. Gatty, FSA (London, 1902).

Baggley, John, *Doors of perception: icons and their spiritual significance* (Crestwood, NY, 1988).

Bainvel, JeanVincent, *Kult Serca Bożego: Teoria i rozwój* (Kraków, 1934) (transl. from French).

Bang, Anton Christian, *Hans Nielsen Hauge og hans Samtid* (Kristiania, 1874).

Bardon, Jonathan, *A history of Ulster* (Belfast, 1992).

Barry, David Thomas, *Psalms and hymns for the church, school and home* (London, 1865).

Bauer, Hans-Joachim, 'Franz Liszts Reformen zur Kirchenmusik', *Kirchenmusikalisches Jahrbuch*, 73 (1989), 63–70.

Baumgarth, C., *Geschichte des Futurismus* (Reinbek, 1966).

Belting, Hans, *Likeness and presence: a history of the image before the age of art* (Chicago & London, 1994).

Blackbourn, David, *Marpingen: apparitions of the Virgin Mary in nineteenth-century Germany* (New York, 1994).

Blancpied, J.-M. (ed.), *Le souvenir de la Mission ou le Salut Assuré aux âmes de bonnes volontés d'après St Alphonse à l'usage des personnes du monde qui veulent assuré leur salut* (Lyon & St-Etienne, 1913).

Bloch, Mark, *Le rois thaumaturges: etude sur le caractère surnaturel attribué à la puissance royale particulièrement en France et en Angleterre* (Paris, 1983).

Blumenberg, Hans, *Die Legitimität der Neuzeit* (Frankfurt, 1966).

Bøe, Alf, *From Gothic revival to functional form* (Oslo, 1957).

Boesch Gajano, S., *La santità* (Roma-Bari, 1999).

Bourdieu, Pierre, 'Genèse et structure du champ religieux', *Revue française de sociologie*, 12:3 (1971), 295–334.

Bourdieu, Pierre, *The logic of practice* (Cambridge, 1990).

Bowen, Desmond, *Souperism: myth or reality? A study in Souperism* (Cork, 1970).

Bowen, Desmond, *The Protestant crusade in Ireland* (Dublin, 1978).

Boylesve SJ, M. De, *Appel a la jeunesse catholique contre l'esprit du siècle* (Paris, 1851).

Braarvig, Jens and Thomas Krogh (eds), *In search of symbols: an explorative study* (Oslo, 1997).

Brekkan, Anja, *Ett religiøst syn. Én motstander. Opplysningsteologiens kritikk til Hans Nielsen Hauge* (Oslo, 1999).

Brewer, John with Gareth Higgins, *Anti-Catholicism in Northern Ireland, 1600–1998: the mote and the beam* (London, 1998).

Brown, Peter, *The cult of the saints* (Chicago, 1981).

Brożyna, Andrea Ebel, *Labour love and prayer: female piety in Ulster religious literature, 1850–1914* (Belfast, 1999).

Buckley, A.D. and Kenneth Anderson, *Brotherhoods in Ireland* (Cultra, 1988).

Buckley, A.D. and Mary Kenney, *Negotiating identity: rhetoric, metaphor and social drama in Northern Ireland* (Washington, DC, 1988).

Busch, Norbert, *Katholische Frömmigkeit und Moderne. Die Sozial-und Mentalitätsgeschichte des herz-Jesu-Kultes in Deutschland zwischen Kulturkampf und Erstem Weltkrieg* (Gütersloh, 1997).

Byron, Georges, 'Franz Liszt et la dévotion à la croix: Via Crucis', *La Maison-Dieu*, 171 (1987), 99–109.

Caffiero, Marina, 'Dall'esplosione mistica tardo-barocco all'apostolato sociale' in L. Scaraffia and G. Zarri (eds), *Donne e fede. Santità e vita religiosa in Italia* (Roma-Bari, 1994), pp 327–73.

Caffiero, Marina, 'Un santo per le donne: Benedetto Labre e la femminilizzazione del Cattolicesimo tra Settecento e Ottocento', *Memoria. Rivista di storia delle donne*, 30:3 (1990), 89–106.

Caffiero, Marina, *La politica della santità. Nascita di un culto nell'età moderna* (Roma-Bari, 1996).

Caffiero, Marina, *Religione e modernità in Italia (secoli XVII–XIX)* (Pisa, 2000).

Calamari, Barbara and Sandra DiPasqua, *Visions of Mary* (New York, 2004).

Campbell, Colin, *The romantic ethic and the spirit of modern consumerism* (Oxford, 1987).

Campbell, T.A., *The religion of the heart: a study of European religious life in the seventeenth and eighteenth centuries* (Columbia, SC, 1991).

Carroll, M.P, *Irish pilgrimage: Holy Wells and popular Catholic devotion* (Baltimore & London, 1999).

Carruthers, M.J., *The craft of thought: meditation, rhetoric and the making of images, 400–1200* (Cambridge, 1998).

Caspistegui, Francisco Javier, '"Spain's Vendée": Carlist identity in Navarre as a mobilizing model' in Chris Ealham and Michael D. Richards (eds), *The splintering of Spain* (Cambridge, 2005), pp 177–95.

Chadwick, O., *The secularization of the European mind in the nineteenth century* (Cambridge, 1975).

Charru, Philippe and Véronique Fabre, *Voici l'homme: au croisement du 'Miserere' de Georges Rouault et de la 'Via Crucis' de Franz Liszt* (Paris, 2006).

Chateaubriand, Francois-René, *Génie du christianisme* (Paris, 1802).

Chazelle, C.M., 'Pictures, books and the illiterate: Pope Gregory I's letters to Serenus of Marseille', *Word and Image*, 6:2 (1990), 138–53.

Christoffersen, Svein Aage (ed.), *Hans Nielsen Hauge og det moderne Norge* (KULT's skriftserie, 48) (Oslo, 1996).

Cicero, Marcus Tullius, *On the ideal orator (De oratore)*, trans. with intr., notes, appendixes, glossary, and indexes by J.M. May and Jakob Wisse (New York, 2001).

Cingria, A., 'La décadence de l'art sacré', *Cahiers Vaudoirs* (Lausanne, 1917).

Clark, David, *Between pulpit and pew: folk religion in a North Yorkshire fishing village* (Cambridge, 1982).

Clark, W. Augustus, *Sacred hymns, for the use of the elect family of Jesus, in this militant state* (London, 1782).

Clemente, Josep Carles, *Raros, heterodoxos, disidentes y viñetas del Carlismo* (Madrid, 2005).

Codex Iuris Canonici 1917, *c*.1164.

Connerton, Paul, *How societies remember* (Cambridge, 1989).

Connolly, Gerard, 'Irish and Catholic: myth or reality? Another sort of Irish and the renewal of the clerical profession among Catholics in England, 1791–1918' in Roger Swift and Sheridan Gilley (eds), *The Irish in the Victorian city* (London, 1985).

Connolly, Sean J., *Priests and people in pre-Famine Ireland, 1780–1845* (Dublin, 1982).

Coro, Francisco Rodríguez de, et al., *Los Carlistas, 1800–1876* (Vitoria, 1991).

Corish, Patrick J., *Maynooth College, 1795–1995* (Dublin, 1995).

Cox, Jeffrey, 'Master narratives of long-term religious change' in Hugh McLeod (ed.), *The decline of Christendom in Western Europe* (Cambridge, 2003), pp 201–17.

Cressy, David, *Bonfires and bells: national memory and the Protestant calendar in Elizabethan and Stuart England* (London, 1989).

Cribb, Joe, 'Medaglie cristiane e croci usate in Cina', *Medaglia*, 15 (1978), 21–39.

Crown of Jesus music (London, 1864).

Cruz, Rafael, 'Old symbols, new meanings: mobilizing the rebellion in the summer of 1936', in Chris Ealham and Michael D. Richards (eds), *The splintering of Spain* (Cambridge, 2005), pp 159–76.

Csikszentmihalyi, Mihaly and Eugene Rochberg-Halton, *The meaning of things: domestic symbols and the self* (Cambridge, 1981).

Csikszentmihalyi, Mihaly, 'Why we need things' in Steven Lubar and David Kingery (eds), *History from things: essays on material culture* (Washington, DC, 1993), pp 20–9.

Dawson, Christopher, 'The secularization of Western culture' (1943) in Gerald J. Russello (ed.), *Christianity and European culture: selections from the work of Christopher Dawson* (Washington, DC, 1998), pp 170–81.

De Certeau, M., *L'écriture de l'histoire* (Paris, 1975).

De Palma, F., 'Il modello laicale di Anna Maria Taigi' in E. Fattorini (ed.), *Santi, culti, simboli nell'età della secolarizzazione (1815–1915)* (Torino, 1997), pp 529–46.

de Zedelgem, P. Amédée, OFM, 'Aperçu historique sur la devotion au chemin de la croix', *Collectanea Franciscana*, 19 (1949), 45–142.

de Zedelgem, P. Amédée, OFM, *Saggio storico sulla devozione alla Via Crucis: evocazione e rappresentazione degli episodi e dei luoghi della Passione di Cristo: saggi introduttivi*, ed. A. Barbero and P. Magro (Ponzano, 2004).

Decreta Synodi Plenariae Episcoporum Hiberniae apud Thurles habita Anno MDCCCL (Dublin, 1851).

Delehaye, H., *Sanctus: essai sur le culte des saints dans l'antiquité* (Bruxelles, 1927) (Subsidia hagiographica, 17).

Delooz, P., *Sociologie et canonisations* (Liège, 1969).

Demus, O., *Byzantine church decoration* (London, 1976).

Devlin, Judith, *The superstitious mind: French peasants and the supernatural in the nineteenth century* (New Haven, CT, 1987).

Dirvin, Joseph, *Saint Catherine Laboure of the Miraculous Medal* (1958), Online source: http://www.ewtn.com/library/MARY/CATLABOU.HTM, accessed 18 August 2008.

'Domestic and Apostolic Labours, vol. 1' (1851–68) (Dublin).

Domokos, Zsusanna, 'The performance practice of the Cappella Sistina as reflected in Liszt's church music', *Studia Musicologica Academiae Scientarum Hungaricae*, 41 (2000), 389–406.

Doolan S., *La redecouverte de l'icone: la vie et l'oevre de Leonide Ouspensky* (Paris, 2001).

Driskel, M.P., *Representing belief: religion, art and society in nineteenth-century France* (Philadelphia, PA, 1992).

Drumm, Michael, 'Neither pagan nor Protestant? Irish Catholicism since the Reformation' in Denis Carroll (ed.), *Religion in Ireland: past, present and future* (Dublin, 1999).

Duffy, Eamon, *The stripping of the altars: traditional religion in England, c.1400–c.1580* (New Haven, CT, & London, 1982).

Duffy, Eamon, *Faith of our fathers: reflection on Catholic tradition* (London, 2004).

Duggan, Laurence G., 'Was art really the "book of the illiterate"?', *Word and Image*, 5:3 (1989), 227–51.

Durkheim, E., *Les formes élementaires de la vie religieuse* (Paris, 1912).

Editorial 'Gammel og ny hedendom', *Skandinavisk Kirketidende for katholske Christne*, 1 (København, 1861).

Eisenstadt, S.N., *Fondamentalismo e modernità. Eterodossie, utopismo, giacobinismo nella costruzione dei movimenti fondamentalisti* (Roma-Bari, 1994).

Eliassen, S.G., 'Gerhard Seeberg – en prest og hans menighet' in Arne Bugge Amundsen (ed.), *Presetne-lærer, Kollega, Lovbryter. Studier i Østfolds prestehistorie på 1700–og 1800-tallet* (Sarpsborg, 1992).

Eriksen, Anne and Anne Stensvold, *Maria-kult og helgendyrkelse i moderne katolisisme* (Oslo, 2002).

Feldbæk, Ole, *Danmark-Norge, 1380–1814 4. Nærhed og adskillelse 1720–1814* (Oslo, 1998).

Fernow, Fernow, *Leben des Künstlers Asmus Jakob Carstens* (2nd ed., Hanover, 1867).

Fet, Jostein, *Lesande bønder. Litterær kultur i norske allmugesamfunn før 1840* (Oslo, 1995).

Fielding, Steven, *Class and ethnicity: Irish Catholics in England, 1880–1939* (Buckingham, 1993).

Florenskii, P., 'On the icon', *Eastern Churches Review*, 8:11 (1976), 11–37.

Fortescue, Fortescue, *The ceremonies of the Roman Rite described* (London, 1917).

Franciosi SJ, X. De, *Le dévotion au sacré-coeur de Jésus et au saint-coeur de Marie: notions doctrinales et pratiques* (Paris, 1878).

Freedberg, David, *The power of images: studies in the history and theory of response* (Chicago, 1991).

Friligkos, Ioannis, *O agiografos Kwnstantinos Fanelis kai to ergo tou* (Athina, 2005).

Frye, Northrop, *The great code: the Bible and literature* (New York, 1982).

Furseth, Inger, *People, faith and transition: a cmparative study of social and religious movements in Norway, 1780s–1905* (Oslo, 1999).

Gell, Alfred, *Art and agency: an anthropological theory* (Oxford, 1998).

Georgiadou–Kountoura, E., *Thriskeutika Themata sti neoelliniki zwgrafiki* (Thessaloniki, 1984).

Germann, G., *Neugotik. Geschichte ihrer Architekturtheorie* (Stuttgart, 1974).

Goetz, W., 'Historismus. Ein Versuch zur Definition des Begriffes', *Zeitschrift des Deutschen Vereins für Kunstwissenschaft*, 24 (1970), 196–212.

Gother, John, *Instructions and devotions for hearing Mass* (1699).

Gotor, M., *I beati dei papi. Santità, Inquisizione e obbedienza in età moderna* (Firenze, 2002).

Gundersen, T.R., '"Disse enfoldige ord": Hans Nielsen Hauges forfatterskap' in Egil Børre Johnsen and Trond Berg Eriksen (eds), *Norsk litteraturhistorie. Sakprosa fra 1750 til 1995* I (Oslo, 1998).

Gundersen, T.R., *Om å ta Ordet. Retorikk og utsigelse i den unge Hans Nielsen Hauges forfatterskap* (Sakprosa 3) (Oslo, 2001).

Hagen, Ursula, *Die Wallfahrtsmedaillen des Rheinlandes in Geschichte und Volksleben* (Köln, 1973).

Hall, James, *Hall's dictionary of signs and symbols in art* (London, 1992).

Halle, David, *Inside culture: art and class in the American home* (Chicago, 1993).

Hamburger, Klara, 'Program and Hungarian idiom in the sacred music of Liszt' in Michael Saffle and James Deaville (eds), *New light on Liszt and his music: essays in honour of Alan Walker's 65th Birthday*, Analecta Lisztiana II (Stuyvesant, 1997), pp 239–51.

Harford, George et al. (eds), *The prayer book dictionary* (London, 1925).

Harris, Ruth, *Lourdes: body and spirit in the secular age* (New York, 1999).

Hartigan, Maurice, 'The religious life of the Catholic laity of Dublin, 1920–40' in James Kelly and Dáire Keogh (eds), *History of the Catholic diocese of Dublin* (Dublin, 2000), pp 331–44.

Hauge, H.N., *Brev*. Ingolf Kvamen (ed.), I–IV (Oslo, 1971–6).

Hauge, H.N., *Skrifter*. Hans Ording (ed.), I–VIII (Oslo, 1947–54).

Hazard, P., *La crise de la conscience européene (1680–1715)* (Paris, 1935).

Hedley, J.C., *The Holy Eucharist* (London, 1907).

Hefling, Charles 'The state services' in Hefling Charles and Cynthia Shattuck (eds), *The Oxford Guide to the Book of Common Prayer: a worldwide survey* (Oxford, 2006).

Heggtveit, H.G., *Den norske Kirke i det nittende Aarhundrede* I-II (Kristiania, 1905–20).

Heimann, Mary, 'Catholic revivalism in worship and devotion' in Sheridan Gilley and Brian Stanley (eds), *The Cambridge History of Christianity: world Christianities, c.1815–c.1914*, 8 (Cambridge, 2006), pp 70–83.

Heimann, Mary, *Catholic devotion in Victorian England* (Oxford, 1975).

Heinemann, E.G., *Franz Liszts Auseinandersetuzung mit der geistlichen Musik. Zum Konflikt von Kunst und Engagement* (Munich, 1978).

Heinemann, Michael, 'Bach: Liszt' in Michael Heinemann, Hans-Joachim Hinrichsen and Joachim Lüdtke (eds), *Bach und die Nachwelt*, 2: 1850–1900 (Laaber, 1999), pp 127–62.

Hempton, David and Myrtle Hill, *Evangelical Protestantism in Ulster society, 1740–1890* (London, 1992).

Hervicu-Léger, Danièle, *Religion as a chain of memory* (Cambridge, 1993).

Herzig, Yvonne, *Süddeutsche sakrale Skulptur im Historismus. Die Erberle'sche Kunstwerkstätte Gebr. Mezger* (Petersberg, 2001).

Hill, Cecil, 'Liszt's Via Crucis', *Music Review*, 25 (1964), 202–8.

Hodgkins, Geoffrey (ed.), *The best of me: a Gerontius centenary companion* (Richmansworth, 1999).

Hollein, C. and M., *Religion Macht Kunst. Die Nazarener. Katalog zur Ausstellung in der Schirn Kunsthalle Frankfurt* (Köln, 2005).

Hvattum , M., *Gottfried Semper and the problem of historicism* (Cambridge, 2004).

Hymns by Frederick William Faber DD, new ed. (London, 1861).

James, Liz (1996), *Light and colour in Byzantine art* (Oxford, 1996).

Jarman, Neil, *Material conflicts: parades and visual displays in Northern Ireland* (Oxford, 1999).

Jenkins, Richard, *Re-thinking ethnicity: arguments and explorations* (London, 1997).

John, Marquess of Bute, *The Roman breviary* (2 vols, Edinburgh, 1889).

Julian, John, *A dictionary of hymnology, setting forth the origin and history of Christian hymns of all ages and nations* (London, 1892, 1908).

Karakatsani, A., 'I kosmiki zwgrafiki toy Kontoglou', *Oi Ellinies zwgrafoi, tom. II, 20th century* (Athina, 1976), pp 219–20.

Kaufmann, Suzanne, 'Selling Lourdes: pilgrimage, tourism and the mass-marketing of the sacred in nineteenth-century France' in Shirley Baranowski and Ellen Furlough (eds), *Being elsewhere: tourism, consumer culture and identity in modern Europe and North America* (Ann Arbor, MI, 2001), pp 63–88.

Kaufmann, Suzanne, *Consuming visions: mass culture and the Lourdes shrine* (Ithaca, 2005).

Kavanagh, Patrick, *Tarry Flynn* (London, 1948).

Keach, Benjamin, *Antichrist stormed; or, Mystery Babylon, the great whore and great city, proved to be the present Church of Rome. Wherein are all objections answered* (London, 1689).

Keach, Benjamin, *Spiritual melody, containing near three hundred sacred hymns* (London, 1691).

Keach, Benjamin, *War with the devil: or the young man's conflict with the powers of darkness: in a dialogue. discovering the corruption and vanity of youth, the horrible nature of sin and the deplorable condition of fallen-man. Also a definition, power and rule of conscience and the nature of true conversion* (3rd impression, London, 1675).

Keenan, Desmond, *The Catholic Church in nineteenth-century Ireland: a sociological study* (Dublin, 1983).

Kennedy, G.A., *Classical rhetoric and its Christian and secular tradition from ancient to modern times* (Chapel Hill, NC, 1980).

Keogh, Dáire, '"The pattern of the flock": John Thomas Troy, 1786–1823' in James Kelly and Dáire Keogh (eds), *History of the Catholic diocese of Dublin* (Dublin, 2000).

Kierkegaard, Søren, *Samlede værker*, 19 (København, 1991).

King, E. Frances, *Material religion and popular culture* (New York, 2010).

Kjeldsen, Jens, 'Visuel retorik' (PhD, U. Bergen, 2002).

Kleinberg, A., *Prophets in their own country: living saints and the making of sainthood in the later Middle Ages* (Chicago, 1992).

Klenze, Leo von, *Anweisung zur Architectur des christlichen Cultus* (München, 1822/4).

Knapp, Ulrich, 'Restauratio Ecclesiae. Die Erneuerung einer Kirchenlandschaft' in Ulrich Knapp (ed.), *Restauratio Ecclesiae. Das Bistum Hildesheim im 19. Jahrhundert* (Hildesheim, 2000).

Koht, Halvdan, *Norsk bondereising. Fyrebuing til bondepolitikken* (Oslo, 1926).

Kontoglou, Fotis, 'I byzantini zwgrafiki kai I alithini tis aksia' in F. Kontoglou, *Ponemeni Rwmmiosuni* (Athina, 1974).

Kontoglou, Fotis, *Ekfrasis tis Orthodoxou eikonografias* (Athina, 1979).

Kontoglou, Fotis, *Pros agiografon Euaggelon Mayrikakin* (Athina, 1997).

Kontoglou, Fotis, *Thalasses, kaikia, karavokurides* (Athina, 1978).

Kordis, Georgios, *Ierotypws: I eikonologia tou ieroy Fwtiou kai I texni tis meteikonomaxikis periodou* (Athina, 2002).

Kordis, Georgios, *Paradosi kai dimiourgia sto eikastiko ergo toy Foti Kontoglou* (Athina, 2007).

Krins, Hubert, *Die Kunst der Beuroner Schule* (Beuroner Kunstverlag, 1998).

Kselman, Thomas A., *Miracles and prophecies in nineteenth-century France* (New Brunswick, NJ, 1983).

Kubik, Jan, *The power of symbols and the symbols of power: the rise of solidarity and the fall of state socialism in Poland* (Philadelphia, PA, 1994).

Lagrée, Michel, 'The impact of technology on Catholicism in France (1850–1950)' in Hugh McLeod (ed.), *The decline of Christendom in Western Europe* (Cambridge, 2003).

Lamentabili sane exitu, decree of Pope Pius X, 7 July 1907: Acta sacretae sedis, 40 (1907), 470–8.

Langlois, Claude, *Le catholicisme au féminin: les congrégations françaises à supérieure générale au XIXᵉ siècle* (Paris, 1984).

Larkin, Emmet and Hermann Freudenberger (eds), *A Redemptorist missionary in Ireland, 1851–1854. Memoir by Joseph Prost CSsR* (Cork, 1998).

Larkin, Emmet 'The Devotional Revolution, 1850–1875' in Emmet Larkin, *The historical dimension of Irish Catholicism* (Dublin, 1984), pp 57–91.

Larkin, Emmet, 'The Devotional Revolution in Ireland, 1850–75', *American Historical Review*, 77:3 (June 1972), 625–52.

Larkin, Emmet, 'The parish mission movement, 1850–1880' in Brendan Bradshaw and Dáire Keogh (eds), *Christianity in Ireland: revisiting the story* (Dublin, 2002), pp 195–204.

Laugerud, Henning, 'Det hagioskopiske blikk: Bilder, syn og erkjennelse i høy- og senmiddelalder' (PhD, U. Bergen, 2005).

Laurentin, René and P. Roche, *Catherine Labouré et la médaille miraculeuse: documents authentiques 1830–1876* (Paris, 1976).

Laurentin, René, *Lourdes: histoire authentique* (Paris, 2002).

Le paroissien romain (Paris, 1860).

Lewis, Clive Staples, *The discarded image: an introduction to medieval and Renaissance literature* (Cambridge, 1964).

Lindbeck, Anders, 'Presteskapet sitt syn på Hans Nielsen Hauges religiøse vekkelse i 1804' (MA, U. Bergen, 1999).

Lisle Phillipps, Ambrose, *The Catholick Christian's complete manual* (London, 1847).

Llorente, Angel, *Arte e ideología en el franquismo (1936–1951)* (Madrid, 1995).

Loftus, Belinda, *Mirrors: orange and green* (Dundrum, 1994).

Loftus, Belinda, *Mirrors: William III and Mother Ireland* (Dundrum, 1990).

Luzzatto, S., *Padre Pio. Miracoli e politica nell'Italia del Novecento* (Torino, 2007).

Maclaren, S.F., *La magnificenza e il suo doppio. Il pensiero estetico di Giovanni Battista Piranesi* (Milano, 2005).

Manual of Our Lady of Perpetual Succour (London, 1944).

Marx-Weber, Magda, 'Die Musik zur Kreuzwegandacht von Casciolini bis Liszt', *Kirchenmusikalisches Jahrbuch*, 73 (1989), 51–70.

Massenkeil, Günther, 'Das weihnachtliche Stabat Mater in dem Oratorium "Christus" von Franz Liszt' in M. Dobberstein (ed.), *Artes liberales. Karlheinz Schlager zum 60. Geburtstag*, Eichstätter Abhandlungen zur Musikwissenschaft, 13 (Eichstätt, 1998), pp 283–9.

Mathew, G., *Byzantine aesthetics* (London, 1963).

McConvery, Brendan, 'Hell-fire and poitín: Redemptorist missions in the Irish Free State, 1922–36', *History Ireland*, 8 (2000), 18–22.

McConvery, Brendan, 'Some aspects of Redemptorist missions in the new Irish state (1920–1937)', *Spicelegium Historicum Congregationis Ss Redemptoris*, 47 (1999), 105–25.

McDannell, Colleen, *Material Christianity: religion and popular culture in America* (New Haven, CT, 1995).

McGrail, Peter, *First Communion: ritual, church and popular religious identity* (Aldershot, 2007).

McNamara, Francis, CSsR (ed.), *Mission keepsake: devotions and prayers taken chiefly from the writings of St Alphonsus* (Dublin, 1932).

Metken, S., 'Nazarener und nazarenisch – Popularisierung und Trivialisierung eines Kunstideals' in Klaus Gallwitz (ed.), *Die Nazarener*, Catalogue.

Meulemeester, Maurice de, *Bibliographie Générale des Ecrivans Rédemptoristes*, i (Louvain, 1933).

Miller, Daniel, *Material culture and mass consumption* (Oxford, 1987).

Miller, D.W., 'Irish Catholicism and the Great Famine', *Journal of Social History*, 9:1 (1975), 81–98.

Miller, D.W., 'Mass attendance in Ireland in 1834' in S.J. Brown and David Miller (eds), *Piety and power in Ireland, 1760–1960: essays in honour of Emmet Larkin* (Belfast & Notre Dame, IN, 2000), pp 158–79.

Miller, J.M., CSB, 'Sacramentals in Catholic theology' in Ann Ball (ed.), *The how-to book of sacramentals* (Huntington, IN, 2005), pp 9–19.

Missions in Ireland by the Fathers of Charity, 1848–1854 (Dublin, 1855).

Missionsbuchlein fur Junglinge und Jungfrauen. Ein Unterrichs- und Andachtsbuch als bestandige Hausmission (15th Auflage. Munich, 1909).

Mitchell, C., 'The religious content of ethnic identities', *Sociology*, 40:6 (2006), pp 1135–52.

Moffit, Miriam, *Soupers and jumpers: the Protestant missions in Connemara* (Dublin, 2008).

Moffitt, Miriam, *The society for Irish church missions to the Roman Catholics, 1849–50* (Manchester, 2010).

Mokrzycki, Bronisław (ed.), *Zawierzyliśmy Miłości: Kult Najświętszego Serca Jezusowego* (Kraków, 1972).

Molland, Einar, *Norges kirkehistorie i det 19. århundre* I (Oslo, 1979).

Moser, Roland, 'Unitonie – Pluritonie – Omnitonie: Zur harmonischen Gedankenwelt in der *Via crucis* von Franz Liszt', *Basler Jahrbuch für historische Musikpraxis*, 21 (1997), 129–42.

Murpyh, James, 'The role of Vincentian parish missions in the "Irish Counter-Reformation" of the mid-nineteenth century', *Irish Historical Studies*, 24:94 (1984), 152–71.

Neame, Alan, *The happening at Lourdes or the sociology of the grotto* (London, 1968).

New Catholic Encyclopedia (NCE) (1967).

New Redemptorist Mission Book (Baltimore, MD, 1911).

Newman, Henry, *Loss and gain: the story of a convert* (London, 1891).

Newman, John Henry, *The dream of Gerontius* (Oxford, 2001).

Newport, K.G.C., *Apocalypse and millennium: studies in biblical exegesis* (Cambridge, 2000).

Nic Ghiolla Phadraig, Máire, 'The power of the Catholic Church in the Republic of Ireland' in P. Clancy et al. (eds), *Irish society: sociological perspectives* (Dublin, 1995), pp 593–619.

Nolan, Barbara, *The gothic visionary perspective* (Princeton, NJ, 1977).

Nolan, Mary Lee and Sidney Nolan, *Christian pilgrimage in modern Western Europe* (Chapel Hill, NC, 1989).

O'Dwyer, Peter, OCarm, *Mary: a history of devotion in Ireland* (Dublin, 1988).

O'Halloran, Leo, *Prayer Book for Women* (Dublin, 1957).

O'Halloran, Leo, *Prayer Book for Boys* (Dublin, 1956).

O'Halloran, Leo, *Prayer Book for Men* (Dublin, 1952).

O'Neill, Robert, *Cardinal Herbert Vaughan, archbishop of Westminster, bishop of Salford, founder of the Mill Hill Missionaries* (London, 1995).

Olivetti, Marco M., 'Le problème de la sécularisation inépuisable' in E. Castelli (ed.), *L'Herméneutique de la secularisation* (Paris, 1976), pp 73–86.

Olszewsky, Hans-Josef, 'Liszt, Franz Ritter von' in Friedrich Wilhelm Bautz (ed.), *Biographisch-Bibliographisches Kirchenlexikon*, 5 (Herzberg, 1993).

Onsell, M., *Ausdruck und Wirklichkeit. Versuch über den Historismus in der Baukunst* (Braunschweig/Wiesbaden, 1981).

Organ für christliche Kunst (Köln, 1852), no. 2.

Ott, Ludwig, *Fundamentals of Catholic dogma* (St Louis, MO, 1964).

Ouspensky, Lossky V., *The meaning of icons* (Crestwood, NY, 1983).

Ouspensky L., *Theology of the icon* (Crestwood, NY, 1978).

Ozolin, Nicholas, 'The theology of the icon', *St Vladimır's Theological Quarterly*, 31:4 (1987), 297–308.

Panowsky, Erwin, *Gothic architecture and scholasticism* (Latrobe, 1951).

Pattison, Stephen, *Seeing things* (London, 2007).

Pelikan, Jaroslav, *The Christian tradition: a history of the development of doctrine*, 5 (Chicago, 1989).

Perry, Nicholas and Loreto Echeverría, *Under the heel of Mary* (London, 1988).

Pesch, O.H., 'Musik als Glaubenszeugnis: Anmerkungen zu Bach, Beethoven, Bruckner, Strawinsky und anderen' in Michael Kessler (ed.), *Fides quaerens intellectum: Beiträge zur Fundamentaltheologie. Festschrift Max Seckler* (Tübingen, 1992), pp 467–94.

Plumb, Brian, 'Hymnbooks revisited', *North West Catholic History*, 27 (2000), 68–91.

Pocknell, Pauline, 'Liszt and Pius IX: the politico-religious connection' in Michael Saffle and Rossana Dalmonte (eds), *Liszt and the birth of modern Europe: music as a mirror of religious, political, cultural and aesthetic transformations*, Analecta Lisztiana, III (Hillsdale, 2003).

Pontalier, Fr C. de, *Le trésor du Chrétien* (2nd ed., Paris, 1785).

Pope, Barbara Corrado, 'Immaculate and powerful: the Marian revival in the nineteenth century' in C.W. Atkinson et al. (eds), *Immaculate and powerful: the female in sacred image and social reality* (London, 1987), pp 173–200.

Prieto, Dario, 'Los investigadores reivindican la figura de Carlos Sáenz de Tejada', *El Mundo*, 6251 (28 Jan. 2007), 64.

Psalms, hymns and passages of scripture for Christian worship (London, 1894).

Pugin, A.W.N., *An apology for the revival of Christian architecture in England* (London, 1843).

Pugin, A.W.N., *Contrasts; or, A parallel between the noble edifices of the Middle Ages and corresponding buildings of the present day; shewing the present decay of taste* (Reading, 1836).

Rapin, René SJ, *La Foy des dernieres siecles* (Amsterdam, 1695).

Redemptorist hymn book and prayers (Dublin, 1946).

Redepenning, Dorothea, 'Meditative Musik: Bemerkungen zu einigen späten geistlichen Kompositionen Franz Liszts', *Hamburger Jahrbuch für Musikwissenschaft*, 8 (1985), 185–201.

Reichensperger, August, *Die christlich-germanische Baukunst und ihr Verhältnis zur Gegenwart* (Trier, 1845).

Reid, Alcuin, OSB, *The organic development of the liturgy* (Farnborough, 2004).

Reinhard, W., 'Gegenreformation als Modernisierung? Prolegomena zu einer Theorie des konfessionellen Zeitalters', *Archiv für Reformationgeschichte*, 68 (1977), 226–52.

Remembrance of the Mission preached by Redemptorist Fathers at Ballinabrackey Church, September 1888. Box N: *Early Home Missions*. Redemptorist Provincial Archives, Dublin.

Ricoeur, Paul, 'L'herméneutique de la secularisation' in E. Castelli (ed.), *L'Herméneutique de la secularisation* (Paris, 1976).

Ringbom, Sixten, *Icon to narrative: the rise of the dramatic close-up in fifteenth-century devotional painting* (Åbo, 1965).

Rolston, Bill, *Politics and painting: murals and conflict in Northern Ireland* (Cranbury, 1991).

S. Léonard de Saint-Maurice, *Via crucis; ou, Méthode pratique du chemin de la croix* (Tournai, 1852).

Sacred hymns, for the use of the elect family of Jesus, in this militant state; by W. Augustus Clark (London, 1782).

Sacrosanctum Concilium (Constitution on the Sacred Liturgy), 4 Dec. 1963.

Saffle, Michael, 'Liszt and Cecilianism: the evidence of documents and scores' in Hubert Unverricht (ed.), *Der Caecilianismus: Anfänge – Grundlagen – Wirkungen*, Eichstätter Abhandlungen zur Musikwissenschaft, 5 (Tützing, 1988), pp 203–13.

Saint Alphonse of Liguori, *Esercizio della via crucis*, see: http://www.preces-latinae.org/thesaurus/Filius/ExercitumVC.html.

Sanders, Hanne, *Bondevekkelse og sekularisering. En protestantisk folkelig kultur i Danmark og Sverige, 1820–1850* (Stockholm, 1995).

Santino, Jack, *Signs of war and peace* (New York, 2001).

Santuario Nacional, *El Santuario Nacional de la Gran Promesa* (Valladolid, 1963).

Schieder, Martin, *Jenseits der Aufklärung* (Berlin, 1997).

Schindler, Herbert, *Nazarener – Romantischer Geist und christliche Kunst im 19. Jahrhundert* (Regensburg, 1982).

Schlegel, Friedrich, 'Rede über die Mythologie', *Athenaeum*, 1:1 (Berlin, 1800).

Schlegel, Friedrich, *Ansichten und Ideen von der christlichen Kunst* (1823) (Paderborn, 1959).

Schwoerer, Lois G. 'Celebrating the Glorious Revolution, 1689–1989', *Albion: a Quarterly Concerned with British Studies*, 22:1 (spring 1990), 1–20.

Seland, Eli Heldaas, '19th-century devotional medals' in Henning Laugerud and Laura Katrine Skinnebach (eds), *Instruments of devotion: the practices and objects of religious piety from the late middle ages to the 20th century* (Aarhus, 2007), pp 157–72.

Semper, Gottfried, *Der Stil in den technischen und tektonischen Künsten oder Praktische Ästhetik*, I–II (München, 1860, 1863).

Sharpe, John, *Reapers of the harvest: the Redemptorists in Great Britain and Ireland, 1843–1898* (Dublin, 1989).

Sichler, Jean, 'La *Via Crucis* de Franz Liszt', *Transversalités*, 69 (1999), 61–7.

Skandinavisk Kirketidende for katholske Christne, 4/1856 (København, 1856).

Skullerud, Åge, *Bondeopposisjonen og religionsfriheten i 1840–årene* (Oslo, 1971).

Songs of gladness: a hymn book for the young (London, c.1905).

Sorokin, Pitirim A., *Altruistic love: a study of American 'good neighbours' and Christian saints* (Boston, MA, 1950).

Sperber, Jonathan, *Popular Catholicism in nineteenth-century Germany* (Princeton, NJ, 1984).

Stebbing, George, *Thirty ways of hearing Mass* (London, 1913).

Stowell, Hugh, *A selection of psalms and hymns suited to the services of the Church of England* (London, 1854).

Stratton, Suzann L., *The Immaculate Conception in Spanish art* (Cambridge, 1994).

Talarico, Marco, *Der Kreuzweg Jesu in historischer Authentizität und katholischer Frömmigkeit*, Ästhetik – Theologie – Liturgik 25 (Münster, 2004).

Tanquerey, A., *Doctrine and devotion* (Tournai, 1933).

Taylor, Charles, *A secular age* (Cambridge, MA, 2007).

The Divine Office for the use of the laity: (the Mass for every day of the year, vespers and compline) (London, 1763).

The garden of the soul; or, A manual of spiritual exercises and instructions for Christians who (living in the world) aspire to devotion (London, 1740).

The hymnes and songs of the church. Divided into two parts. The first part comprehends the canon-icall hymnes and such parcels of Holy Scriptures, as may properly be sung: with some other ancient songs and creeds. The second part consists of spirituall songs, appropriated to the several times and occasions observable in the Church of England (London, 1623); *Halelujah or, Britans second remembrancer, bringing to remembrance (in praisefull and poenitentiall hymns, spirituall songs and morall-odes) meditations, advancing the glory of God, in the practice of pietie and virtue; and applied to easie tunes to be sung in families &c* (London, 1641; Spencer Society, 1879).

The Mission Book. Instructions and prayers to preserve the fruits of the mission, drawn chiefly from the writings of St Alphonsus Maria de Liguori, new and revised ed. (Dublin, 1891; new and rev. 12th ed., Dublin, 1916).

The national Orange and Protestant minstrel: being a collection of constitutional and protestant songs, hymns, toasts, sentiments and recitations, original and select. Bradford: printed and published by squire auty, at the Orange and Blue Banner office (Kirkgate, 1853).

The New Catholic Dictionary (London, 1929).

The New Mission Book of the Redemptorist Fathers by Very Revd F. Girardey CSsR (St Louis, MI, 1911; repr. 1928).

The Notre Dame Hymn Tune Book. Comp. and arranged by F.N. Birtchenall and Moir Brown (Liverpool, 1905).

The Office of the Holy Week according to the Latin Missal and Breviary (London, 1738).

The official handbook of the Legion of Mary (Dublin, 1962).

The path to heaven (1862).

The Protestant hymn book: for use at Protestant meetings, conferences and lectures (London, 1894).

The psalms of David imitated in the language of the New Testament, by I. Watts (London, 1719).

The Roman Catholic 'dedication of England' to the Virgin Mary as 'Our Lady's Dowry'. A manifesto to the people of Great Britain. By an Englishman (London, c.1893).

The whole booke of Psalms, collected into English metre by T. Starnhold I. Hopkins & others: conferred with the Ebrue, and apt notes to synge the withal, faithfully perused and allowed according to thordre appointed in the quenes maiesties iniunctions. Very mete to be used of all sortes of people primately for their solace & comfort: laying apart all ungodly songes and ballades, which tende only to the nourishing of vyce and corrupting of youth (London, 1562).

The young Protestant's hymn, 'We won't give up the Bible'; the words written and adapted by a clergyman of the Church of England; the music arranged for three voices, with symphonies and a separate accompaniment for the piano forte, by W.H. Kearns, organist of the Verulam Episcopal Chapel, Lambeth (London).

Thurston, Herbert, SJ, 'Benediction of the Blessed Sacrament', *Report of the Nineteenth Eucharistic Congress, held at Westminster from 9th to 13th September 1908* (London, 1909).

Toras na Croiche. A.M. Ligouri. Trans. J. MacHale (Dublin, 1873).

Trubetskoi, Eugene, *Icons: theology in color* (Crestwood, NY, 1973).

Turner, Victor and Edith Turner, *Image and pilgrimage in Christian culture: anthropological perspectives* (New York, 1995).

Vauchez, André, *La sainteté en Occident* (Rome, 1981).

Vezzosi, E., 'Mediatrici etniche e cittadine: le Maestre Pie Filippini negli Stati Uniti' in E. Fattorini (ed.), *Santi, culti, simboli nell'età della secolarizzazione (1815–1915)* (Torino, 1997), pp 495–514.

Walker, Alan, *Franz Liszt: the final years, 1861–1886,* 3 (London, 1996).

Warner, Marina, *Alone of all her sex: the myth and the cult of the Virgin Mary* (London, 1976).

Watson, Francis, 'Theology and music', *Scottish Journal of Theology*, 51 (1998), 435–63.

Webb, D., *An inquiry into the beauties of painting; and into the merits of the most celebrated painters, ancient and modern* (London, 1769).

Weber, Max, *Gesammelte Aufsätze zur Wissenschaftslehre* (Tübingen, 1922).

Weber, Max, *Wissenschaft als Beruf* (München, 1919).

Weinstein, D. and R.M. Bell (eds), *Saints and society: the two worlds of Western Christendom, 1000–1700* (Chicago, 1982).

Williamson, Philip, 'State prayers, fasts and thanskgivings: public worship in Britain, 1830–1897', *Past and Present*, 200 (August 2008), 121–70.

Wilson, Stephen (ed.), *Saints and their cults: studies in religious sociology, folklore and history* (Cambridge, 1983).

Wilson, Walter, *The history and antiquities of dissenting churches and meeting houses in London, Westminster and Southwark; including the lives of their ministers from the rise of nonconformity to the present time* (London, 1810).

Wittgeinstein, Ludwig, *Philosophical investigations*, transl. G.E.M. Anscombe (Oxford, 2001).

Xuggopoulos, A., *Sxediasma istorias tis Thriskeutikis zwgrafikis meta tin alwsi* (Athina, 1957).

Yates, Frances A., *The art of memory* (London, 2007).

Young, Percy M., *Elgar, Newman and the dream of Gerontius: in the tradition of English Catholicism* (Aldershot, 1995).

Zarri, Gabriella, *Le sante vive. Profezie di corte e devozione femminile tra '400 e '500* (Torino, 1990).

Zemon Davis, N., *Women on the margins: three seventeenth-century Lives* (Cambridge, MA, 1995).

Zias, Nikos, *Fotis Kontoglou zwgrafos* (Athina, 1991).

Zias, Nikos, 'Neoelliniki ekklisiastiki zwgrafiki', *Syntaxi*, 24 (1987).

Zundel, Maurice, *Splendour of the liturgy* (London, 1941).

Ørstavik, Lars, 'Haugianismens sorte epidemi'. Studier i Hauge-ovringa på. Sunnmore, 1799–1805' (MA, U Bergen, 1982)

WEB SOURCES

www.chapellenotredamedelamedaillemiraculeuse.com/EN/B3.asp, accessed 28 Aug. 2008.

www.lourdes-france.org/, accessed 18 Aug. 2008.

www.ewtn.com/library/councils/trent25.htm#2, accessed 6 Aug. 2008.

www.newadvent.org/fathers/3819.htm, accessed 6 Aug. 2008.

www.newadvent.org/cathen/07674d.htm, accessed 27 Aug. 2008.

www.youtube.com/watch?v=C2pF5XhNSJk, accessed 28 Aug. 2008.

www.vatican.va/roman_curia/tribunals/apost_penit/documents/rc_trib_appen_doc_20071121_decreto-lourdes_en.html, accessed 10 May 2010.

Index